Misbegotten Muses

American University Studies

Series IX
History

Vol. 32

PETER LANG
New York · Bern · Frankfurt am Main · Paris

Richard C. Poulsen

Misbegotten Muses
History and Anti-History

PETER LANG
New York · Bern · Frankfurt am Main · Paris

Library of Congress Cataloging-in-Publication Data

Poulsen, Richard C.
  Misbegotten muses : history and anti-history / Richard C. Poulsen.

  p. cm. — (American university studies. Series IX, History ;
vol. 32)
  Bibliography: p.
  1. History—Methodology.   2. History—Philosophy.   I. Title.
II. Series.
D16.P66   1988
901—dc19
ISBN 0-8204-0535-3
ISSN 0740-0462

CIP-Titelaufnahme der Deutschen Bibliothek

Poulsen, Richard C.:
Misbegotten muses : history and anti-history /
Richard C. Poulsen. — New York; Bern; Frank-
furt am Main; Paris: Lang, 1988.
  (American University Studies: Ser. 9,
  History; Vol. 32)
  ISBN 0-8204-0535-3

NE: American University Studies / 09

Printed by Weihert-Druck GmbH, Darmstadt, West Germany

This book is for
Don D. Walker

To speak humanly from the height or from the
  depth
Of human things, that is acutest speech.
        Wallace Stevens
        "Chocorua to Its Neighbor"

Contents

Preface

Empire has created the time of history.
    J. M. Coetzee
    Waiting for the Barbarians

This is a book about time and space—about the space of time. Of what time is, what time has become, and what time is not. Engulfed in a sweep, a movement, of something we perceive as time, of an event against which we gauge our humanity, we search for our place in this system, or we create the system to establish a place for ourselves. This place, this moment in time, is a relative moment. It is a play of perception. So that "the old man in the road would see what he remembered, but the boy's squinting eyes saw only what was there."[1] What we see is what we have been taught to see; and as a human event, the past is a remembered language: we see what we have lived.

But the historical event is a moment of pedagogy, a taught language, a movement in which time is transformed for a visible purpose. History subsumes the remembered language, replacing it with a sense of apocalypse: a set of predetermined events. We assume history encloses, accounts for, time, while it is time that encloses history. History is a most visible icon, around which every major institution of the Western world turns—or seems to turn. Time is as elusive as the space in which it is perceived. To escape history is not easy, since the hierarchy history assumes is the way we have been taught to think. And encased by such thought, we have forgotten the language of time, in which we have all shared, for a moment forgotten or a moment remembered.

If, at times, this book seems cold, it is because it deals, by necessity, with the icy noise of the historical event. But this book, at its core, is warm; it is warm from the heat of human actions, from the voice of the remembered past, from the memory of a lived experience. "I bow to memory, every person's memory. I want to leave memory intact, for it belongs to the man who exists for his freedom."[2]

To deal with a past beyond the influence of historicity is not easy; perceptions and possibilities of such a past have become invisible to cultures whose institutions operate on and define themselves by a chronology which reflects the verities of their respective faces. But there is a time beyond history, even though its existence and its voice seem unattainable. That which remains untaught and uncodified, however, speaks from an expanse (a space) which seems illimitable. And I believe that it is not only right, but necessary, to utter the unattainable. Voices are heard only when they are spoken; silence is the opium of the masses.

Other questions and problems loom in considerations of the space of time. What, for example, is an ethnography? Are human events approached and made clear by the establishment of a proper "data base," the objectivity of the measurements of science? Or is ethnology a poetics? A space? A prejudice? A fabric of human events whose voice (in time), like the idiom of languages, confuses and disrupts a system to which all things are discoverable through measurement?

And what then of truth when weighed against considerations of time? Beyond a chronology, truth begins to vacillate, to shatter, to portray itself in alien forms. Truth seems not the property of a limitation, but the condition of a chaos: a condition whose morphology in the space of time is amorphous. Yet, setting limits for the limitless, and defining those limits both as truth and as an ethnography are omnipresent. What, then, do we see, experience? How much of what we see have we never seen at all? In the space of time, truth's commodity is itself: manifold but not coherent; at once visible and invisible.

> If ever the search for a tranquil belief should end,
> The future might stop emerging out of the past.[3]

So the space of time remains an image—not a dogma:

The old man: saw what he remembered.

The boy: saw only what was there.

What do we *remember*? And what is *there*? Both are illusions of the past; both moments are played out within the space of time, within a context of the experience of existence. These moments form the thrust of this book: the archaeology of space, the anguish of the antithetical.

The essays in this collection grew one-from-another expressly for the book. These essays function as spokes around a central hub, as indicators of multi-direction. They do not flow gently, normally, one to another. Each spoke is discrete, independent, except as it reinforces a position of thesis, a place in the wheel.

The wide range of essays here is not exhaustive, is not meant to be. Each essay samples undisturbed, unruffled dust in a world of historical assumption, a wide-world of assumption.

Chapter One

History and Folklore: Misbegotten Muses

History has no meaning, I contend.
> Karl R. Popper
> *The Open Society and Its Enemies*

The thump and crump of history becoming unstable, crumbling.
> Patrick White
> *The Twyborn Affair*

History is a nightmare from which I am trying to awake.
> James Joyce
> *Ulysses*

None of the "original" three nor the final nine muses of the Greeks and Romans paid homage to folklore, although Clio, muse of history, presided from earliest times over inspiration associated with the past. Perhaps the Romans emulated no muse of folklore because they moved in a society which not only saw little artistic inspiration in folk things, but which also viewed the past in terms of the desacralization of time they had inherited from the Greeks, from historians like Xenophanes, who emptied *mythos* of all religious and metaphysical value.[1] Perhaps there could have been, to these Greeks and Romans after Xenophanes, no muse of folklore, partly because the gap between folklore and history was not one of simple distance, but one of profoundly different world-view.

This possibility seemed especially true to me as I recently endured a session of professional papers in a meeting devoted to folklore. The last speaker of the day, a historian who claims identity with folkloristics, rambled at great length about territorial baseball in the Desert West. Although his topic pointed to a discussion of folk-sport, no such commitment was kept. Instead, "our" historian treated his dutiful listeners to fifty minutes of historical detritus, minutiae gleaned from archives and yellowed newspapers. But his shortcomings were much larger than those growing from boredom; in his attempt to interpret things of the folk with the mind of the historian, he lucidly illustrated the impossibility of such a venture.

We have been persuaded to believe in the implicit and explicit compatibility of history and folklore by scholars who may be praised in the folklore hall of fame, but who were really historians masquerading as students of culture. Alexander Haggerty Krappe, in his oft-quoted and more often emulated *The Science of Folk-lore*, noted that "folk-lore is, in fact has been for a considerable number of years, an historical science. . . . With its sister sciences it may combine, in various ways, to make up the cycle of our knowledge of man's past life."[2] Later, Krappe rightfully asserted that the methodical study of folklore in Europe in the nineteenth century was essentially "a fruit of the Romantic movement."[3] Of course, one of the basic tenets of the romantic movement was glorification of the past, of a past which, when linked with folklore, became present and future as well.

The real problem here is not, as we have been so willing to believe, one of antiquarianism. Rather, the essential problem, when discussing the supposed relation of history and folklore, grows out of the nature of the whole tradition of historical inquiry. Richard M. Dorson has written that history is more than "a sequential series of cause-and-effect relationships"[4]—which is true—but the question he does not satisfactorily answer is, What then is history, and how does it interpret folk materials, other than by placing them in a historical context, a context which some of the greatest minds of the twentieth century have been seriously questioning for decades? Minds like Albert Camus, Jean-Paul Sartre, Jacques Lacan, Claude Lévi-Strauss, Martin Heidegger, Hayden White—and perhaps Henry Nash Smith, whose book *Virgin Land*, despite Dorson's claims,[5] is no more a historical work than is Herman Melville's *Moby Dick*.

As Alan Dundes has argued, American folklorists, in attempting to reconstruct past forms of present folklore, have followed the lead of their

European precursors by looking backwards. "The idea of studying the present to discover the past is entirely in keeping with nineteenth-century historical reconstructionist aims."[6] What this dalliance in the past has produced is the romanticizing of folk belief, which is responsible for the "historical bias"[7] remaining strong not only in American folklore scholarship, but in Western folklore and mythology scholarship generally. Dundes also sees that Dorson is more interested in using history to understand folklore than in using folklore to reconstruct history.[8] Assuming Dundes' judgments are true, what Dorson has done with folklore is more damaging than reconstruction, because history, finally, is not interpretive, but clearly manipulative, as Hayden White, the most rigorous and illuminating philosopher of history this century has known, clearly establishes.[9] In analyzing historical plot structures, White perceives four "modes of emplotment" for historiography: romance, comedy, tragedy, and satire.[10] Because a historian like Michelet is a "romanticist," he interprets or emplots his history of France up to the revolution of 1789 as "romance." This is precisely how history manipulates: the past conforms to a style, not to the fallacious "found data." Extrapolating these problems to folkloristics, it becomes clear that folklorists' attitudes toward history can manipulate narratives more than mere alteration of texts.

The firm hold history retains on the scholarly mind may find explanation in the fact that it has been made palatable to the masses in a way literature, science, and philosophy perhaps can't be, since the re-creation of the past through historiography remakes the past in our image. History is seldom revolutionary. Like journalism, the more banal the history, "the better its chances of being esteemed by the common man."[11] In the selling of history for public consumption (an affliction, in my opinion, which has engulfed folkloristics),[12] the past is generally romanticized, because that is what the public wants and understands—it is then the audience which molds the form historiography will take. Perhaps such a realization prompted Sartre to write, "Therefore if we study the relations of the past to the present in terms of the past, we shall never establish *internal* relations between them,"[13] simply because the past and present may have no logical relationship.

Because history establishes connections which are at best illusory, at worse dishonest,[14] the historical imagination "constitutes the fundamental barrier to any attempt by men in the present to close realistically with their most pressing spiritual problems."[15] And since folklore may contain, exude, and reflect those most pressing problems, history precludes not only the expression of these problems, but also their understanding. By themselves, there is nothing inherently evil in the verbal fictions[16] of historical narratives. Problems develop, however, when we consider history as panacea for the past, as an elixir whose use will enable us to see deeply into the predicaments and meanings of folklore—this simply because historical narratives are rhetorical descriptions of the past. A penchant for interpreting folkloristic events and predicaments historically smacks not simply of antiquarianism, but of a culture which has grown stale[17] through emulation of its own monuments of the past.

This, I believe, is precisely what Dorson attempts when he claims that historical periods in America reflect (or are reflected by) folkloristic concerns, "the values, tensions and anxieties, goals and drives, of [a] period."[18] It is not folk narratives that teach this, but the historians. If, as Dorson suggests, historians are turning "to folklore as a vital source for black, ethnic, urban, and frontier historical writing,"[19] they are transforming the powerful cultural forces of folklore into digestible historical pieces. This is not only undesirable, but impossible. If folklore and history seem, at times, synonymous it is just by chance, just as the fact that two individuals having almost exactly the same dream, each of which may signify different problems and anxieties,[20] is coincidental.

There is no convincing evidence that "American civilization is the product of special historical conditions which in turn breed" special problems of folkloristics.[21] Actually, there is strong evidence to the contrary. Perusal of early journals surrounding the American fur trade, for example, shows that early explorers and travelers perceived the landscape of manifest destiny not from the vantage point of the historian, but through the literary eyes of Fenimore Cooper. Perceptions of what the American landscape was and would become grew largely from the synthesis of myth and story, not special historical conditions.[22] When ornithologist John C. Townsend described the antics of beaver on the banks of the Malade River near present-day Ketchum, Idaho, he alluded to the accuracy of Cooper's descriptions of the animals in *The Last of the Mohicans*, not to scientific or historical attitudes toward the animals.[23]

D. H. Lawrence rightly attributed to Cooper what he called a myth-meaning,[24] a perception of the landscape—the essentially American—which profoundly affected settlement patterns and perceptions of what America is, much more deeply than the verbal fictions of historiography.

Stephen Stern and Simon Bronner have recently accused Dorson and others of committing the "'fallacy of hypostatized proof,' by which the historian substitutes sanctified academic interpretations for actual historical events," thereby rejecting contradictory evidence.[25] But the sins of history against folklore are much greater than Stern and Bronner allow, and these sins are committed not only by the old guard, but also by some of those who consider themselves anthropological folklorists—scientists. For example, in a recently published essay, one folklorist claims that old houses in Utah can tell us much about early Utah history, and implies that the "architectural vocabulary" of folk houses is a frustrating historical dialect.[26] He concludes his essay on "a new architectural understanding" with claims that the potential of "all" old houses is to construct a complete historical record.[27] As I have argued elsewhere,[28] that is precisely what the houses do not tell us, since they are structures whose significance can best be understood against the backdrop of myth and symbol.[29] Yet we persist in our assumptions that folklore is history, the found data of the external world, manifestations of the historical mainstream.

The journals are filled with so-called literary and anthropological approaches to folklore which see the lore as a manifestation of history. New Ph.D.'s in folklore, as Dundes argues, may have no problem reconciling literary and anthropological approaches,[30] but many display a tendency to perceive folklore as history, perhaps because since its inception as a scholarly discipline, folklore was perceived by Krappe and others as history.[31]

Since a persistent threat in contemporary as well as past folkloristics is to lay claim to the world of science, one does well to consider Hayden White's lucid proofs that history is not science;[32] that it is, on the other hand, a stylistic verbalization of the past which emplots events according to the sensibilities of the historian. Interestingly, psychological interpretations of history have been anathema to most historians. White argues that among contemporary historians one senses a growing movement to block serious consideration of the more significant advances in literature, social science, and philosophy, and that the historian is not the mediator between art and science, but "the irredeemable enemy of both."[33]

Solutions to the oppressive problem of history (as it concerns folklorists) will be forthcoming only when we adopt new attitudes toward the past, new theories of history. Norman O. Brown, in a much neglected work, *Life against Death: The Psychoanalytic Meaning of History*, sees that "the actual changes in history neither result from nor correspond to the conscious desires of the human agents who bring them about."[34] In such a view, history as now perceived reacts against the very forces responsible for the creation and perpetration of folklore. Dundes seems, although somewhat ambivalently, to agree with Brown when he muses that the "distinction between folklore as a product of the past and folklore as a reflector of the present has had crucial implications for folklore methodology,"[35] noting also that both anthropological and literary folklorists have unitedly espoused historicity while unitedly ignoring psychological, symbolic approaches.[36]

What folklorists sorely need in order to deal with the problems of historicity is a new approach, a new theory of history, one that places history in its proper perspective to folklore. Suppose that we consider history as an array of "markers" (or signs) which allow the cultural accommodation of folklore (or symbols)—these signs could either be stylistic or "real," as long as they furthered (or impeded) the cultural accommodation of folklore. History then is not a view of the past as it was, but as it must be in order for the deep structures of culture to be perpetrated, destroyed, or expressed. In other words, history is valueless and amoral by itself; it only attains meaning in its relationships, either positive or negative, with culture. History only exists as we would have it, as our culture allows it. It is not folklore that changes, not at least in its expressions of culture, but history which changes, to accommodate culture, in particular folklore. In such a view, folklore becomes what Michel Foucault calls "centuries of continuity, the movements of accumulation and slow saturation, the great silent, motionless bases that traditional history has covered with a thick layer of events."[37]

Folklore is the constant; history is the variable. Profound changes, for example, in Russian history from Czarist to Dialectic times have been noted by many scholars. But how profoundly has the culture in its deep structures (those expressed largely by folklore) changed? Why is anti-Semitism as important a part of contemporary Russian life as it was before the revolution? The answer is simple: history changes; folklore, its modes and manifestations, do not. By the same token, folkloristic perceptions of blacks by Mormons have not appreciably changed since 1978, when blacks were allowed full communion; what has changed is Mormon history regarding black policy, not deeply felt cultural perceptions, for anti-black jokes by Mormons, as a later chapter will show, are as pointed and alive as they were before revelation declared blacks equal to whites.[38] Prejudice (as reflected in folklore) is archetypal, while history is a stereotypic stylistics. Official pronouncements and history may alter, but the violence of prejudice persists in culturally sanctioned forms. Folklore and history exist on levels which are so totally removed in spirit, yet at times so visibly parallel, as to never approach each other in meaning or intent. It is only the façade, the style, of history which seems to approach the deep meanings inherent in folklore.

Likewise, the "history" of the demise of the Sioux, the spiritual problems of the past, can neither be approached nor understood by recourse to history. When Black Elk mourned the circle of his tribe being broken, he talked not of the murder of Sitting Bull or Crazy Horse, nor of the confinement of his people to reservations, all actions approached and touted by historians. Rather, Black Elk saw the destruction of his people as a dissolution of spirit, of the deep structures of the culture disappearing.[39] Doubtless, this spiritual dissolution is largely attributable to the disappearance of the buffalo; but the slaughter of the buffalo, seen from the cultural vantage point of the Sioux, was not a historical problem, but a cultural horror. How can history possibly approach and illuminate the meaning to the Sioux of the disappearance of the buffalo, when history is guided and given life by chronology? As Lévi-Strauss so wisely said, "There is no history without dates."[40] We know that folklore cannot be defined; when will we realize that it cannot be understood by recourse to chronology?

Even the "hard sciences" with their historical equipage have difficulty tracing, chronologically, the working out of major scientific advances. Thomas Kuhn has said, when faced with the problem of retrieving historical data from the movements of science, "Clearly we need a new vocabulary and concepts for analyzing events like the discovery of oxygen";[41] this because history cannot tell us when oxygen was discovered, let alone what the discovery means.

Consequently, "any historical fact," wrote Ernst Cassirer, "however simple it may appear, can only be determined and understood by such a previous analysis of symbols."[42] Because the symbolic precludes the historical, when, for example, one uses symbols to deal with the past, one arrives at new understanding of the past, which simultaneously gives new prospect for the future.[43] Only when we are freed from the burden of history can we extrapolate the meaning of the past to the present. Such ideas, it seems to me, are especially crucial for the study and understanding of folklore. Seen in such a way, the negation of history, through which the past can be approached in genuinely interpretive ways, will lead to the eclecticism requisite for discovery and progress in any field,[44] will lead us to the crossing of boundaries that divide one discipline from another, will allow us the use of illuminating metaphors for organizing our perceptions of reality.[45]

Hayden White sums the importance of coming to terms with cultural problems without the burden of history when he writes:

> Since the second half of the nineteenth century, history has become increasingly the refuge of all of those "sane" men who excel at finding the simple in the complex and the familiar in the strange. This was all very well for an earlier age, but if the present generation needs anything at all it is a willingness to confront heroically the dynamic and disruptive forces in contemporary life.[46]

But perhaps more important for folklorists than simple divestment of history's burden is the reconstruction of new theories of the past,[47] a sense of curiosity and discovery portrayed in a language vital and accessible[48]—a look away from the historic past in which man finds his future guaranteed,[49] a past which reveals itself as metaphorical, but not redundant.

Such a view of the past must be developed, I believe, not in an escape into the confusion of chronology, but through "a steadfast, unflinching look" into the mind, "a shattering experience for anyone seriously committed to the Western traditions of morality and rationality"[50]—those committed to historical explanations of man's motivating forces. Folklore is bred and nurtured by conflict, and it is in the relation between the conscious and the unconscious that conflict lies, the place where symbols are made, the place where folklorists must go (a place thoroughly ahistorical) if they are ever to approach the profundity of folklore. The immense pattern that emerges from the place of conflict is, said Norman O. Brown, hitherto unrecognized by historians, the dialect of neurosis,[51] a point made time and again by Freud, perhaps most meaningfully in *Civilization and Its Discontents*.

Because normal history and historiography allow no movement to the place of conflict, we have, with the historical, pure appearance rather than full being, as Sartre so aptly wrote.[52] When we turn to the place of conflict we transcend the past as well as the future,[53] and are only then able to deal with the spiritual significance of the symbols, a place where history no longer exists[54] because it is only façade, not being, a place without human possibility.[55] That is why our theory of the past must renounce the historical, because the past can only have meaning when it becomes the present, a present of conflict and repression.[56]

I am not suggesting that there is one correct way of looking at, of understanding, the past. What I am suggesting is that in our attempts to find continuity in the past we have glossed over the heart of the matter; we have turned from linguistic determinants (Freud's whole *modus operandi*, and the place of conflict) and found satisfaction in the easily swallowed and softly digestible pleasures of chronology. The mind is not historical, although in the superficialities of cultural backwash, it may seem, and only seem, historically motivated.

Such a view of the past was espoused by American artist Jackson Pollock. Not only did his new view of the past, an acceptance of another kind of history, release art in the United States from its long European bondage,[57] it allowed him to enter the spiritual life of the Navajo—but this came only after a renunciation of normal history, a rejection that dropped technological society and consumption-oriented cultures, which had reduced man to "episodes of the productive machine."[58] This new past to Pollock was symbolic, a past made present in Navajo sandpaintings.

What we (students of culture) must therefore do if we are ever to escape the belief, the supposed cultural necessity, that man can be understood by recourse to history is re-examine and reform the texts of our profession, not merely the texts we employ to teach people about tradition, but the texts we so trustingly collect and store in archives. What do the texts mean? Have they become museum pieces, and therefore icons of the profession, or are they fluid symbols of the place of conflict? Like Pollock, Gary Witherspoon only arrived at the heart (one that proved thoroughly linguistic) of Navajo culture after abandoning the anthropological tools of the trade. We must follow suit.

An example: for several years I collected and "stored" folk-evidence of the motivations behind what I came to call the Mormon Migration Myth. I discovered that despite "historical evidence," folk perceptions of the transcontinental movement of Mormons viewed it as providential,[59] a term scholars for centuries have attached to the Puritan view of history: a providential historiography. To the Puritans, history was not providential; providence was history, was the past, and thus their historiography is not really history at all, but an attempt to chart the mind of God, their perception of the place of conflict.

The same can be said of Mormons who view their history as providential. What, I believe, they envision is not history at all (Mormons are simply using a convenient label), but the place of being in which conflict reigns supreme, the unconscious, the place of repression. In their view of a providential journey through the maw of wilderness, a world-view is conceived, a conscious way of dealing with the conflict is born. Violence and hostility, not the dust of a benevolent historiography, are the authors of the Migration Myth.[60] And as such, history to them becomes signs or markers which allow the cultural expression and accommodation of folklore.

In a reinterpretation of texts, we must probe the depths of the conflict, of the symbols emanating from the unconscious. That is the path we must take to construct a new, culturally viable view of the past and of its relationship to the forces of folklore. Perhaps then a new muse will be born to replace the tyrannies of Clio, a muse whose focus of inspiration will not be bounded by, deadened by, a historically determined view of the past.

Chapter Two

The Enigma
of the Puritan Mind:
Cotton Mather Revisited

For only the history of the symbolic function can allow
us to understand the intellectual condition of man.
Claude Lévi-Strauss
"The Sorcerer and His Magic"

History is the will of a just God who knows us.
Reynolds Price
A Palpable God

Early in his magnum opus, the *Magnalia Christi Americana*, Cotton
Mather, in praise of Edward Hopkins, explained that Hopkins, whose
prayers were not only frequent but fervent, often "fell a *bleeding* at the
nose through the agony of spirit with which he laboured in them."[1] And
in his infamous *The Wonders of the Invisible World*, he repeated a
"published and credible Relation" which told "that very lately in a part
of England, where some of the Neighbourhood were quarrelling, a *Raven*
from the top of a tree very articulately and unaccountably cry'd out,
Read the Third of Colossians and the Fifteenth!"[2] Later in *Wonders* he
explained that the Devil impedes the progress of industry; strong evidence of this truth, he went on to relate, lies in the fact that before the
Children of God came to America, the savages had never seen nails,
boards, knives, or grains of salt.[3]

On the other hand, Cotton Mather was an accomplished and
accepted thinker and "scientist," well known in England, and one of
the few men of his time and religion to be made a member of the Royal

Academy of Science. He also championed the introduction of smallpox vaccine into the colonies, a commitment which led to the fire-bombing of his house in Boston. He, unlike the bulk of his colleagues, also saw the sun as the center of the solar system.

Most students of Puritanism are well versed in the few details I have mentioned so far; I repeat them simply to show, once again, that Cotton Mather was a man of seemingly deep inconsistencies, a man, divine, thinker, scientist, who has been thoroughly damned by virtually all of his critics because of the enigmatic nature of his life and letters, the inexplicable duality of his thoughts and actions.[4]

These scholars have been so vehement in their denunciation of Mather as to raise some suspicion of their own scholarly objectivity. In his usually perceptive work, *The New England Mind*, Perry Miller openly displayed a burning disgust of Mather, claiming that "Cotton Mather in his heart of hearts never doubted that the divinity was a being remarkably like Cotton Mather"[5] and that on most scores Mather fortunately was in the minority.[6] Miller, like most critics both before and after him, took the easiest, least demanding approach possible to Mather: he dismissed him with a sneer. Turning away from the inexplicable Mather, Perry Miller praised Jonathan Edwards' fierce piety, seeing his spirituality as clearly representative of the Puritan norm,[7] Mather, as noted, being only a case for a psychiatrist.

Katherine Anne Porter, whose aborted attempt at a biography of Mather never solidified, bitterly attacked Mather at every hand, accusing him of confusing public opinion with the voice of God;[8] she called the Salem witchcraft proceedings, orchestrated primarily by Mather, a solemn farce.[9] Ultimately, Porter turned Mather's life into a cheap, though tragic, love story, and caricatured him as hypocrite and fool.

In his prize-winning book on the Mathers, Robert Middlekauff admits that Cotton Mather was respected by his contemporaries, but claims the respect was given grudgingly, "except by his close friends and admirers."[10] Further attempting to come to terms with this "bewildering man,"[11] Middlekauff takes his analysis to Samuel Eliot Morison, a "modern scholar" who, claims Middlekauff, understood much of Mather's thought. Morison's analysis of Mather leads to the conclusion that "he was at best the source of a profound revulsion, or at worst of an upset stomach."[12]

A very few scholars have not been so intense in their invectives against Mather. Kenneth Murdock, in a statement which turns to the enigmatic image of the man, writes that "he was apart from his times, not truly representative of them."[13] He also notes that his transports of religious feeling have been interpreted by some as evidence of an unsound mind.[14] But Murdock perceptively sees that our ironical fascination with Mather teaches us that he "defies reduction to the limits of a type."[15] And Barrett Wendell, who remains Mather's most insightful and competent biographer, at least does not accuse Mather of insidious motives when he says that the divine was one of "those who take life in earnest."[16]

Some contemporary critics, although shying from analysis of Mather's mind and motives, seem to see Mather as something more than a confusing stereotype. Sacvan Bercovitch refers to the man's "enormous imaginative intensity" and assesses him as a man of vision.[17] Gustaaf Van Cromphout calls Cotton Mather "the most impressive exemplar of the humanist tradition in American Puritanism."[18]

Even though some of Mather's interpreters allow his vision and humanism, most if not *all* studies of him have attempted meaning through historical avenues, through the mediums of biographical, intellectual and social history. In what I consider the most perceptive piece in print about Cotton Mather, David Levin thoughtfully and accurately points out the mistakes of Mather's would-be interpreters. Speaking as historian, he calls Katherine Anne Porter astonishingly inaccurate.[19] Levin goes on to dispel the grotesque caricature of Mather that has accumulated over the last three hundred years, largely by attacking the historical assumptions of accuracy Mather's critics have claimed. In an insightful passage Levin proposes that

> Mather remains a fascinating problem for modern biography not only because of his importance in colonial New England, his vast range of learning and the prodigious quantity of his writing, or his strange personality, but also because his character and his actions challenge the biographical vocabulary of a hostile age.[20]

This is a significant statement. By "challenge the biographical vocabulary," I assume Levin means we have no words, at least from the point of view of the biographer, to describe and therefore understand

Mather. However, many critics are averse if not openly hostile to approaches to the past from points of view other than the historical. Remember, for example, the great outcry against Freud when he insisted that the past could be illuminated through an analysis of dreams. If we are ever to create a vocabulary sufficient to deal with the complexities of Cotton Mather, it will not be a lexicon based on the historical fallacy,[21] for recourse to history can, I believe, tell us little about the mind not only of Cotton Mather, but of anyone. Yet, once again, *all* of Mather's interpreters, including Levin, have sought Mather's motives and methods through recourse to history. They have been sorely disappointed.

When Perry Miller wrote that Mather's eccentricities "are of value chiefly because they illustrate extravagantly the qualities which his contemporaries possessed to a less bizarre extent,"[22] he was simply judging Mather from a historical perspective in which the minister was compared with what history tells us about other Puritans. And when Miller quickly added that "Cotton Mather was venturing beyond the limits of ordinary Puritan prudence when he actually did *see* an angel,"[23] he was again simply judging Mather according to the "historical norms" of his peers.

Unfortunately, then, Pershing Vartanian is correct when he argues that "Mather's intense piety has fixed his place, perhaps indelibly, in the historical imagination."[24] And in the historical imagination, Mather has simply become a grotesque plaything of the past. Even so, Middlekauff claims that "the outward circumstances of Cotton Mather's life help clarify some of the mystery that envelops his character and his behavior."[25] Past criticism is the best evidence that the "outward circumstances" of Mather's life (those, I assume, which seemingly lend themselves to the historical imagination) do not illuminate our understanding of the motivations, the implications, the logic, if you will, of Cotton Mather's ways.[26]

What historical interpretations of Mather have fostered is what Levin calls "that hateful image of our national demonology,"[27] and he argues that such results are products of a persistent fitting of meager evidence to assumptions that are astonishingly simple-minded. What we have therefore accomplished is the creation in Mather of an icon of all the horrors of Puritanism—a blatant stereotype.[28] I find puzzling, even ludicrous, our persistent scholarly need to re-indict Mather time and again on the historicity of events which, very possibly, none of us understands. This latent historicity has forced obfuscation of his driving forces, not clarification—produced stereotypes rather than archetypes, so to speak. What we are left with is a villain of our own manufacture. "We must not," argues Levin, "cheapen historical art or human reality [the two are very different] with caricature."[29] It is very possible, for example, that Mather's much touted interest in witchcraft has little intellectual importance, other than showing that like most educated men of his day, he believed witches existed.[30]

History cannot probe and illuminate the inward workings of Mather's fascinating psyche. Therefore, we must, if we are to understand him, find other interpretive tools, tools which will lead us *into* rather than *away from* the central problem of Cotton Mather as Puritan divine, as a complex bundle of seemingly irreconcilable differences. Such a tool, I believe, has been given us by Claude Lévi-Strauss in his probing essay "The Sorcerer and His Magic." After studying Mather and his critics for several years, I came upon Lévi-Strauss' article and was immediately impressed by the strong, consistent parallels between the mind and actions of the primitive sorcerer and the mind and actions of Cotton Mather, parallels which, I think, clearly illuminate Mather's actions and motivations as Puritan divine.

We are, I believe, mistaken in viewing the Puritan divines primarily as intellectuals; they were first and foremost ministers, who had important relationships with their congregations and who, as was the case with Mather, were generally thought well of by their parishioners.

As was true for the Puritan ministers, the relationship of the sorcerer to his "audience" was crucial. Speaking of the Kwakiutl Indian sorcerer Quesalid, whom Boas first discussed,[31] Lévi-Strauss, stressing the vital relationship between the shaman (or sorcerer) and his audience, writes that "Quesalid did not become a great shaman because he cured his patients; he cured his patients because he had become a great shaman."[32] Lévi-Strauss then proposes that "the true reason for the defeat of Quesalid's rivals [other sorcerers whose "magic" proved weaker than Quesalid's] must be sought in the attitude of the group rather than in the pattern of the rivals' successes and failures" (p. 180). Quesalid, like Mather, had attained greatness not because of the literal strength of his magic, but because of his strong relationship with his group (or quite literally, his congregation). Without the consent and approval of the group, both the Puritan minister (as was certainly true when one considers the demise of Jonathan Edwards) and the primitive sorcerer are powerless.

An important consideration when weighing the relationship of the sorcerer and his believers, and one which was certainly true for Cotton Mather, especially when considering lapses of "logic" and empirical inconsistencies in *Wonders of the Invisible World*, is the *fact* that to the congregation "historical" inconsistencies are not consequential. (Many Mather scholars have built weighty cases of indictment against him for lack of coherence in detail and method. However, magic is often no respecter of imposed detail.) Speaking of another sorcerer, this time a Brazilian Nambicuara, Lévi-Strauss tells of his own fieldwork in 1938, during which he observed the shaman obviously caught in a "lie," a lie which in no way diminished his stature among his own. One night, the shaman failed to return to camp from his daily activities of hunting and fishing. The band worried, then became certain of his death. Late into the evening the shaman was discovered crouching two hundred yards outside camp, "disheveled and without his belt, necklaces, and armbands." After some persuasion, he told the group that during the afternoon he had been caught in a storm and carried off by thunder to a site several miles distant, completely stripped, and then returned to the spot where he was later found. "The next day," writes Lévi-Strauss, "the thunder victim had recovered his joviality and, what is more, all his ornaments" (pp. 169–70). This obvious deception caused no lapse of faith in his followers, just as the fact that Mather's weak excuses (our judgments) in defending his actions during the Salem witchcraft frenzy in no way cost him his congregation. To the sorcerer's believers, transportation by thunder "belonged to the realm of real experience" (p. 171), in which such inconsistencies have no bearing on the shaman's veracity. To his congregation, Cotton Mather was a pillar of strength whose power, in large part, was derived from the very people who adored him.

What we moderns face here is a puzzling duality which our historicity of thought has not equipped us to deal with or understand. We see, therefore, "that the psychology of the sorcerer [which was, according to his critics, Cotton Mather's main distinguishing characteristic] is not simple" (p. 178). We are faced with two thought processes, which Lévi-Strauss calls normal and pathological. "From any non-scientific perspective (and here we can exclude no society)," he writes, "pathological and normal thought processes are complementary rather than opposed."[33] Herein, it seems to me, is a key to the understanding of Mather (as well as of his congregation). Normal (or empirical) thought and pathological (or emotional) thought in the Puritan world-view are complementary.[34] Thus Mather could on the one hand champion the introduction of smallpox vaccine into Boston, and on the other dwell hellishly on remarkable providences and religious marvels. He was not inconsistent; he was simply exercising both kinds of thinking, which his congregation of believers fully expected, and which indeed formed the basis of Puritan belief. For the primitive group involved in collective participation in shamanistic curing, a balance is established between normal and pathological thought. For the Puritan, a collective sharing of piety produced a unity of belief in much the same way. Our main problem in dealing with Mather is that we cannot put ourselves in the place of his congregation. Perhaps, to a degree, Barrett Wendell (as priest) could; and perhaps this is why he has glimpsed the motivations of Cotton Mather better than any of his other interpreters. What we need in order to come to terms with the anomaly of Cotton Mather is an anthropological and folkloristic understanding of New England rather than a historical gloss. Simply stated, Cotton Mather's mind is beyond historicity.

The problems of history in dealing with so complex a figure as Mather are not much alleviated by attempting, as Lévi-Strauss so perceptively shows in his analysis of the sorcerer, to deal with his so-called intellect. It is the symbolic function of folk belief—the condition of the folk mind—and its understanding which will probe the depths of Mather's mysteries.

Speaking again of the sorcerer, Lévi-Strauss claims that "the more sincere among them, believe in their calling" (p. 179). Not only does the shaman believe in his calling, he actually relives the events of his ministry "in all their vividness, originality, and violence" (p. 181). To moderns, this intense re-experiencing of past events, especially as displayed by Cotton Mather in his reliance on an elemental folk belief to interpret the subtleties of witchcraft,[35] is little more than a morbid, deranged preoccupation with history. But this is not so. Mather's reliance on the past to deal with present and future was not only expected by his congregation, but also came from the marrow of biblical tradition, in which past events, and past events alone, can interpret present and future. Thus, when Lévi-Strauss describes the shaman's relation with the past, he seems to be talking pointedly of Mather himself. We see the sorcerer,

> with a mixture of cunning and good faith, progressively construct the impersonation which is thrust upon him—chiefly by drawing on his knowledge and his memories, improvising somewhat, but above all living his role and seeking, through his manipulations and the ritual he builds from bits and pieces, the experience of a calling which is, at least theoretically, open to all. (P. 174)

If Cotton Mather seems more intense than his fellow ministers, it was because he believed more deeply than they did. The continuous recalling of his knowledge and memories served not only to establish his special and elect relationship to God, but also to firmly establish him as the shepherd of his flock, a flock kept from scattering by experiencing the intensity of its pastor's faith and knowledge. We should therefore take Kenneth Murdock quite literally when he writes that the story of Mather's "professional career is simply that of a devoted minister of one of the two or three largest churches in the American colonies."[36] Mather's intense reciprocity to his church established him not as deranged intellectual, but as shaman.

Such "unity" was implied by Barrett Wendell when he wrote that Mather "often saw things not as they were but as he would have had them."[37] However, Wendell interpreted Mather's intensity of spirit as evidence that he was "a constant victim of a mental or moral disorder whose normal tendency is towards the growth of unwitting credulity and fraud."[38] This may be true. It is, however, instructive to remember that Quesalid, the Kwakiutl sorcerer, became a shaman from a quest to expose the lies and incongruities of other sorcerers. He knew full well, in the beginning at least, that when he pulled a bit of blood-soaked feather from his own mouth, he was not producing the mysterious sickness of his patient, but only a feather soaked with his own blood. As his tribesmen began to honor him as one possessing great magic (great because it cured them), he began to see himself in a different light. He continued to know, we assume, that the feather was only a feather.

Or did he? Was there a point when the feather, because of the adulation of his tribesmen, became something more than a feather: a symbol of his intense relationship with his congregation, a manifestation of the unity and will (although grounded in fraud) of his mind and attitudes toward the people he served so well? If one takes Middlekauff literally, one sees that Mather's relationship with God's creations was precisely that of Quesalid's to the feather. One of Mather's techniques, says Middlekauff, "was the spiritualization of ordinary objects, extracting the holy significance from the creatures."[39] "Hence the relentless activities," Middlekauff later notes, "of his inner and outer life and his attempts to extract meaning from the most trifling events."[40] A bloody feather in the mouth; a devil with the feet of a cock, the body of a monkey: both are manifestations of a unity of thought and action which transforms a chaotic universe into comprehendible, vitally real units of pure magic. If only because of the possibility of these things actually happening and existing, they, to the congregation and the shaman–minister, belong to the realm of reality (p. 171), and therefore imply a unity of thought and action rather than a morbid fragmentation of a disturbed mind.

What the magic of the minister and the sorcerer accomplishes is the transformation of the chaotic, the unknown, into humanly predictable patterns, into a reality of belief and meaning exemplified by the abilities of the religious figure. As Lévi-Strauss explains, "The choice is not between this system and another, but between the magical system and no system at all—that is, chaos" (p. 174). But all this becomes clear only when one remembers that without the minister–congregation tie, all this magic is nothing more than the basest insanity. Therefore, "the efficacy of magic implies a belief in magic" (p. 168); if the magic works, if it transforms chaos into cosmos, then the only choice is to believe.

Although such a system seems foreign to twentieth-century rationality, this essential method of seeing and believing parallels the development of modern science (p. 176). Thus, Mather's commitment to science, when viewed together with the efficacy of Puritan magic as well as the implicit belief of the congregation in the minister as magician, is not at all out of place in the midst of his other actions and beliefs. All empirical knowledge, because it transforms chaos into reality by revealing evidence of a living God, is a sweet unity of spirit, both in the back-country of early twentieth-century Brazil and in the streets and spaces of late seventeenth-century Boston.

What the Puritan minister and the primitive shaman in their respective intensities have thus created is world-view, a system of belief and action—a reality which grows directly from what Lévi-Strauss calls the "shamanistic complex," a system which closely involves the relationship between the shaman, his patient, and "the public," who also participate in the cure. Such a system is one of unified action and belief when viewed from the inside. When seen from the outside, across the expanse of time and cultural change, the system is only madness. But the shaman-istic complex of the Puritan world, which revolved about the relations of the minister and his congregation, was one of unity and implicit belief, a system which Cotton Mather not only understood perfectly, but in which he functioned literally as its major proponent, unifying both normal and pathological thought into a coherent system of belief based largely on the times and needs of Puritan culture. For when the efficacy of a theistic universe began to erode in the acid bath of Deism and literal and empirical realities, only one type of thought persisted; the other was swallowed by the past in the long march toward a thoroughly measurable world.

Any approach to Cotton Mather, whether benevolent or malevolent, whether tending to vilify or exonerate, must remain ineffectual as long as it is grounded in the belief that history can explain the actions of so complex a character. For all his careful analysis of Mather and his critics, David Levin's approach to the enigmatic life of Mather is still based on the assumption that history will ultimately, when studied closely and long enough, reveal the intricacies of Mather's mind. There is, I believe, careful evidence to the contrary. It is the *timeless* analysis by genuine anthropological and folkloristic tools which reveals the complexity and unity of Mather's mind; and almost ironically, Mather can best be understood by comparisons to mental activities and attitudes far removed from Puritan New England by the immensities of time and space, but as close to her in psychological perspective and religious belief as the social customs and politics of Old England.

Chapter Three

Violence and the Sacred:
Mormon Jokes about Blacks

Interpretation is nothing but the possibility of error.
Paul de Man
Blindness and Insight

Summer 1978 marked one of the most profound changes Mormonism has experienced since its inception. Hailed as a major "revelation," an announcement issued by the church's supreme body, the First Presidency, proclaimed that "all worthy male members" could now be endowed with the male-only priesthood; this dictum was generally interpreted as an extension of the priesthood to blacks. According to two Mormon historians, the announcement of the priesthood revelation "was received, almost universally, with elation."[1] While a "universal elation" may have been expressed among the Mormon intelligentsia, this elation was not expressed generally among the rank and file.

On the contrary, narratives formed as jokes by the masses displayed and perpetrated a vicious cycle of biting, racially prejudiced invective, statements levelled directly at the Black Brother. These jokes were heartily circulated even by passive bearers of tradition, a fact which clearly establishes the intensity and importance of these narrative forms to the folk. As Freud noted, "Under the influence of strong purposes even those who otherwise have the least aptitude for it become capable of making jokes."[2]

I have grouped the jokes in several major categories, all of which are deeply involved with sacred cultural as well as doctrinal practices among Mormons. For the sake of illustration, I will give an example of one joke from each of these several categories.

1. *Moroni jokes*. A rather famous "landmark" on Mormon temples (perhaps especially the one in Salt Lake City) is a gold-leaf statue of a Book of Mormon prophet, Moroni. This statue, generically, has become an iconographic representation of temples themselves. One joke about the Moroni statue ran:

> Did you hear what they are going to do to the Salt Lake Temple now that they have given the priesthood to the blacks?
>
> They're going to replace Moroni with a gold statue of Louis Armstrong.

2. *Temple jokes*. These jokes involved not simply an icon of the temple, but often the holy practices carried on within the temples. Such jokes played on common mainstream-America black stereotypes, but set them in a context of sacrality.

> Have you heard that they are going to remodel the St. George Temple again [a temple, newly remodeled, in southern Utah]?
>
> No! What are they going to do now?
>
> They are going to add chicken coops out back.

3. *Clorox baptism jokes*. Mormons baptize by total immersion in water. The following joke focused on future baptism of blacks. In the Mormon bureaucracy, a bishop functions much as a Catholic priest, and a ward is a spatial unit similar to a diocese:

> Bishop A: Now that the blacks can hold the priesthood, I am afraid that there is going to be a lot of contention in my ward as we baptize them.
>
> Bishop B: Oh, we have already figured out a solution to that problem in my ward.
>
> Bishop A: Really, what is it?
>
> Bishop B: We just pour bleach into the baptismal font first.

4. *Watermelon jokes*. This joke-type was the most widely told joke which played, generally, on a black stereotype, the supposed exuberant enjoyment of watermelon:

> Did you hear about the bishop's storehouse [a repository for goods dispensed through the Mormon welfare system] in Atlanta, Georgia?
>
> They have a new inventory of just watermelon and hominy grits.

5. *Seagull jokes*. In a popular Mormon miracle, to which a monument was erected in the temple block in Salt Lake City, seagulls descended on hordes of crickets in the early days of the church, saving the grain crop and therefore the Utah Mormons. The following joke focused on the seagull as salvific bird:

Today we give the priesthood to blacks, but do you know what the Mormons did when the first blacks walked into the Salt Lake Valley?

Prayed for bigger seagulls.

6. *Slave jokes*. These jokes involved a play on another black stereotype, but in the image of sacrality. Mormons believe that during the Millennium (when the devil will be chained, and peace will be the "order of the day" on earth for one thousand years), the New Jerusalem will be established in Jackson County, Missouri—and will be populated by Mormons, most of whom will have to travel there from Utah— perhaps even on foot because of the horrors of the apocalypse:

Do you know why they gave the blacks the priesthood?

They knew they needed someone to carry the luggage in the Millennium.

7. *Tithing jokes*. Faithful Mormons pay ten percent of their gross income to the church. Again, in the context of sacrality, these jokes played on the rigors of the faithful, plus the social problems involved in the federal integration program:

Have you heard the new commandment?

We're now supposed to pay twelve percent tithing. The extra two percent is to bus the blacks.

8. *Guess Who's Coming to Priesthood jokes*. These widely told jokes played on the social and thematic implications presented in a movie titled *Guess Who's Coming to Dinner*, in which a white, upper-class girl brings a black companion home not only to dinner, but to marry:[3]

Have you heard about the new movie the Mormons made on June 9, 1978?

It's called *Guess Who's Coming to Priesthood*. [Priesthood here refers to a Sunday meeting attended only by priesthood holders.]

9. *Hymn-change jokes*. The Mormon hymnal is an intense religio–cultural phenomenon which needs serious scholarly attention—its cultural importance is not unlike that of *The Bay Psalm Book* to American Puritans. One of the most popular hymns among Mormons, which deals with the travail, both temporal and spiritual, Mormon pioneers experienced while moving west, is called "Come, Come, Ye Saints":

> Since the blacks received the priesthood, some of the LDS [Latter-day Saint] hymns have been re-named. Now it's "Come, Come, Ye Saints, Doo-da, Doo-da."

10. *Knock-knock jokes*. The principal figure in these jokes was either a Mormon bishop or a Mormon home teacher (a lay member who visits certain families in his ward each month). The "play" (or perhaps a better term is Freud's "joke-work") here was on the stereotype of black dialect:

> Knock, knock.
>
> Who's there?
>
> Isa.
>
> Isa who?
>
> Isa your new bishop.

or

> You know the Millennium has arrived when there is a knock at your door and you hear: "Let us in, brother, we is yo' home teachers."

11. *Blacks and the priesthood jokes*. This group of jokes focused directly on the "painful predicament" of blacks actually receiving the priesthood. In Mormondom, the sacrament is distributed ("passed") each Sunday to members during a service called sacrament meeting. The sacrament is passed by deacons, priesthood bearers who are generally between the age of twelve and fourteen.

> Do you know why they haven't let the blacks pass the sacrament yet?
>
> Because they jive on down the aisle and ask, "Who'uns of you honkies haven't had the chance at this here bread?"

Other miscellaneous jokes such as

Do you know what LDS [Latter-day Saint] stands for?

Light and Dark Saints.

were in wide circulation for perhaps a year after the 1978 announcement, but the "types" discussed above were predominant.

Interpretation of the jokes mentioned so far, and others of the type, is no easy matter, even for one in touch with the culture. The joke is as complex a form as legend, folktales—even belletristic fiction; and meaningful, measured interpretations of the type are scarce. With these jokes, in their context of sacrality, it certainly seems true that they merely afford an opportunity for Mormons to express the fact that "an accepted pattern [of supposed racial tolerance] has no necessity."[4] Culturally, the view of "no necessity" is terrifying: a culture is actually "dismembered" by the joke-work. Such self-annihilation expresses the type of nihilism I discuss in chapter five.

Although Freud distinguished between what he called non-tendentious (or innocent) jokes and tendentious (or hostile) jokes, he later claimed that "jokes, even if the thought contained in them is non-tendentious and thus only serves theoretical intellectual interests, are in fact never non-tendentious."[5] This idea seems especially significant when attempting interpretation of Mormon black jokes, if one remembers that Freud carefully, compellingly established the point that a joke becomes more pleasurable as it becomes more tendentious, and that tendentious jokes "must have sources of pleasure at their disposal to which innocent jokes have no access."[6] With an increase of hostility in the joke-work comes an increase of pleasure. The joke therefore becomes a "spontaneous symbol"[7] of pleasure embodied in a context of hostility.

This experience of pleasure, which may lie at the core of all jokes, but which is certainly a major factor in the jokes of this study, is likely grounded in the experience of decrying the necessity of a social fabric on the one hand while proving the vibrant nature of the pleasure of hostility on the other. This achieves a kind of consonance, "a consonance between different realms of experience," which becomes "a source of profound satisfaction":[8] pleasure. In essence, an alternate structure, however fleeting or whispered, is proven as sturdy as the belabored structure of society, and is achieved through the pleasurable contrast to an expectation.[9]

This creation of an alternate structure is compelling; it insinuates a view in which spontaneous pleasure builds an institution as formidable as the tried and obvious ways of the culture. This is precisely the reason why "a new joke," as Freud wrote, "acts almost like an event of universal interest; it is passed from one person to another like the news of the latest victory."[10] The new joke, in its spontaneity, is in fact a victory over the strictures of repression, and ironically (or appropriately) establishes a repression of its own not unlike that imposed by the culture it momentarily replaces. Pleasure is therefore liberated as the imposed inhibitions of society are shed.[11] But the implied victory of the jokes of this study is twofold: victory over the threat of disruption in the status quo (by black inroads in the sacred), and victory over those who have imposed the pain of change (prominent leaders of the Mormon church).

There is no question that stereotypes form and perpetrate prejudice.[12] Actually, prejudice itself is a stereotype searching for form. Such stereotyping is one of the most obvious, pressing "qualities" of Mormon black jokes, and jokes generally. Jokes are real in their creation of structure, but as illogical in that creation as the repressions imposed by the culture. Through stereotypes, the otherwise unknown actualities of the joked-upon group are experienced as the real:[13] stereotypes become the living truths emulated and found pleasurable in the joke-work.

There are several implications of this ethnic stereotyping. One involves, through the deprecation of the out-group, an enhancement of the in-group's self-image.[14] And although such deprecation and subsequent enhancement are obvious in the jokes of this study, the image is complex and fleeting. What, for example, is the image the in-group attempts? Is it one of self-aggrandizement, and what we mundanely express as "hostility," or is it the realization of an image through the pleasure of tendentiousness? An image which touts the experience of pleasure as the fleeting image of status quo? "It is the participatory tendency in humor which enables it to contribute to group solidarity."[15] And through such participation an image is drawn. Thus Mary Douglas writes that "the joke works only when it mirrors social forms; it exists by virtue of its congruence with the social structure."[16] The social structure at the point of the joke-work, however, is an image of pleasure, an enigmatic human condition.

But pleasure also implies catharsis. Freud wrote: "By making our enemy small, inferior, despicable or comic, we achieve . . . the enjoyment of overcoming him."[17] Such enjoyment is grounded, perhaps, not largely in the transformation of the enemy to that which is despicable, but in the experience of pleasure, a pleasure realized only in ritual cleansing, in the catharsis of the joke-work. Such possibilities become more pressing if we consider that "the need for catharsis through humor is related to historical circumstances."[18] Events of the past (which are synonymously events of the present) act as events to trigger the desire for pleasure, the desire for pleasure through catharsis. Historicity in this sense is important as a vehicle to ensure that stereotypes remain current within a culture. "Whenever in the social situation," writes Douglas, "dominance is liable to be subverted, the joke is the natural and necessary expression, since the structure of the joke parallels the structure of the situation."[19] The joke (most pointedly those of this study) parallels the structure of the situation because it is precisely the closeness of the situation to the stereotype which has recalled it and made it operable. The reason the joke-structure is so profound and necessary is that it replaces the imposed structure with its mirror-image, a spontaneous stereotype.

Such stereotyping leads to places other than the pleasure (hostility) of catharsis. "Essentially, a joke is an anti-rite."[20] It is an anti-rite because it destroys (in pleasure) the order of hierarchy. "The message of a standard rite is that the ordained patterns of social life are inescapable. The message of a joke is that they are escapable."[21] When the standard rites of culture jar the status quo, the mirror-image of the joke-work demands, creates, a structure which re-establishes the possibility of order and therefore the possibility of pleasure.

The anti-rite, the mirror-image, questions (if only briefly, and flirtingly) the very right of the guardians of the culture to exist, to dictate change in the status quo, since the structures of pleasure formed by the anti-rite are as "normal" as the "enduring" structures of dominance. Such quest for pleasure is, I think, of great importance in Mormon black jokes. The joke therefore "consists of challenging [and belittling] a dominant structure."[22] Américo Paredes reported such mirror-image functions among Mexican–Americans:

It is this double nature of our texts that makes them especially interesting. In the satirizing of folk medicine and *curandero* belief tales they express a mocking rejection of Mexican folk culture; in their expression of resentment toward American culture they show a strong sense of identification with the Mexican folk.[23]

The fluid nature of jokes (which, by the way, accounts for great difficulties in interpretation) allows them to both mock and support simultaneously.[24] Such duality is beyond paradox—paradox simply meaning something contrary to expectation. Jokes are more than paradoxical; they embody forms of narrative which both destroy and give pleasure with the same breath, which as anti-rite or mirror-image build and yet destroy—not contrary to expectation, but precisely functioning as the body of all expectation: the image of pleasure.

In the image of pleasure is not a renunciation, but a retrieval of what was lost in the stirrings of the status quo.[25] In the retrieval of the image found in pleasure, the status quo is re-formed (although the reformation is transitory), and the hierarchy suffers. This accounts for the great subversiveness of jokes: the mind of the folk is always impervious (in flashes, at least) to the dictates of the body politic. We count rebellion against authority as a merit, said Freud. "Tendentious jokes are highly suitable for attacks on the great, the dignified, the mighty, who are protected by internal inhibitions and external circumstances from direct disparagement."[26]

Obviously, the jokes of this study create images of pleasure through tendentious weaponry used against both blacks and the purveyors of society: the leaders of the church. But this is not the only posture the jokes assume. Douglas argues that "the joke form rarely lies in the utterance alone, but that it can be identified in the total social situation."[27] Concerning Mormon black jokes, the total social situation involves images of pleasure within the enveloping context of sacrality: of the strictures of Mormonism, which has provided the world-view within which the jokes operate and develop.

To understand the stark immediacy of violence (tendentiousness) within the confines of the sacred, we need to look beyond a close, empirical, often short-sighted analysis of jokes themselves to implications of socially sanctioned violence, in which the mirror of pleasure reaches fruition. In his probing work on the birth of the prison, Michel Foucault, writing of the searching, segmented, immobile institution of panopticism says that in the institutions of spectacle, of temples, theatres, circuses, public life, festivals, sensual proximity, "blood flowed, society found new vigour and formed for a moment a single great body."[28] Violence is a measure of unification, a structure of the image of pleasure, the news of a late, important victory which concerns the entire culture, and which is an act of universal interest because (either rite or anti-rite) it has created an image of stability. Within the context of sacrality, that image, perhaps, attains an even greater degree of the sacred than that supplied by the institution, because the object of the mirror-image is the realization of pleasure, a structure that must endlessly re-occur to maintain not only perspective, but sanity.

René Girard's controversial work, which approaches ritual and sacrifice from fresh perspectives, illuminates not only the meaning of cultural sacrifice, but the importance of violence within structures of sacrality. According to Girard, "The role of sacrifice is to stem this rising tide of indiscriminate substitutions and redirect violence into 'proper' channels."[29] Thus violence within the sacred is an institution which, in its ambivalence, not only protects categories within the culture of dominance, but which focuses violence (pleasure) in ways (through narrative forms, for example) that speed the creation of an image. Sacrificial rites then pacify, settle, and unite.[30] But sacrifice need not, often does not, assume literal, tangible forms. Clearly, narrative units, like the jokes of this study, which slay an image of that which is reprehensible, are distinct forms of cultural sacrifice, in which violence (pleasure) is used as unifier and pacifier—themselves units of the sacred, not the profane. The functional duality of pharmakos–sparagmos among the Greeks was not unlike the play of Mormon black jokes within the dominant culture. Both systems lead toward a rejuvenation of the culture through the experience of sacrifice. In Euripides' *Medea* the savage form of sacrifice is not unlike the joke-work. This is distilled in the nurse's statement about the rage of Medea: "I am sure her anger will not subside until it has found a victim. Let us pray that the victim is at least one of our enemies."[31]

In the rage of a culture, on its most elemental level, against change and the movement of institutions, the joke-work seems a lucid form of sacrifice, of the dissolution of an enemy for the salvation of forms that would otherwise crumble. Such possibilities seem especially poignant if one considers Girard's statement about the relation of religion and violence:

> Religion invariably strives to subdue violence, to keep it from running wild. Paradoxically, the religious and moral authorities in a community attempt to instill nonviolence, as an active force into daily life and as a mediating force into ritual life, through the application of violence.[32]

Systems of violence are therefore self-perpetuating, and in Mormon black jokes are sentiments, stereotypes, which are acknowledged by the culture, but which cannot be expressed in an institutional milieu. The joke-work, in its violence, allows expression of truths which, perhaps, cannot be expressed otherwise. Thus, about religion Girard can say that in its broadest sense, it is "another term for that obscurity that surrounds man's efforts to defend himself by curative or preventative means against his own violence."[33] In the religious context, the joke is a vehicle which demands an expression of violence (pleasure), which the culture-at-large must deny.

"Violence," writes Girard, "is the heart and secret soul of the sacred."[34] This verity in part accounts for the intense delight Mormons on virtually all levels (including the intelligentsia) took in telling the jokes, in pursuing prescribed courses of violence in a context of suppression that quite literally demanded the jokes be told, that pleasure be realized.

In 1934 H. A. Wolff and others wrote, "The truth is that our understanding of the entire problem of humor is vague and uncertain."[35] This truth persists. As Thomas Kuhn has so brilliantly illustrated,[36] the discoveries of science are not cumulative; knowledge is not expressed or experienced through the amassing of details whose only logical relationship may be that we demand they express a logic. This is precisely what Girard assumes when he writes that "there is no reason to believe that advances in scholarship will, by the process of continuous enrichment so dear to the positivist cause, increase our understanding."[37] Girard writes of understanding the great dramatic tragedies; I assume the same can be said of the interpretation of jokes.

When Mary Douglas defines the joke as a play upon form, she moves beyond positivist enrichment to the difficult problems of genuine interpretation. She goes on to suggest that a joke "brings into relation disparate elements in such a way that one accepted pattern is challenged by the appearance of another which in some way was hidden in the first."[38] Because of this, she confesses, she finds Freud's definition of the joke highly satisfactory. I concur. Jokes can be appreciated only when viewed as integral units in the entirety of social situations, as forms of violence which lead to the express pleasure of both building and destroying, of the rite and anti-rite experienced simultaneously. Jokes unleash "the energy of the subconscious against the control of the conscious."[39] What jokes then give those who express and those who enjoy them are "glimpses of truth which escapes through the mesh of structured [historical] concepts."[40] Reacting against structure, they are units of anti-structure, whose presence ironically nurtures the culture.

The joke is therefore an irony of enigmatic proportions, proportions which were realized by Victor Turner in his "study" of the joke rite among the Ndembu of Zambia. In the middle of the sacred moment of religion (in which Kavula, the great white spirit, is paid homage) joke-work becomes part of the ritual. The joke-work in this context, says Turner, hints at unfathomable mysteries. He says, "We have in Chihamba the local expression of a universal-human problem, that of expressing what cannot be *thought of*, in view of thought's subjugation to essences."[41] Turner's discoveries, I believe, are not only the most illuminating statements (besides Freud's) about the meaning of the joke-work generally, but also imply an interpretive scheme for dealing with Mormon black jokes.

It is true that joking in the context of sacrality, as Girard implies, is a portrayal of violence and sacrifice, but it is also true that the mystery of such behavior continues to elude us. The unfathomable mysteries lie within the core of the narrative process, of the language of mythology,[42] a language we have been slow to interpret. The enigma of language Turner approaches is that thought (perhaps the logical, the rational, the need to make lasting connections) is subjugated to essences (the desire for, need of, hostility–pleasure, which resides beyond the rational), because thought cannot express the propensity of human beings for violence. This perhaps is why the joke-work is so totally beyond the control of even the most repressive institutions; actually, the more repressive the institution, the more vibrant the joke-work becomes, because the essential is beyond the rational; the essential is honed by its play against the rational. That is why, as Freud wrote, "a good joke makes, as it were, a *total* impression of enjoyment on us."[43]

A good joke, in this context, is a hostile joke, one that clearly expresses the essences, which clearly institutes (in the core of Mormon black jokes) a system of sacrifice whose expression is a totality of joy, a euphoria of play upon form, of the release of a spontaneous symbol. The jokes themselves are extremely complex and many-faceted; and beyond the expressions of hostility (pleasure) toward blacks, and toward the institution of repression, they mouth the unthinkable in a system which worships primarily that which can be thought.

When Freud wrote, "Dreams serve predominantly for the avoidance of unpleasure, jokes for the attainment of pleasure; but all our mental activities converge in these two aims,"[44] he approached the astounding importance of jokes to a culture; and in the context of Mormon joke-work, the sacrifice is again experienced through elemental forms of the word, of that which expresses both the thought and the unthought, and of the play between them. Like the world of the Puritan mind, a world of modern joke-work is beyond interpretation through historical means.

Chapter Four

Speech as Liminality:
A Language of Mythos

> As members of society, most of us see only what we expect to see, and what we expect to see is what we are conditioned to see when we have learned the definitions and classifications of our culture.
>> Victor Turner
>> *The Forest of Symbols*

> Yet I felt uneasily that I was always on the outside looking in, for I was constantly aware of the thudding of ritual drums in the vicinity of my camp.
>> Victor Turner
>> *The Ritual Process*

> Myths are made for the imagination to breathe life into them.
>> Albert Camus
>> *The Myth of Sisyphus*

Lévi-Strauss judged correctly when he wrote that as anthropologists turned from the study of primitive religion (a prime ground for studies of myth and mythological systems), amateurs from other disciplines turned this field of study, this reference point, into their own private playground.[1] And so everyone writes about myth. This piece, I hope, will not simply be another doodle on the playground. For although anthropologists, according to Lévi-Strauss, abandoned the study as a wasteland, and although sundry others have written about myth, there are few serious studies of the field which attempt genuine interpretation.

One of the most prominent attitudes toward myth, and one which antedated serious anthropological concern about mythos, was the deification of the Greeks and the simultaneous freezing of the archaic past of Greek mythology into a static form which, because of its stasis in the mind of the "classical scholar," has been dubbed literature, indeed some of the finest, if not the finest literature we know. This process of stasis is precisely analagous to John Milton's attitude toward good books: as "the precious lifeblood of a master spirit, embalmed and treasured up on purpose to a life beyond life."[2] This embalming process, the reification of Greek myth into literary texts, has done more to hamper a serious study of myth than the ravings of a thousand amateurs on the playground of primitive religion. Lévi-Strauss himself is guilty of paying obeisance to the embalming process when he says his perception of the Oedipus myth, his arrangement of mythemes, "would be improved with the help of a specialist in Greek mythology."[3] Specialists in Greek mythology tend to be notoriously narrow-minded in their embalming of Greek myths.[4]

Other major mythographers who may not happen to be specialists in Greek mythology often pattern their own reification of mythos after the philosophy of embalming which underlies prevalent attitudes toward Greek artifacts, both material and verbal. For example, when Mircea Eliade implies that fairy tales are camouflaged or fallen myths,[5] he employs the "theory" of *gesunkenes Kulturgut*, which sees folklore as bastard forms of high-cultural narratives, forms which are sunken and debased. The high-cultural narratives are virtually always attributed to the Greeks. So we have an unalterable diadem of Greek ethnicity frozen as artifact and brought forward into modern culture as the status quo, the literature, of mythological systems. For mythology, the Greek system remains our arbitrary, our celestialized base of reference.

Stephen C. Pepper, in his book *World Hypotheses*, perhaps gives us a possibility for explaining this deification of stasis. After dismissing animism and mysticism as inadequate world hypotheses, Pepper poses four theories which he claims account for all lasting or worthwhile hypotheses. These are formism, mechanism, contextualism, and organicism. In my opinion, Pepper's categories are so broad and so inclusive as to border on the meaningless, but there is a lesson to be learned from his hypotheses. Pepper claims that each of these hypotheses has at its core a root metaphor which supplies each theory with its meaning, both, I assume, cultural and philosophical. The root metaphor for formism is *similarity*; that for mechanism is *the machine*. Both contextualism and organicism, however, take a common root metaphor: *the historic event or process*. An interesting metaphor in its own right grows from Pepper's perceptions: we (in Western society) live in a world conceived in and created by historicity. History in actuality has become our modern metaphor for truth: in science, in art, in mythological systems. And as purveyor of truth, this time-based metaphor naturally promises a sure-knowledge of beginnings: a right vision of the way things were.

So even the anthropologists are obsessed with beginnings. And it is true that within the narrative form of a myth, of that which, from a traditional point of view, teaches of the beginnings, of the gods and the heroes, and provides models for cultural conduct, *the beginning* is crucial. But are we talking of a beginning which is grounded in time, in a perception of the past in which chronology is vital, or are we dealing with a world that instead of being conceived in time is conceived in language? If, within the mythological system, we are dealing with language, its subtleties and implications, rather than time, we have the possibility of a new approach to mythography, one which deifies no system (because systems are always conceived in time), but which focuses on the fluid word, not the past event, as perpetrator and nurturer of mythical systems.

Unlike the folktale, the myth has no explicit morphology. But Propp was able to supply a morphology for the folktale only when he insisted that "as long as no correct morphological study exists, there can be no correct historical study."[6] This means, simply, that morphology precludes history, that there can be no history, no origins,[7] without a morphology. This is a crucial problem, since with origins and history we are dealing with time; but quite the opposite is true for morphology; morphological problems are problems of language (as Propp so clearly showed), and a morphology for myth (if indeed one exists as it does on the same level as the folktale) can be discovered, or invented, only through recourse to a language of mythos. Myth has no morphology because it has no language, and it has no language because we have obscured the possibility for discovering that language by insisting, either implicitly or explicitly, that myth is a historical phenomenon.

But by a language of myth I do not mean the linguistic reductionism of phoneme–morpheme, and their supposed translation into the mythemes theorized by Lévi-Strauss. Such reductionism has not led to a clarification of myth, but rather to its obfuscation. Denotation, says Roland Barthes, gathers all meaning around it in a circle, and by that very process permeates the world as exclusive, as a static system. "If we base denotation on truth, on objectivity, on law," he writes, "it is because we are still in awe of the prestige of linguistics, which, until today, has been reducing language to the sentence and its lexical and syntactical components."[8] From the beginning of his landmark essay "The Structural Study of Myth," Lévi-Strauss is guilty of a constant reductionism.

After arguing that "myth cannot simply be treated as language if its specific problems are to be solved, [because] myth *is* language," and to be known it must be told,[9] Lévi-Strauss promptly reverts to a discussion of myth as a *linguistic* rather than a *language* expression,[10] stating that we should look for the mytheme (basic mythical unit of meaning) on the sentence level.[11] Unfortunately, what Lévi-Strauss' analysis of myth leads to is a rather simplistic reductionism, a dispersion of the language of myth. By the end of his essay he seems to have totally abandoned language—as a system of signs, or even lexical units—in favor of mathematics. That is why Lévi-Strauss does not give us a morphology of myth; he is, in a sense, swallowed by his own analysis: the language of myth becomes subservient to linguistic enumeration.

We therefore smart under the lack of a morphology of myth, of a view of the meaning of and possibilities for a language of mythology, at least from *traditional* points of view. There are reasons for this lack. Mary Douglas claims that that which cannot be clearly classified in traditional terms or which falls between classificatory boundaries is almost universally regarded as polluting and dangerous.[12] In other words, if we look for meaning in areas or places which have not been codified or canonized, such activity is highly suspect, and will likely be regarded with genuine hostility. Such, however, is always the nature of real discovery; it seldom makes people comfortable—its illumination must always be at odds with the status quo. Some notable thinkers, both anthropologist and non-anthropologist, have led us to a point of discovery of a language of myth.

Because of his resentment over seeing nature and history confused at every turn, Roland Barthes turned from a traditional perception of myth and concluded that myth is a language.[13] This, however, is not the morphemic language Lévi-Strauss attributes to myth, for as Barthes later noted, myth is depoliticized speech,[14] or, one might say, language which is completely beyond the possibility of political overtures or consequences, *political* in this case meaning those aims of an institution, any institution, which are made to serve the express purposes of the institution, rather than the culture or the individual. Myth then is a language which is not self-serving, which creates movable structures which only have meaning within the auspices of the culture and for each individual of the culture. Myth, and the world-view it creates, is always apolitical, because its truth is based upon the internal needs of a culture, not the external demands of a bureaucracy. Myth, of course, can be exploited by Politicians (used in the broadest sense), but only if it is frozen in the past and thus endowed with a historicity. If it is not historicized, it cannot become political; its speech therefore is natural and unself-assuming, but at the same time profoundly existential.

The profundity of the language of myth is clearly illustrated by Gary Witherspoon in his *Language and Art in the Navajo Universe*. According to Witherspoon, the Navajo universe is totally a product of language, is totally subsumed and consumed on the cultural and the existential level by language. The Navajo language, shows Witherspoon, is a language of constant motion, and that motion is reflected and reinforced in the visible mythology. "To the Navajos," writes Witherspoon, "the earth is a living being, and it has an inner form who is Earth Woman, another one of the names of Changing Woman."[15] Among the Navajo, Changing Woman is the Earth Mother figure, and as her name implies, she is conceived in motion, in the process of organic change and movement. At this level, it is the language itself which forms and perpetrates the mythology. This is likely also true with mainstream American culture and its concomitant mythology, although the status quo may be stasis.[16]

The point is that myth is language—that myth is determined and given meaning by a particular language system. That, however, does not mean that as interpreters we have a language of mythology, like we have a language of the folktale. If and when we have a language of myth, we will have a morphology of myth. It is the world actualized through language[17] that becomes the world of mythology.

But the language of mythology is depoliticized. According to Victor Turner, "Members of despised or outlawed ethnic and cultural groups play major roles in myths and popular tales as representatives or expressions of universal human values."[18] This "sentiment for humanity," continues Turner, represents the poor and the deformed and appears to symbolize the moral values of communitas against the supreme power of political rulers. Myth, at this instant, is stripped of all illusions of power, is a voice for that which is essentially human, which brings us to a crucial point: the essence of myth, its language, is found where we least expect it, between systems of power, at a place where humanity excels.

Such a place Victor Turner has called liminal, after van Gennep's term *liminal rite*, which referred to rites of transition,[19] or rites of the threshold. These are rites which lie between rites of incorporation and rites of separation. Turner calls this liminal period a state of ambiguity in which past and future become superfluous.[20] This, I believe, is the formative state of myth, in which language *becomes*, so to speak, on a mythical level. Turner further discusses this liminal area as a place expressed by a rich variety of symbols, which means it is an essential place of language, since the prime function of language is to form symbols.[21] Since this place is fraught with meaning, although (or because) it is a middle ground or threshold, it is frequently likened to death, to being in the womb, to wilderness, to darkness.[22]

This is the area in which language becomes critical to the culture and to the individual because it is absolutely depoliticized. "Liminality, marginality, and structural inferiority," writes Turner, "are conditions in which are frequently generated myths, symbols, rituals, philosophical systems, and works of art."[23] It is the absolute level of creativity because it is the place where language is most powerful, is most seminal, because its interests are totally beyond the need to politicize, to build structures for their own sake; it is the place at which language revolves about its own essential nature, a place without a name, a place of absolute anti-structure, in which a crucial dialectic is formed with the culture at large.[24] It is the place where an I–Thou relationship between the individual and his culture is established, a place which (through language) binds the individual to his culture in a system devoid of politics.

This is why the neophyte in liminality must be a tabula rasa,[25] because it is at this place that he indeed learns not only a new language, but a language which contains the essence of his culture. In contrasting liminality with what he calls the status system, Turner constructs a series of binary opposites to express the difference between the threshold and the overt structure. He refers, rightfully, to the liminal state as an anonymous stage, its opposite being systems of nomenclature.[26] But it is precisely this anonymous state, this movement between, which establishes the depoliticized nomenclature most crucial to a culture—in this sense, the nomenclature of myth. It is an area of formation beyond the mytheme, where language in its totality incorporates that whose meaning is quintessential. It is through mythic systems, for example, that the vast array of life forms surrounding a culture are named, and thus given meaning.[27] "The savage mind totalizes"[28] not because it is constructing a world from mythemic units, but because the language of myth, spoken by the culture and developed in liminality, incorporates the world-view in an area devoid of structure, and thus devoid, on its elemental level, of linguistics. Liminality establishes communitas[29] because the liminal is a language state.

Community, as it continues as a structure and becomes the status quo, may become a political entity—that is, an entity whose structure defines its own meaning, but it remains apolitical as long as it derives its force from the liminal. The affinity of man for man, expressed perhaps most lucidly through his mythos, seems an innate, apolitical attraction—what draws man to other man as I-to-Thou is devoid of politics. Thus there is both a political force or power (perhaps best defined as a sense of historicity) and an apolitical, mythic force which forms communitas. The latter, however, forms the language of community; the former creates a power structure.

These systems may and do exist side by side, simultaneously in a sense. But they should not be confused. Historical systems (as systems of structural power) are only incidental to the force of communitas growing from liminality. Phases of history are only homologous to phases of liminality because a culture on the level of structure attempts to create a form which gives a secular voice to myth. This is not possible, but the two may be easily confused. When the power structure provides a pseudo-voice to mythos, we see the total exploitation and destruction of the myth, since it is wrenched from liminality and given political form. As Turner notes, "Time and history, however, bring structure into their social life and legalism into their cultural output."[30] What remains at this point is not *gesunkenes Kulturgut*, not a culture fallen from grace, but a mythic voice which has been stilled, a system of totality which has been politicized. Myth as depoliticized speech speaks to all men; nationalism is only possible within politico–historical systems. Because it is a voice which speaks to all men, liminality is "the Nay to all positive (or political) structural assertions."[31] Turner notes, "In human history, I see a continuous tension between structure and communitas at all levels and scale of complexity."[32] This is so, once again, because the historical system is a political system, a system for itself, a history *for*, not *of*, while communitas as it grows from liminality is a voice for all men.

In my opinion, the most brilliant spokesman for liminality, although he does not use the term, is Michel Foucault. In all of his works, Foucault sees the binding, driving force of culture as language. When a culture is exploited, when myth is transformed into a power structure, it is always through a perversion, a politicizing of language. Therefore, when we look above or below the threshold, the liminas, we do see forms of order,[33] but the order is an illusion of what is most deeply cultural. Thus, says Foucault, "it is only in the blank spaces of this grid [or form] that order manifests itself in depth as though already there, waiting in silence for the moment of its expression."[34] It is therefore this middle region, because it is language in essence, which liberates order itself, which gives expression to the actual values of a culture. "This middle region, then, in so far as it makes manifest the modes of being of order, can be posited as the most fundamental of all."[35] This middle region becomes the pure experience of order because, once again, it speaks for all men; it is language as actuality. It is "propertyless, occupationless, liminal."[36] But if the force to conserve outweighs the growth of anti-structure, if the historical, the national, the political take precedence over the liminal, myth is fragmented because its language is dispersed.

Liminality therefore contains and exudes the life of a culture. It is that area in which symbols are created, and these symbols are the language of myth. When symbols are transformed into, are exploited for, the political, then and only then is there a possibility for the historical. History and mythology are *always* antithetical. Prehistory becomes history through the exploitation of the liminal, the reification of a language for all men to a language for the few.

Perhaps it is impossible to establish a morphology for mythos, at least of the order Propp supplied the folktale with form. If mythos is the language of the liminal, the place where symbols are produced in the context of culture, then perhaps it has no appreciable form, since form itself involves the politicizing of events and feelings. At any rate, the language of myth cannot be quantified, since it is beyond the morphemic. Mythemes are therefore politicized units of a language. We can never analyze myth scientifically, because it exists only as symbol. It was Lévi-Strauss' euphoria for the computer which caused him to miss the mark, to look beyond the tissues of language to structural forms which only approximate mythos.

It was and continues to be that same euphoria, the urge to embalm texts, to transform the liminal into an icon of elitism, which has deified the Greeks. What we therefore have in the Greek mythology most of us know are historicized and politicized texts which form a status quo, a structure of absolute non-meaning. To approach the meaning of mythos, its language and therefore its world-view, we need to look deeply into the liminal, into the dark and fertile areas of meaning we have traditionally ignored. Both Jung and Freud have taught us more about myth than the structuralists, because they looked into liminality, a living morphology.

Until we approach the area between the ordering codes and reflections upon order itself, we will, as Turner says, "see only what we expect to see, and what we expect to see is what we are conditioned to see when we have learned the definitions and classifications of our culture."[37] We will learn little about the language of mythos until we divest ourselves of power, a politics of power, and turn to the actualities of language.

Chapter Five

Nihilism on the Plains:
A Language of Tradition

> The only being which can be called free is the being
> which nihilates its being.
>   Jean-Paul Sartre
>   *Existentialism and Human Emotions*

> It is the tyranny of hidden prejudices that makes us
> deaf to the language that speaks to us in tradition.
>   Hans-Georg Gadamer
>   *Truth and Method*

I have written elsewhere of the sweetness of the Canadian plains—
how I was thrust into that vast landscape by institutions of power, whose
all-seeing, all-searching eyes demanded an accounting of an immigrant
experience, of an experience likely etched in logs and their ordered symmetry in traditional houses. What I accounted for was quite different,
I find, from what I learned; the archive is largely a repository of misperceptions.

Out of the effusive Canadian experience, and quite apart from the
business of professional headhunter—data collector, chronologist of
culture—came a force which bushed me: the slow realization that details
are not cumulative, that the universe is only predictable insofar as we
demand it speak of predictability. As the innumerable details of my
plains experience began to die, to slowly recede into the oblivion of the
mind's archive, I began to realize how little of what I had seen and
done was important, important to me as a student of culture; in short,
I experienced a shock of denied sensibilities, a realization that the mind
subordinates on its own.

Figure 1: The unhewn log "L" house, built about 1890

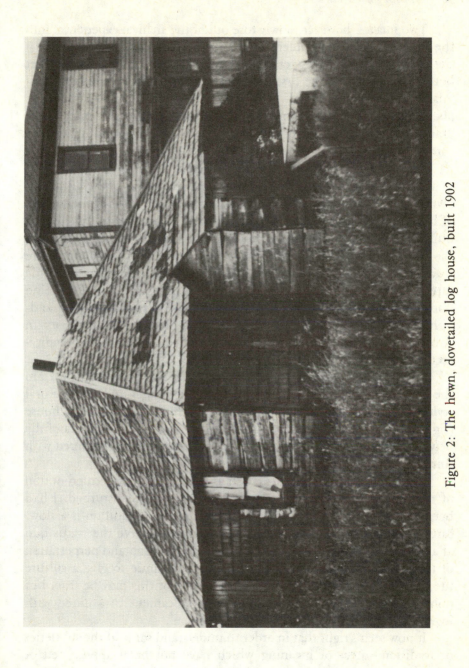

Figure 2: The hewn, dovetailed log house, built 1902

Two images, however, slowly rose out of the archival experience, into the realm of genuine problem; one I have called cultural invisibility;[1] the other is of a different, yet perhaps related problem. I lost sleep over both; I rid myself of the first only by writing about it—the latter still gnaws. With the expanse of years I have felt increasingly uncomfortable about an afternoon I spent in central Alberta talking with a man whose grandfather and father had built traditional log houses within a stone's throw of each other.

About eight miles east of Bashaw, Alberta, these houses stand, both in the process of decay, disintegration. According to Darrel Pearson, owner of the land on which the houses rest, and inheritor of the lineage of both the builders, his grandfather came to Alberta from Ireland and built the log "L" house (fig. 1) around 1890, shortly after his arrival in the New World. The structure is what most students of folk architecture would call rough: logs saddle-notched, unhewn, protruding rafters, wide interstices between the logs, which require much "chinking." Since no traditional horizontal log architecture exists in Ireland, Darrel's grandfather must have learned his craft of building from neighbors in Alberta; his structure is thus a product of immediate and perhaps radical acculturation.

Around 1902 Darrel Pearson's father built a log house not far from the one his own father had raised; but the appearance and architectural style of the two are virtually opposite. Darrel's father built a house (fig. 2) with a high hip roof. The logs in this house were carefully hewn and dovetailed, and the structure was evidently once covered with shingles. The son in no way built like his father.

Problematic here is the fact (then and now) that my accrued notion of tradition, its method and properties, was strongly disturbed. I had been carefully nurtured on assumptions which said tradition is a slow, careful, non-radical process which attempts to preserve the status quo at all cost; that culture was based on the accumulation and perpetration of traditional forms, forms which gave and continue to give a culture life, meaning, and an order of stability. Some of this may be true, but none of it, in my opinion, explains the predicament I was faced with in Alberta, which continues to haunt me.

It now seems right that in order to understand some of the subtleties of tradition—areas of meaning which have not been appreciated or interpreted—one needs to move outside traditional assumptions about tradition, which have perhaps become, more than the immense force of tradition itself, the status quo of traditional events. Alexis de Tocqueville, says Marshall McLuhan, "was a highly literate aristocrat who was quite able to be detached from the values and assumptions of typography. That is why he alone understood the grammar of typography."[2] Like de Tocqueville, we must detach ourselves from traditional notions of tradition, notions which are grounded in a thoroughgoing historicity, before we can approach tradition on its own common ground. Before this is possible, however, we need to examine, and when appropriate divest ourselves of, perceptions which hold us from genuine interpretation.

A striking reality one is immediately confronted with when "reviewing" the immensity of material in print which deals or purports to deal with tradition is that tradition is often viewed from a religious perspective, especially when associated with the Judeo–Christian universe. Actually, the terms *religion* and *tradition* often seem to be used synonymously. In an early work on tradition, one Christian apologist claimed that traditions are ancient doctrines with authority only slightly less than the scriptures themselves,[3] and that tradition in a broader sense means that the holy scriptures contain all things necessary for salvation.[4] The writer also suggested that tradition may be adorned with cultural politics when he claimed that true tradition is a great proof against popery.[5]

Centuries later, Jewish thinker Walter Benjamin said: "I am convinced that tradition is the medium in which the student is continually transformed into the teacher."[6] This is a rhetorically and culturally pleasing statement, but the force of tradition here is religious, a force which cannot extrude the teacher from a religious context. In Judaism (and this is certainly true in the millennialism of Christianity as well) religion came to be closely associated with history, and thereby with tradition. When Jewish tour guides in Jerusalem use the Old Testament as a topographical guide, as a friend of mine recently reported, they are viewing the land and its associated traditions as products of history.

According to one scholar, historical attitudes toward tradition by Jews have created some difficult and disturbing problems: "Secularism and historicism began to affect Jewish thinking, and the stable world of tradition" began to crumble.[7] Furthermore, "the attempt to understand the Jewish tradition from a historical perspective soon turned out to contain a major threat to the survival of that tradition."[8] Obviously, tradition and history are not necessarily compatible, and are synonymous only because we make them so, because we demand that they assume a similar posture toward the past.

Therefore, definitions of tradition which claim that its force, its cultural strength, "lies in its reconciliation of reason and experience in a *lived history*,"[9] oversimplify the meaning and importance of history, and simply supply us with a standard gloss which arms us, once again, with a sense of tradition, which is actually a sense of history. A sense of tradition, however, is not a sense of historical reality.[10]

There are also doomsday writers who would have us believe that one of the ills of modernity, the sense of alienation evident in the deification of juvenility, lies in "a disparagement of tradition and the values formerly believed to be implicit in a knowledge of history."[11] But history and tradition are not the same, and to attempt to restore the meaning of tradition through recourse to history is dangerous and subversive: Adolf Hitler's rise to power in Germany was accomplished by successfully confusing tradition and history in the minds of many Germans. If cultural change can cause a failure of the past to inform the future[12] (but not necessarily a corresponding loss of tradition), then the historical past is not tradition and is not necessarily traditional.

It is certainly true that tradition maintains a link, or certain kinds of links, between past and future, and that these relationships are vital,[13] but tradition is not history, although it has much to do with the past. Unlike history, tradition does not have a fixed or static quality,[14] but a confusion of the historical with the traditional may cause tradition to appear static, when it is actually a living, moving, changing force. Repetition does not imply stasis. On the contrary, the force of repetition ensures that a culture moves to fruition, not necessarily in a linear fashion—perhaps in a fashion which closely resembles the movement and change of biological forms. The habitual action[15] of tradition is habitual in the sense that it ensures movement, not that it maintains dogma in stasis. "The word *tradition* derives from the Latin *tradere* which means to transfer or deliver,"[16] the root-meaning of the word explicitly assuming continuous motion.

Likely, there are also limitless types of tradition within a context of motion. "We are beginning to see," writes J. G. A. Pocock, "that it may take place in a variety of ways and give rise to a variety of mental phenomena."[17] This because tradition is not based on or nurtured by the stasis of historicity, but because tradition and its motivations are based upon both the consciousness and the unconsciousness of the group, and of the individuals within the group, who are not subsumed by the group but who instead lend their voices to the establishment of tradition within the group (but not without the individual)—negation of the individual leads to a death of culture. It is surely true that individual behavior within a folk group is determined by and involves the family or the group at large,[18] but without the individual, tradition is meaningless. (I am referring to the individual as a biological entity as well as a spiritual entity; indeed, his traditional role in some cultures is more strongly determined by his biology than by his spirituality.)

In much printed material that claims to deal with tradition directly, the word and its implications are taken for granted. These studies are generally narrow and unilluminated in their approach and findings, because they fail to come to grips with tradition's essences.[19] This because so many "interpreters" assume that tradition and history are the same, and that to understand the history of a people is to understand their traditions. Unlike perceptions of history which read doom in repetition, the repetitions of tradition, divorced from systems of political power,[20] are not dooming, but redeeming. *Human* nature is a flowing constant in which man produces himself[21]—largely through participation in traditional processes and events.

Peter Berger and Thomas Luckmann argue that "the self cannot be adequately understood apart from the particular social context in which [it was] shaped."[22] An implication here is that tradition, in large measure, determines what the self is. This is not a historical process, but an anthropological one, for the authors later illustrate that only after "habitualizations and typifications" are undertaken in the common life of individuals do such typifications become historicized.[23] History, then, in basic human relations is an institution which is established after the fact, a politicized structure which reifies the past for its own sake, not for the sake of cultural movement and validity. It is not modernity nor the confrontation with newness and change which annoys tradition, but rather the process of historicity. Modernity and tradition are not antithetical;[24] the two are often congruent and mutually reinforcing, because the process of tradition is equipped to deal with the process of change. Tradition might be defined as the cultural accommodation of change. It is the not-said, the unstated force that ensures the survival of culture, an unconscious force which illuminates the experience of humanity.

According to Paul de Man, "Moments of genuine humanity . . . are moments at which all anteriority vanishes, annihilated by the power of an absolute forgetting."[25] Such a statement, it seems to me, is a lucid description of the force of tradition, a force which involves the dual processes of annihilation and forgetting. de Man goes on to evaluate such processes as a radical rejection of history, but claims that such a rejection is not only justified but necessary to the fulfillment of our human destiny and as the condition for action. The process of annihilation and forgetting is part of the language of tradition; we are blinded to it by our historical biases and our failure to seriously consider, on cultural levels, the immense importance of the unconscious. Such phenomena cannot be accounted for nor assessed by historicity. That is why "social order is not part of the 'nature of things,' and [why] it cannot be derived from the 'laws of nature.'"[26] Social order is determined not by the laws of normal history or normal science,[27] but by moments, processes, of genuine humanity. These moments are virtually always at odds with structures of rationality.

In the process of tradition, in which the individual is not forgotten, the focus of transmission wavers nonetheless between the individual and his society. What the individual abnegates to society is transmitted to all of its members—ideally at least. Thus, "no individual internalizes the totality of what is objectivated as reality in his society, not even if the society and its world are relatively simple ones."[28] This concept is significant because it clearly illustrates the prime necessity to cultural validity of what the individual cannot internalize, or annihilates and forgets. Seen in this light, this new light, the process of nihilism, denial and rejection, is one of the vibrant forces of tradition, is perhaps the most crucial part of tradition's speech, for without nihilation on the cultural level, stasis becomes the status quo; history becomes the prime cause or determinant of cultural action; and the culture moves to (or stops at) oblivion.

Berger and Luckmann have written perceptively of the meaning and importance of nihilism to the perpetration and establishment of culture.

On one level, nihilation is used to liquidate that which impinges upon the universe of the culture, thus in a sense denying reality to that which defies or defiles the universe. As such, nihilation becomes a mediating force between change and the perpetration of culture—that is, it becomes therapeutic for the culture at large, not as an establisher of stasis, but as a protector of cultural viability. Change is inevitable; nihilation controls and channels change so that it will not become unbearable, or so that the culture will not be destroyed from within or without. Say Berger and Luckmann, "Sometimes, alas, circumstances force one to remain on friendly terms with barbarians."[29]

Of course, recognition and establishment as literal imperatives are also important to the life and meaning of the culture, but nihilation is also essential to make sense of the individual's journey toward the great truth of living, vibrant, interhuman relations.[30] Ongoing destruction of elements and institutions within a culture are crucial to its well-being. However, nihilation needn't be radical—and in fact, from the point of view of the destroying culture, seldom is. Simply speaking, in order to remain healthy, the culture must continually prune itself. Without nihilation, the "network of face-to-face groups" of traditional societies[31] will disintegrate. In large part, it is nihilation which serves "to bring home to every individual his dependence on everything about him, and the absolute limitations that flow from this dependence."[32] Such limitations are only absolute, once again, in that they define the movement and purpose of culture. While the maintenance of cultural consistency involves the process of nihilation, so does the procedure of re-socialization, in which "the past is reinterpreted to conform to the present reality, with the tendency to retroject into the past various elements that were subjectively unavailable at the time."[33] Without nihilation, such a process would be impossible.

It may be argued, then, that nihilation is a crucial force of cultural maintenance, and I believe this complex force accounts largely for what I observed and experienced in Alberta when I was confronted with what seemed an enigmatic problem of radical cultural change.

I have no way of knowing the minds of the Pearsons who constructed houses of logs on the northern plains—I only know about them from what the buildings say.[34] I believe, however, that Darrel Pearson's father could not (not "would not") have told me why he did not build a house like his father's; few people have given voice to their unconscious, almost as few take it seriously. To ask a person to bring to consciousness what exists on a subliminal level is to demand a great sacrifice, a great expense of spirit. It is rather akin to asking a person why he has two legs: the answer will most often be couched in religion or theosophy rather than biology, because we understand little if anything of the intricacies of such problems. It is one thing to know we have two legs; it is quite another to know why. So Mr. Pearson might have explained to me that he wanted to do something different than his father did, or that he didn't like the shape of his father's house—or more likely, he would have no good, no rationally conscious answer at all; for what I believe he was involved in was the process of cultural nihilation, of saying with tools, and through wood, that culture must progress.

I am not describing a process of artistic innovation, although nihilation probably plays an important role there also. What I am describing is the other half of tradition, the half that demands the denial of certain cultural institutions in order for others to exist. It is quite possible, even probable, that Mr. Pearson was influenced by the smooth dovetailing and hewing of logs he observed in the products of Scandinavian and Eastern European immigrants, the neatness and coherence they brought to their buildings. But in constructing a building with strong Scandinavian antecedents, he was denying the tradition established by his father (even though that tradition had not been long in the land) as much as he was accepting another aspect of tradition in the surrounding built environment.

For years I thought this denial, this affront to romantic ideals of tradition, of the close, careful and loving work between father and son, was a puzzle without explanation. And I believe that from points of view which conceive tradition as a highly visible, highly institutional, thoroughly historical phenomenon, this puzzle indeed has no explanation. But when one views tradition not only as a careful building, but also as a careful destruction of events and forms within a culture, the puzzle has a solution. Nihilation is as crucial to the survival of culture (and therefore of the individual) as is overt affirmation; in fact, nihilation itself is an affirmation not only of those aspects of culture which are retained, but also of the process of change itself. It is the force of nihilism within a culture which accommodates the need for change, for transition, for movement into the world of cultural meaning: the world of traditional truth.

According to Berger and Luckmann, "The process of transmission simply strengthens the parents' sense of reality."[35] By "reality," they mean the historical and the objective, and they later note that the institutionalization of the objective and the historical have coercive power over the individual. I believe they are right in assuming that transmission, the movement of tradition, strengthens the parents' sense of reality, but I also believe that on the level of genuine tradition this sense of reality antedates the objectivity of external historicity—that it is this cultural force, impervious to the coerciveness of history, but in tune with, indeed partly created by, the life-giving force of cultural nihilism, that ensures a culture's continued existence within a world of change and great unsurety. Thus, the language of nihilism, if we listen closely, speaks as clearly and forcefully as the language of legitimation, of the building up of cultural verities. Change can only be accommodated by destruction; this is clearly evident in the nihilism of the Pearson log house, a force we can only understand when we divest ourselves of the tyranny of hidden prejudices, of the cloak of historicity that makes us deaf to the language that speaks to us in tradition.

Chapter Six

The Equilibrium
of Presence: Or the Unity
# of Bosom Serpentry

> The functionaries themselves told them that the
> legend of his strange illness was true, that he couldn't
> receive them because toads had proliferated in his
> belly.
>
> Gabriel García Márquez
> *The Autumn of the Patriarch*

Several years ago I attempted analysis of a phenomenon among American Puritans and Utah Mormons that I came to call bosom serpentry, largely because of Nathaniel Hawthorne's tale "Egotism; or, The Bosom Serpent," in which a young man is tortured by an unwanted guest living inside his body.[1] Before the article was published, I read it before a group comprised largely of folklorists and historians.

After my presentation, a friend questioned whether the phenomenon, condition, of bosom serpentry couldn't be explained through recourse to the wiles of the human gastrointestinal system, to the widespread malady of intestinal parasites. He went on to relate an experience of his own: he had eaten uncooked fish in Scandinavia, and had contracted, nurtured, a tapeworm which grew to an immense length; the creature he eventually passed (after beginning medication) resembled a serpent.

What my friend turned to in his need for explanation was essentially the whole Western system of rationality, a system which promises that all real problems of the human organism can be explained through recourse to science, to the careful, methodical explanation of the world we know, the world we touch and smell. And yet some explanations seem insufficient to cope with, appreciate, the immense pervasiveness of certain folk, certain mythological images. It is one problem to be able to explain, prove, that animals like frogs, toads, newts, lizards, sala- manders, snakes cannot exist, let alone thrive, in human gastric juices; it is quite a different task to explain why such beliefs, even in the face of modern science, persist. Yet they do persist, despite "our" protestations.

On September 26, 1952, a long-time Utah resident named Minnie Akelund Maxfield signed an affidavit in which she told of an experience as a young girl when she drank water from an irrigation ditch, felt something queer slip down her throat, and subsequently became very sick. Weeks later it became apparent (when she was taken to a folk healer) that she had a living being within. After being treated with certain remedies, both physical (blood root) and spiritual (prayer and fasting), she vomited up a snake, still living, which was five-and-a-half or six inches long.

Through the whole of Ms. Akelund's narrative are certain persistent motifs (length of creature, method of ingestion, method of expulsion), that accompany most of these narratives which have been dubbed "belief tales." I believe, however, that in our exuberance to label these tales, to codify and therefore clarify them within an empirical system we find pleasing and believable, we have overlooked crucial images or metaphors: metaphors which allow access to a level of meaning inherent in these narratives which interpreters have never approached.

Many of the tales of bosom serpents[2] (if not most) involve the mouth of the "victim," the serpent or serpent-like creature itself, and a body of water. Such tales and images are as replete in antiquity as they have been in recent times, the major images being virtually unchanged. In 1563 Englishman Thomas Hill, referring to Pliny and a famous physician, Marcus Gatinaria, wrote that burning old shoes in a garden would pro- duce a smoke which would dispel that type of serpent which enters men's mouths when they are asleep in the summer. These serpents, said Hill, have even been made to exit the body when subjected to this magical smoke, as was the case with a man of Flanders, whose "bosom serpent" left him via the fundament when the smoke of old shoes was administered.[3] Although a body of water is not a major image in this narrative, the mouth and the serpent are. In many of the tales, the serpent is enticed to leave the body by being offered a bowl of milk or a bowl of water, or occasionally certain other delicacies. Perhaps the enticing presence of a vessel of liquid has, in these tales, replaced the natural body of water. At any rate, the serpent is usually closely identified with liquid.[4]

Such identification persists in a Chinese folktale, "The Infection."[5] In this narrative, a young, beautiful girl is plagued with an infection which is manifest by disgusting open sores and foul breath. Near death, she develops an agonizing thirst; she drinks all the liquid she can find, but her thirst remains unquenched. Finally, she sees an old cracked wine jug into which a fiery red snake has fallen. She then drinks the entire contents of the jug, and collapses on the floor. A friend, Ma, thinking she is dead, places her on a bed. "Because she had drunk the wine and the snake," the tale runs, "the ulcers disappeared, and eventually she was cured."[6] As in other tales from various parts of the world, both ancient and contemporary, the serpent passes from or with the liquid into the host. Although the snake in the Chinese tale is an elixir of health, in most of the stories he is a parasite, but usually one who does not cause irreparable damage.

The association of serpents (usually sacred) with bodies of water is a persistent image in folk belief. Sir James George Frazer noted that "the Akikuyu of British East Africa worship the snake of a certain river, and at intervals of several years they marry the snake-god to women, but especially to young girls."[7] The phallic-nature of the serpent seems obvious in this tale, and is an important aspect of the bosom serpentry narratives. Frazer went on to relate that in a well-known world-folktale a monster, sometimes described as a serpent, inhabits the water of a sea, a lake, or a fountain. In some versions he is a serpent or a dragon who takes possession of the springs of water, and allows use of the water only if he is provided with a human victim.[8]

Frazer was clearly puzzled by the fantastic nature of these stories, as he insisted that it would "be a mistake to dismiss all these tales as pure inventions of the story-teller." They probably reflect, he speculated, a *real custom* of sacrificing humans to water spirits, who are very often conceived as great serpents or dragons.[9] Like most of the explicators of the phenomenon of bosom serpentry, Frazer attempted interpretation by insisting the tales must have antecedents in literal practice, that is, practice which has an empiricism and a history.

Lévi-Strauss, however, wrote of the belief being associated with sorcery in Australia—ultimately, the belief being totemic. In parts of southeast Australia totemism takes form as the "belief in mythical snakes which live inside the body of the sorcerer."[10] Since totemism is an insistence upon the ultimate compatibility (of the spirit and of the body) between man and nature, we begin to see another image, connection, between man and serpent, one that transcends political, empirical, and historical systems to assume a stance toward nature which denies the "discontinuity between man and nature which Judeo–Christian thought has held to be essential."[11] In such a context the serpent becomes a natural form (whether loved or feared) not necessarily foreign to the body (and soul) of the sorcerer. As Lévi-Strauss explains, "the zoological species appears as a mediating term between the soul of the species and that of the sorcerer"[12]—the purpose of the relationship being communion, an establishment of presence, a communion which, in its manifestations in folk belief, whether they be overtly totemic or not, has transcended, antedated, the political, the historical, and the empirical. And in such a transcendence, we see in the narratives of bosom serpentry a problem (need, desire, predicament) which totally defies Western traditions of rationality and perceptions of truth.

These narratives, then, lie like alien kernels of meaning at the heart of a culture which can no longer explain their existence, tenacity, because its tools of explication are forged by history and empiricism. Such dismal failure to interpret a cultural phenomenon, symbol, of a ubiquity and antiquity which astound, is clearly revealed by Michel Foucault in his landmark work, *Madness and Civilization*.

Dealing with the relationship between doctors and patients during the age of reason, Foucault discusses the confrontation of reason with unreason—a crisis, he says, "which marks the point at which illusion, turned back upon itself, will open to the dazzlement of truth."[13] At such a moment, or opening, the point is the suppression of disease. "A ruse," writes Foucault, "which surreptitiously alters the autonomous operation of the delirium, and which, ceaselessly confirming it, does not bind it to its own truth without at the same time linking it to the necessity for its own suppression."[14] What, then, is necessary for the illumination of truth (reason) is the suppression of non-reason (madness).

Foucault further notes that the simplest example of this method of suppression is the guise employed with "delirious" patients "who imagine they perceive within their bodies an object or an extraordinary animal."[15] When a patient believed he was inhabited by a living animal, the physician pretended to have withdrawn it; if the animal happened to be in the stomach, one could, by use of a purgative, produce a desired effect, and throw the animal into a basin without the patient noticing.[16]

Several points are crucial here: one who claims to be inhabited by a living animal is mad; the abode (for example, the stomach) is described in specific anatomical terms; and the cure is effected through a ruse. The "cure" produced here is, of course, one of historical and empirical application—and if the historical and the empirical are not, or cannot, be satisfied by the pathology of a preposterous disease, then the explanation was (is?) madness.

The problem with such an approach, both then and now, is that the reality of the bosom serpent lies beyond the access of historicity or empiricism; it is a reality which exists within the truths of dream, myth, and psyche, completely devoid of historical, political, and empirical antecedents; we deny such possibilities only because we have been taught to look for all answers within the confines of the Western system of rationality. Myth, however, is no respecter of systems, and continues to thrive despite the fact that it is frozen into texts of history and pseudo-literature by archivists and antiquarians. There is a level of liminality through which history and science cannot pass.

Remembering that the unconscious is not autobiographical, a point strongly made by both Freud and Jung, we move into the level of mythical liminality when we consider Freud's discovery that "many of the beasts which are used as genital symbols in mythology and folklore play the same part in dreams . . . above all those most important symbols of the male organ—snakes."[17] The penis, on the liminal level, has no history because it is not a historical entity. Assuming serpents, both in dreams and mythical systems, are phallic images, and that in such a context as bosom serpentry they may symbolize exactly a fulfillment of wish, their mythical meaning is of a deeply human and therefore ahistorical nature.

Like Freud, Jung related several dreams of his patients which involved the entering of the body by a serpent. One dreamer complained that a snake was stuck in her throat,[18] and another related a "fantasy" that "she was a snake which wound itself round her mother and finally crawled right into her."[19] Bosom serpentry on the level of the dream is an expression of deep human aspiration and desire, as well as fear. Jung claimed that "the unconscious insinuates itself in the form of a snake if the conscious mind is afraid of the compensating tendency of the unconscious."[20] The serpent then becomes a symbol of compensation, in a sense a symbol of the totality of presence, as is true among the Australian sorcerers. Implications here are profound: in the experience of the bosom serpent, no matter how the moment is expressed in folk belief, or mythology, an equilibrium of the spirit and the body is reached, in which the wish moves to fruition, thus joining the conscious and the unconscious.

This perhaps explains not only the tenacity of the narratives, but also their persistence into historical time: there is so little within the system of Western rationality which unites the conscious and the unconscious, that whatever attempts that union must be esteemed as invaluable. But the spiritual value of the bosom serpent lies not within the auspices of a historico–empirical mind-set, but beyond the entire mechanism of comfortable Western consciousness, which is why the narratives *always* seem insane, ludicrous, untrue.

The serpent, then, in the context of the essentially-human, is sacred and benevolent (although not painless) because he is the restorer of equilibrium, the guardian of the sacred waters.[21] Such a cyclical renewal, guarantor of equilibrium, was evident in the relationship in parts of Europe between the Serpent and the Son. "The Serpent, incarnate in the sacred serpents which were the ghosts of the dead, sent the winds." And subsequently the Son (who ushered in the light of the moon) was reborn every year, destroyed the serpent, winning the supreme Goddess' love. Appropriately, her love destroyed him, and from his ashes was born another serpent which, at Easter, laid the *glain* or red egg which she ate, so that the Son was reborn to her as a child once more—establishing the great round of renewal and stability.[22]

According to Lévi-Strauss, a similar possibility for the renewal of equilibrium exists among the Tallensi of the northern Gold Coast. This equilibrium is perpetuated through the renewal of a relationship between the living and the ancestors. "The python, for example, is particularly sacred in the territory guarded by a certain clan." It is a totem, and is protected not merely from prohibition, but because it is an ancestor, and to kill it would be tantamount to murder; this is true because the ancestors, their human descendants, and the resident animals are united by a territorial link.[23] Thus, "the ancestors . . . are spiritually present in the social life of their descendants in the same way as the sacred animals are present in sacred pools or in the locality in which the group is identified."[24] Clearly, the link between sacred serpents and sacred waters is one of prime importance in the maintenance of cultural, spiritual equilibrium; and the entry of the serpent from the water into the body completes a coherent round of totality, which may be seen as the entry of the phallus as life-perpetuator, but which symbolically establishes the importance and existence of an equilibrium that cannot, perhaps, be expressed in a more meaningful way, because here man and nature become one, a united presence.

When viewed as a problem of history, as a product of the limitations of both time and place, tales of bosom serpentry must be dismissed (as is true of much folk belief from the vantage point of empiricists) as chronological impossibilities, or as curiosities fondled by the wild imaginations of the *canaille*. When viewed as a problem of empiricism, there is always a logical explanation (within the auspices of Western culture) if we only look long enough, with real intent; thus by association, bosom serpents are actually tapeworms or other biological verities which the folk, in their charming way, have transformed into serpents.

However, when narratives of bosom serpents are approached on their own terms, on the level of mythic actuality, we find a vibrant equilibrium, a creation of cultural presence, inherent in the "play" between serpent, water, and human, a play which is so serious, so completely beyond the historical, the political, and the empirical, that it buttresses the very foundations of culture, of the human need to transform the universe to a perfect system of spiritual perpetuation, a system which can be constantly retrieved through the medium of the narrative, the language of symbol.

Chapter Seven

The Hero
as Cultural Mirror:
Metaphor versus History

What is a hero? The one who has the last word.
Roland Barthes
A Lover's Discourse

Perceptions of the hero have busied scholars for decades; the looming bulk of texts intending explanation, assuming solution, at once astounds and dismays. Yet only a scant few of these works have attained a degree of permanence, have endured the oblivion of old books.

One book of endurance is Joseph Campbell's *The Hero with a Thousand Faces*. Campbell continues to inform, because the essence of hero-ness cannot be discovered through formulae which reduce him/her to a series of propositions, but by philosophers in touch with the rhythms of humanity. "There is," writes Campbell, "no final system for the interpretation of myths, and there will never be any such thing."[1] Heroization, or the heroic process, is a living dance whose subtlety of movement and intricacy of desire have eluded the most persistent of scholars.

In the main, those who reduce the hero to a list of descriptive actions and predicaments function primarily as historians. In a plea for nationalism (which is always accomplished through historicism), one zealot wrote that "a nation that cannot evoke the spirit of its dead heroes and the birth of new ones, in a time of crisis, is doomed."[2] Such pronouncements view the hero primarily as a political tool to be used in times the moralist deems necessary, times during which a vigorous nationalism parasitizes the hero or the supposed hero.

Other perceptions may not focus so explicitly on the historical norm, but most, nevertheless, do circle the hero with an aura of historicity. One problem laid frequently at the feet of the hero is that of emulation—that is, can the hero be understood or judged by apprising the degree to which he inspires emulation? But emulation, of course, is a relative term based not only upon the values of a culture, but also upon the point of view of the interpreter. So when Roger D. Abrahams writes that "Anglo–American folk cultures in the United States have produced few figures whose actions call for heroic emulation,"[3] he is making a judgment based on his own perceptions as scholar, perceptions which place *emulation* in a historical context: the sweep of Anglo–American folk culture in the United States.

Later, Abrahams speaks of a list of characteristics which assume creation (elucidation) of the hero-grown-old; he claims that "these heroes are characteristic of a land in which there is no longer any frontier."[4] The very question of a frontier in America, however, has been and continues to be one fraught with historicism. Frederick Jackson Turner may have traced, with tools of the historian, the disappearance of an American frontier in 1892, but to Everyman, living in the depths of landscape, and defining his frontier by the backdrop of hill, forest, sea, or desert, the frontier persisted, as did his perception of the heroic. The frontier is a reflection of a mindset, not the number of human inhabitants per square mile. The hero in America has grown not from maincurrents in American thought, but from the deeper, more subtle maincurrents of American non-thought: the longing of mythos.

In a cryptic piece titled "(PC + CB) × SD (R + I + E) = HERO," Michael Owen Jones' formula for heroization includes a Credulous Biographer (CB).[5] Problematic here is the notion, which I will discuss later, of the biographer: biographers write biographies, which are histories, and there is no reliable, convincing evidence that the hero grows from, or is a product of, historical circumstances. Likewise, when Pete Axthelm says that "America has grown too rich, too confused or too sophisticated for heroes,"[6] he grounds his comment in the supposed historical mainstream, the nationalistic spirit which (for purposes of its own revival), views America as a place of decay.

Rather closely aligned with Axthelm's view is that of Orrin E. Klapp, who sees the hero as a "jack—to lift people above where they would be without the model."[7] Klapp is a religionist who views the "damned human race" as poorly equipped to save itself, needing the hero as bootstrap–savior. Other attitudes, perhaps not unlike Klapp's, focus on the personal attributes of the hero that will, in one sense or another, save the culture from itself, qualities "that we instantly recognize as true to human life and worth human attention,"[8] although some see the major task of the hero as "doing something a mortal cannot do."[9] Another writer sees the cowboy hero, part of a mythic construct of America's past, existing "in the first place because of a superior act of marketing."[10]

Northrop Frye saw the presence of a hero in literature as so compelling and essential that he classified fictions, "not morally, but by the hero's power of action."[11] This array of actions led, in turn, to a classification of five hero-types. Attempts to classify by enumeration have overwhelmed us with lists of heroes, traits, tasks: some of the equipage of the hero, but not the hero himself. Lord Raglan, despite the fact that his book *The Hero* spends virtually its whole length denying that tradition is history, is remembered and cited for his list of hero-traits. According to Raglan, "a belief in the historicity of tradition is the outcome of a wish to believe rather than of a critical study of the facts."[12] And, he concluded, those most consumed by the wish to believe were classical folklorists like Gomme and Lang,[13] scholars who, at all cost, attempted to establish and re-establish their romantic notions of the folk and of the lore, notions which led to the historization of the hero.

Ironically, we have been blinded to a most crucial slice of Raglan's hero-discussion by lists of what seem archetypal hero traits. But the traits, said Raglan so often, are meaningless if they are viewed as historical. Perhaps the reason most writers dealing with the hero attempt an image of hero-ness through construction of a list is due to the compulsion of historicity, the need to establish a perceived reality, a reality only possible within the hierarchy of a structure: which brings us face to face with an imminent question: does the guise of the hero present us with an *actuality* of historical suppositions, or the *verisimilitude* of mythic perceptions?

If, as I believe, we must deal not with a supposed historicity, but with the verisimilitude of archetypal, yet fluctuating, events, we must divest ourselves of the impediments which have kept us from seeing the hero in an image of wholeness, impediments which have substituted the list for the thing not-perceived.

Despite some rather apparent shortcomings in his work, Raglan attempted to at least stir the imagination beyond the stasis of his list, to perceive the hero as an anti-historical image, as a metaphor not of time but of being. "It should be clear," he wrote, "that the veracity and earnestness of a narrator and the vividness and verisimilitude of a narrative are no criteria of historicity."[14]

Our consuming passion to transform all events into the historical Raglan attributed to a lack of mental perspective, from which we all suffer. "We judge every event by its consequences," he wrote, "and assume that those consequences must have seemed just as inevitable to those who took part in it as they do to ourselves."[15] At the point of the hero, consequences *become* a set of historical propositions, which, in order to make such a magnanimous cultural phenomenon as the hero comprehensible, arrest him in time with a list. We cannot, asserted Raglan, separate our interest in history from our books.[16] History is the product not of time per se, nor of the past, but of certain perceptions frozen in print, encapsulated within the most formidable icons of Western civilization. Since the hero exists outside of books (but not outside language), he exists outside history, and the tools of history can therefore not approach the essence of hero-ness. And therefore, according to Raglan, "tradition never preserves historical facts,"[17] and "a belief in the historicity of tradition is the outcome of a wish to believe rather than of a critical study of the facts."[18]

A careful reading of Raglan's book soon shows him, I suppose ironically, to be a historian, to simply be about the business of proving that the folk are incapable of historicizing. We are, however, not dealing with the veracity of the memory of unlettered peasants (a memory Raglan sees as completely faulty), but with another way of thinking, a way of thinking which, unlike historization, has given birth to the hero. Heroes are imagined through a kind of thought Jung called "fantasy-thinking,"[19] which is spontaneous (and therefore vivid), effortless, unconscious, and subjective—a kind of creative reverie on the communal level. Through fantasy-thinking, heroes are given verisimilitude by being clothed with what might be called illusions of reality: illusions which through their own subjective reverie give life to what history can only kill.

Raglan provided a lucid example of this reverie in what he calls a "history of the Devil." Originally, says Raglan, the Devil was a ritual character who wore the horns of a bull or goat—perhaps a fertility image embodied in a divine king. Later, the horns came to stand for the old king, their actual wearer, rather than the new king, or future wearer, the horned man becoming the antagonist of the hero. "Eventually he stepped out of the ritual into real life, and became, what to millions he still is, a figure far more real than any historical character has ever been to anyone."[20] I am not so concerned here with the veracity of Raglan's ritual-assertions as I am their importance for the power of verisimilitude; it is precisely the Devil's lack of historicity, even in the context of Judeo–Christian doctrine, which infuses him with his omnipresent cultural meaning: he is indeed the most powerful and the most colorful member of the godhead. He is a product of the reverie of fantasy-thinking.

The same is true of other heroes (or anti-heroes?) as well. "The attempt to make Robin Hood a historical character," says Raglan, "not merely involves us in endless anachronisms and other absurdities, but renders the known facts of his cult completely inexplicable."[21] With heroes, history and politics create figments *for* the group rather than images *of* the group, but this distinction between the actuality of history and the verisimilitude of tradition has become incredibly blurred, since the veracity of historic events is one of the givens of modern culture. "There is nowhere any valid evidence to connect the traditional narrative with historical fact."[22]

Only a few scholars besides Raglan have glimpsed the transitory nature of history as it relates to the hero. Although he is wrong in limiting the perception-of-the-hero-as-historical-entity as an American problem, William Savage muses that "perhaps only in America would anyone suppose that heroes should adhere faithfully to history. . . . it is precisely the hero's remoteness in time which enhances his heroic image."[23] He believes the cowboy hero endures because he is "divorced from history,"[24] not because he reflects a historical actuality. Similarly, Paul Hutton has shown, at the point of George Armstrong Custer, that as the values of society change, so does its vision of history.[25] Since history as human actuality has no base of authenticity, Hutton should have used the term *past* instead of *history*. The past of fantasy-thinking changes because it is a past *of* culture; it becomes static only when it becomes a history *for* culture. "History was still blind when the first heroes prevailed,"[26] because the verisimilitude of the hero has nothing to do with history. The static reductionism of history can never move with the living dance of the fantasy-thought hero.

In his essay on the hero, Michael Owen Jones mentions the "persona demanded by the group"[27]—that is, the verisimilitude the culture has thought into the hero. The persona of verisimilitude is the main, perhaps the only, constant exuded by the hero, and exists in a timeless state of flux. When dealing with heroes of the recent past, flesh and blood still twitching, most interpeters assume the problems, the actuality, of this hero are different than with those long dead. It is a simple problem of confusing verisimilitude with the supposed actuality of historical events. In his verisimilitude, the hero is timeless because he is a mirror of the culture which has thought him into being.

The culture mirror, the thought perceptions of hero-ness, are not problems of time, but of the essence of human-ness. That is why the heroes both Campbell and Raglan described are strikingly the same from place to place: hero-thought transcends time; it is a problem of nascent metaphor. Raglan and others who have sought the hero through structures and unbending patterns have failed, perhaps partly because they see the folk as debased, as deriving their perceptions from the belletristic pronouncements of high culture, to deal with the hero as deep cultural metaphor. But that is what he is. Raglan committed a grave error when he wrote that "since interest in the past is induced solely by books, the savage can take no interest in the past; the events of the past are, in fact, completely lost." History and the past are again not synonymous; the past of the savage is metaphoric, not scientific. And it is precisely at this point that Raglan ultimately fails to illuminate the meaning, the essence of hero-ness: he is a historian to whom metaphor has no actuality. When he calls tradition fourth-hand evidence,[28] he continues to insist that there is only one kind of truth: that of the reductionists, who automatically equate history with fact. He sees certain beliefs of a ritual nature as being imported and localized "wherever there was a suitable site and a suitable hero."[29] In such a view, heroes are impositions rather than cultural images.

This mirror of the culture, this essence of hero-ness, is seldom one of perfection, of that which transcends humanity, but it always reflects endurance, the ability or curse to suffer beyond the bounds of normality. Thus Campbell calls the hero "the man of self-achieved submission."[30] The submission, of course, may be self-achieved, but the purpose of the submission is to illuminate the hero-thinking culture. It is through fantasy-thinking, cultural projection, that the hero becomes "the vessel into whom the ethos of a culture" is thrust,[31] not through an indigenous act the hero performs by himself. Personal traits are virtually unimportant for the hero[32] because he is an empty vessel, a mirror of unerring reflection.

But he is also much more than a reflector. According to Robert Plant Armstrong, "A sculpture, for example, may be asserted to have potency and thus to accomplish good, yet at the same time forcefully constitute the abstraction derived from the contemplation of the form or significance of a hero."[33] What Armstrong implies by "the abstraction derived from contemplation" is the sweetness of metaphor, the elusive profundity of what he calls affect, or an affecting presence. The affecting presence is a thing in itself,[34] self-contained, self-perpetuating, eternally asserting itself in our presence.[35] The affecting presence "is not a conceptualization, nor does it in any intrinsic respect refer to anything at all."[36] This is, I believe, precisely the meaning a hero assumes for his culture: the essence of the hero is profoundly metaphoric, with referent turning not outward but inward. The hero is so incredibly tenacious because he is the empty vessel filled with affect, with that essence a culture holds most dear because it is the ultimate product of fantasy-thinking, a reverie which creates a self-perpetuating elixir.

That is not to suggest that the process of heroization is artifactual, is one of stasis—it may only seem that way when viewed from the vantage point of historicity, from beyond the auspices of fantasy-thinking. The hero is so incredibly hard "to figure" because he continually eludes the strictures of static thinking, of thinking that would freeze him in time, thus endowing him with a historicity. Heroes are precious only because they are figures of affect, beyond (although closely allied with) even the immensely powerful cultural symbol. The hero is an empty vessel endowed with affective language.

Let us take, for example, a somewhat recent American hero who still seems close enough in time to be clothed with flesh and blood: Jesse James. There is little question that James has been one of the most

widely celebrated heroes in "recent" American experience. His heroization has been established in several narrative forms. Don Ward, in a
publication marking the centennial of James' death, writes that the
death of the hero-to-become "insured that he would become one of
America's best loved heroes,"[37] but he also puzzles, as do others writing
of the outlaw, that there seems to be no discernible reason why folk
imagination focussed on Jesse. There is no discernible reason for such
a focus because the process of heroization lies beyond the empirical–
historical, in the realm of symbol and affect. Jesse's alliterative name,
assassination by treachery, and other events may be partly responsible
for his widespread popularity, but his status as hero draws not from
historical circumstances and situations, but the affecting presence of
a vessel made full by the culture. The outlaw-hero is heroicized not
because "he must be endowed with traits that confirm his nobility of
character,"[38] but because of his ability to reflect inherent cultural values;
the process of heroization is "an expansion of consciousness and there-
with of being,"[39] not a process measurable in or by conventional time,
not of things become, but things becoming.

   Cultures move constantly, and their heroes keep pace with that
movement—mirrors shifting continually. Says Raglan, "The wearing of
an imitation sword may be just as significant as the wearing of a real
one."[40] Crucial here is the essence of sword-ness: not its actuality as
weapon, but its ability as affecting symbol. An essence of hero-ness is
perceived, internalized as symbol plus affect, which together form the
mirror. Heroes keep pace with the movement of culture through an
affective shift: the fluidity of feeling and desire, the movement of and
with the culture of a presence which illuminates its own being. The traits
of the hero, the enumeration of lists, arrest his movement *with* the
culture, and describe only that which is nonessential; these lists never
describe the affecting presence of a hero, nor do they approach a
metaphor of symbols. Symbols become only things when they are
historicized, and affect sifts unnoticed into oblivion. It is the affective shift that accounts for the immense variety of symbols, not the
enumeration of dead images. Heroes have much in common because the
human spirit, mind, and ethos are strikingly similar wherever they are
found, and these things are borne forward in the heroic vessel through
the affective shift.

In his insistence that the hero is a product not of the book, but of tradition, Raglan chides certain character studies which fail to recognize that words supposedly spoken by the hero "are not those of heroes but of poets."[41] Heroes have no words, yet Roland Barthes says: "What is a hero? The one who has the last word."[42] What Barthes assumes with the word *word* is not an entity of actuality retrievable by the tools of history, but one whose verisimilitude, moved and made imminent by the affective shift, continues to mouth the most profound values a culture can live through the experience of fantasy-thinking. It is this "grammar of symbols"[43] we must learn before we can illuminate and be illuminated by a presence of the heroes, an illumination which radiates beyond lists of reductionism and movements of historical exactitude to the metaphors of being.

Chapter Eight

Legend:
An Image in Time

It is necessary to possess the center of the image with our whole soul.
>   Gaston Bachelard
>   *The Poetics of Reverie*

Is the past a story we are persuaded to believe, in the teeth of the life we endure in the present?
>   Wright Morris
>   *Plains Song*

Whatever we had missed, we possessed together the precious, the incommunicable past.
>   Willa Cather
>   *My Antonia*

Legend descends from the Latin *legendus*, gerundive of *legere*: to read. To read the past, certain events in or of the past, seems the business of legend, of those narrative forms which continue to elude the grasp of those who would catalogue and classify—even interpret. There is no other narrative form, either oral or written, around which has accumulated such an immense heap of bland, obtuse discourse—a language that attempts to pickle living texts in a backwash of antiquated perceptions and sterile methodology. Legend, therefore, has assumed a death-image which threatens to choke and stifle interpretation, and which negates a crucial narrative form by forcing it into the ambivalence of historicity.

Scholars have been hesitant to call most legend "scholarship" what it seems to me to be: uninformed and unilluminated. This lack of honesty among interpreters has led to a severe problem: the continuous (and reoccurring) pile-up of bad ideas and shortsighted analysis, whose accumulation and reoccurrence clogs and obliterates the narratives. Thus legend scholarship, if it is ever to elucidate, must largely be a process of divestment, of the scraping away of layers of scholarly sediment.

Such problems have been evident elsewhere. For example, historians and purveyors of popular culture have so completely covered the American cowboy with layers of illusions and half-perceptions, that to know what he was, essentially, and what he did, essentially, are virtual impossibilities.[1] There are, I realize, many levels of the actual, but some seem to be only about the business of precluding interpretation. Very similar problems have persisted, shows Gary Witherspoon,[2] with perceptions of the Navajo. Scholars themselves, with half-truths and intellectual reductionism, have buried The Indian in dark layers of misperceptions.

Likewise, most of our assumptions about legend have been based on faulty premises. The formidable problem of narrative and its nature needs to be more fully and imaginatively explored. Before we can ask, What is legend? we need to ask, What is narrative?—and pursue the answer to that question tenaciously. In what is perhaps the most visible work on narrative to date, Robert Scholes and Robert Kellogg claim that "the evolution of forms within the narrative tradition is a process analogous in some ways to biological evolution."[3] There is, however, nothing compelling to cause us to believe that narrative forms have evolved like species within biological systems. Actually, Scholes and Kellogg's assumptions (even their use of the biological analogue) grow from the historical tradition which assumes that movement through space can be understood by charting a simultaneous movement through time, through a time which indeed is evolutionary, in which morals and ideals (and therefore language) progress toward, or digress from, a system of eminent worth: the time of historicity. These facts of perception are obvious when one considers Scholes and Kellogg's discussion of empirical narrative, which they divide into the historical and the mimetic. They say that "the historical component owes its allegiance specifically to truth of fact and to the actual past rather than to a traditional version of the past."[4] As I discuss in chapter one, a term like *actual past* is the most relative of perceptions; the *actual pasts* of the historians are themselves based on individual perceptions, not on the stasis of fact.

Scholes and Kellogg are correct, however, when they say that "inevitably the critic seeks to impose such familiar categories as myth, legend, and folktale on a body of texts which defies classification in such terms."[5] This resistance to classification is based on the nature of language and on the nature of society. Although Alan Dundes, I think, betrays a basic misunderstanding of narrative when he writes that "new problems in society create new legends,"[6] he nonetheless does recognize the fact that legend is not a static entity which conforms to narrow scholarly definitions and determinations.

Gary Witherspoon claims that "all cultures are constructed from and based on a single metaphysical premise which is axiomatic, unexplainable, and unprovable."[7] If Witherspoon is correct (and the work of other sensitive interpreters like Robert Plant Armstrong indicates that he is right), we may never construct adequate empirical approximations of what legends, or other narrative forms, for that matter, really are. Witherspoon also admirably shows that the axiomatic, cultural premise is language-based, is the point from which narrative emanates. Legend, finally, will not allow interpretation in empirical terms.

Such assertions, of course, call into question the value and purpose of traditional scholarship, not only at the point of legend, but whenever that scholarship approaches a language-based problem. What such scholarship attempts is the reduction of the problem to its component parts; if the problem has no component parts, as Witherspoon and others believe, what we are left with is nothing: a mound of icons which betray the very thing they promise to explain. Such reductionism is evident even in Scholes and Kellogg's useful book, when they write that "behind the epic lie a variety of narrative forms, such as sacred myth, quasi-historical legend [whatever that may be], and fictional folktale, which have coalesced into a traditional narrative which is an amalgam of myth, history, and fiction."[8] Folklorists and anthropologists are virtually always guilty of such reductionism on almost every hand; it has, unfortunately, become the major marker of the trade. Such statements as: "The informant [people become as mechanistic as their narratives] continually rationalizes his partial belief in the superstition, and the memorate helps him to maintain his belief. . . . the legend provides a definite place, a real family, and concrete details. . . . indicates the total degree of belief . . . provides evidence which . . ."⁹ betray a world choking on its own mechanization.

In one of her many publications about legend, Linda Dégh has written that one important trait of the type is its "tendency to be more communal than any other folklore genre in its compositon and performance."[10] I believe that communitas exists on several levels, but it is one thing to claim that legend is more communal than other narrative forms, quite a different (if not impossible) task to show such communality within the context of the narrative itself. Scholars persist in making nonempirical (unverifiable) statements under the cloak of empiricism. Richard M. Dorson was one of the worst offenders. In an oft-repeated claim, he wrote that "the vitality of American folk legends is directly related to the epochs of American history."[11] What is an epoch of American history? An epoch of American history is an event which exists in the mind of the historian, not in the geography of human events. It may be, seems to be, that legends incorporate a degree of the historical event, of historicity, of what seems to be the empirical truth of past events, of what is actually the human perspective of verisimilitude, but there is no reliable evidence that reveals legends marking time with historical epochs, just as there is no reliable evidence that shows there is such a thing as a historical epoch.

Other reductionist perceptions of legend range from claims that legends are more secular than sacred,[12] to archival deductions that "although extremely uneven, the records are adequate for broad generalizations."[13] It is not possible to assess the supposed sacrality or secularity of legends without dealing with the incredibly complex problems of their meanings and of time, problems which have occupied scholars like Mircea Eliade for a lifetime. We have uncritically accepted uncritical statements about time as truth when they are at best illusions; and claims that the evenness or unevenness of an archive can have anything whatsoever to do with deep and meaningful perceptions of any narrative form are another kind of illusion. Indexes and archives can be valuable for making possible the sense of an image, but by themselves they are valueless, and often very misleading, since we assume that when a group of homogenous narratives are assembled together they tell us something. Interpretation lies in the mind of the interpreter, not within the narrative itself, or in its collection.

Even Alan Dundes seems more concerned with the espousal of a method than in the interpretation of legends when he *preaches* for a psychoanalytic interpretation of legend. His statement that folktales are outside *true time* while *myth* and *legend* are in true time is as uncritical and in some ways as naive as William Bascom's statement quoted earlier. I seriously doubt that anyone has shown that such a thing as untrue time is perceived by people during a narrative event. Further, considering recent discoveries about time and the nature of the universe, is there, even in the empirical world, such a thing as untrue time? Surely, Freud himself clearly illustrated that dream-time, which is perceived on certain conscious levels as the most untrue and unreliable of times, is the most crucial and determinate of all times.

Some scholars, however, have pointed toward new and interesting directions the pursuit of legend-meaning might take us. Robert A. Georges, who cautions that we may be unable to see the forest of legend because of the trees,[14] dispels traditional definitions of legend (such as: a legend is a story or narrative, set in the recent or historical past, that is believed to be true by those by whom and to whom it is communicated) as unsound.[15] He notes that, on the contrary, "legends are frequently conceived to be remote or antihistorical rather than recent or historical."[16] He calls for a reassessment and re-evaluation of legend in which standard notions of *time* and *truth* are rejected. Such standard notions, as discussed earlier, remove us from legend interpretation, as does a rather persistent refusal by narrative scholars to deal with the deep meanings of language.

Américo Paredes sees legends as important because they provide "symbols that embody the social aspirations of the group."[17] Since language is symbolic and metaphoric (and therefore at least partly a product of repression),[18] and since legend is a narrative form, these symbols surely assume and portray certain elemental human needs and activities. But the interpretation of legend, if we take it seriously, must lead us back to the nature of language and of the narrative moment.

In his call for a new concept of legend, Robert Georges suggests we seek that concept "in the nature and structure of the sets of relationships that underlie and are implicit in what we call legends. . . . for legends appear to be metaphorizations of basic kinds of relationship sets."[19] I believe that Georges is right in his suggestion that legend is basically metaphoric, but wrong in suggesting that those metaphors are based on structural principles. Structuralism as a critical movement has not come to terms with the basic nature of language: structures do not reveal metaphors: expressions of repressions. To understand legend we need to approach the function of language in time, of the expression of metaphor as it relates to human events and subsequent perceptions of their meanings.

I resist a new definition of legend. Definitions are exclusive; they build barriers and boundaries where none exist. What I offer is simply a perception: legend is the establishment (or re-establishment) of an image in time. It may be that legends at their core embody certain primordial images that for reasons (deeply unconscious) known only to the culture, or which are known within the culture, portray and reinforce crucial metaphors; the sheer tenacity of the legends almost attests to this probability. If such images exist, and I hope to suggest that they do by discussing a particular legend, their re-establishment within the culture is crucial. We have, I believe, come to call the clothing of the re-establishment "history" because we are ill-equipped to deal with the fluctuation of images in time. We perceive them as being destroyed or discarded, while subsequently new legends are created, when they are actually only being refitted so that they may continue their metaphorization.

The Vanishing Hitchhiker legend, for example, can be clothed in the guise of goddess,[20] saint, young girl; legend is no respecter of persons because it is an image in time, not a historicized bit of narrative grounded in real or imagined empirical experience. Although Frazer considered legends false history,[21] his work nonetheless has transcended and endured—has moved beyond narrow limitations—because Frazer could feel a metaphor. The compelling force of *The Golden Bough* is due not to its immense accumulation of details, but to the image of the priest and the holy tree. His work is not historical, but metaphoric—and the same is true of legend: legends owe their tenacity to their images, their metaphorizations. When Jacob Grimm said legend has almost the authority of history,[22] he betrayed the fact that he, like most of his fellows even to the present, was a historian rather than a student of culture, not a student of language, not a student of metaphor.

Consider a specific, well-defined, rather widely collected legend like the Death Car. The basic narrative event in this legend involves the purchase of a new automobile and a subsequent accident in which the owner is trapped in the car and killed, yet the car is virtually unharmed— or the owner commits suicide within the car. Several days pass before the body is discovered; meanwhile, putrefaction leaves an odor in the car which cannot be eradicated. The car is sold, returned because of the smell, resold, returned . . . until a final image pictures the car, beautiful, new, undamaged, standing abandoned on the used car lot, unsold and unsalable. Although the legend has been widely collected, relatively little has been written about it,[23] when compared, at least, with the Vanishing Hitchhiker legend, which also involves an automobile.

There are other legends, seemingly grounded in the "distant past, the near past, and the real present," which are quite similar, metaphorically, to the Death Car narratives, not in their supposed historicity, but in their presentation of an image in time, the image being an expression not of the historical, but of the anti-historical. Thus, when Patrick Mullen claims that "establishing the setting [of a legend] in the distant past aids in maintaining belief in the legend by making it 'historical' and giving it an air of fact,"[24] he is discussing precisely what a legend does not do. Likewise, when Richard M. Dorson claimed to have discovered the real event, the primordial experience which led to the Death Car legend, he was speaking as historian, not as folklorist, not as one concerned with the nature of narrative,[25] for primordial experiences are not discoverable through empirical interviews or by a tracing of supposed historical events.

Although the Death Car legend per se is not recorded in Thompson's *Motif-Index*,[26] numerous narrative moments are recorded there, moments which do seem to embody the same image (established or re-established in time) which comprise what we call the Death Car legend. All of these narrative moments (motifs) associate evil, as the devil or a witch, or other ominous figure with a vehicle made by hands. The remarkable persistence of evil associated with man-made modes of transportation pervades the index, as though unnatural movement or conveyance (unnatural meaning that which does not exist in nature) is fraught with danger. That is not to suggest that things in nature are not associated with malevolence, for they are (E276, ghosts haunt tree; E278, ghosts haunt spring); but narrative moments involving vehicles usually involve evil of some essence or configuration, as though evil were defined in and made real by an effusion of motion.[27]

If it is the essence of movement which prompts the portrayal of the Death Car image (or vehicle) in time, then the legend has little to do with the automobile, but with the movement inherent in the vehicle built by hands. The death car itself may be a desacralized (because it is simply, at this point at least, a convenient cultural icon) image of the bewitching or of the essence of evil, the image in time being the narration of certain levels of evil: the vehicle the provider of movement, conveyance of verisimilitude in time. Thus, the vehicle undergoes constant transformations, not because of historical events, but because of the modes of conveyance a culture assumes, while the image of evil, the establishment or re-establishment of the image in time, is constant. The vehicle may be a cart, a wagon, a ship, an automobile, while the image remains a constant brought forward in time by the fluctuating forms of the vehicle.

And there is evidence that the forms of the vehicle continue to fluctuate while the image remains constant. In an article concerning what I called the Ghost Ship,[28] I rather naively discussed a legend among airline personnel which I now believe is not a new legend at all, but simply another fluctuation of the Death Car form, the image in time remaining constant. The legend involves a jet plane which crashes, killing several people, most notably the captain, who returns to haunt the plane after it is restored to service. The nature of the ghost depends on the nature a culture ascribes to evil, but as with the death car, death ship, and other vehicles in the sweep of human events, the airplane functions primarily to bring the image forward in time; it is not the image, only its vehicle, which, like the Death Car, ends its haunted movement by standing abandoned—in this case in an obscure hangar somewhere in the United States—after having portrayed not an image of the historical, but of the anti-historical, a primordial image re-established in time.

A flurry of motifs and micro-motifs surround the central image of evil in the Death Car legend and its blood relatives. These motifs shift, disappear, fluctuate, according to shifting cultural values and perceptions, but the deep image persists, created and re-created in time, the essence of a narrative event, an event encircled by and dependent upon an image of seeming indestructibility.

Chapter Nine

The Journey of Renewal: Cultural Migration as Mythic Event

> But all he wanted—all any of them wanted—was history of a certain order, like the scalps hanging across the hall from her father's things.
> Wright Morris
> *Ceremony in Lone Tree*

> The horizon is, rather, something into which we move and that moves with us.
> Hans-Georg Gadamer
> *Truth and Method*

Knowing why people move is not easy. Migratory habits of *Homo sapiens*, whether biological or epistemological, seem at least as complex as other species. The scientific study of the migratory habits of, say, birds remains only descriptive; yet we know more about why birds move, their patterns of fluctuation, than we do about the migratory impulses, patterns, paths, of humans. Virtually, even literally, all of the studies of human migration stand firmly ensconced in a view prompted by historicism, whether the view is assumed by historian, sociologist, anthropologist, geographer, or political scientist. About "peasant emigrants," William A. Douglass has noted that they have been treated by social historians and anthropologists as mindless reactors to uncontrollable circumstances, "and hence as victims of history."[1] However, views of migrations almost without exception treat all peoples and groups of peoples as victims of history.

One manifestation of this victimage leaps from the dehumanization of the person and his group by the very language of the human sciences. "Migration," writes one ethnologist, "has long been the subject of considerable sociological attention. The tendency has been to divide the study of migration into a few broad fields of inquiry although, in dealing with such a complex social phenomenon, these fields cannot in any sense be considered discrete."[2] All peoples and all migrations are victimized by the nascent historicity of such discourse. And within the context, the world, of such discourse, interpretation, let alone illumination, is impossible. Our very language betrays a sense of victimage that far outweighs the supposed laws and circumstances that govern the flow of humans from one place to another place, and this discourse confines them to a movement conceived in and determined by historical systems.

Another researcher writes:

> The data on which this report is based were gleaned from over 1500 detailed interviews with over 300 different African industrial workers in five South African industries located on the Witwatersrand; from observations, structured and unstructured, of over 1000 Africans at work in these same firms; from extensive discussions with all levels . . . ; from intimate personal association with my African research associates whose ideas as well as field work contributed enormously to my own insights into "African" industrial life.[3]

And yet he fails to show how or why the accumulation of these various data, which attempt to ground a complex human phenomenon in time and place, are consequential, how they speak an understanding of human migrations. Some researchers, however, have found "low correlation between migration and unemployment as well as levels of income where in fact a high correlation would be expected. . . ."[4] This essential inconclusiveness perhaps indicates that the essential meaning of human events must always elude the facts, that facts are illusions of measurement which portray the mind of the researcher, not the condition of the thing observed. Facts, under these conditions, become cultural and intellectual impediments. It is the *fact* that the historization of migrations embraces, and in which it attempts to fulfill its own illusion.

I have little doubt that, at least in the Western world, "migration, especially in modern times, is a major symptom of basic social change."[5] But I do doubt that those systems of social change can be understood by charting the course of historical events, by measuring an illusion of reality rather than feeling the pulse of a significant human event.

E. Carpenter told of an Eskimo woman who, in 1772, stole passage on a vessel, alone, essentially starving. When found, she was engaged in the production of "art"—of material symbols. Even when life seemed reduced to nothing, the artistic remained essential.[6] It is such motivations and activities as these that empiricity cannot account for. Likewise, in modern culture the phenomenon we call genius—radical departure from accepted norms of action and intelligence—cannot be accounted for by a systematized study of the body or the mind: genius is non-rational, and yet it assumes the highest degree of rationality modern culture can "experience."

Such paradoxes are always evident in genuine human problems—historicism and empiricity make them seem homogenous. When an immigrant, cultural migrant, said after moving from Europe to the New World that "our imagination had run away with our judgement," the glamour was gone, they were left with nothing but a piece of land from which nothing could be coaxed except by the brutality of labor,[7] he was speaking not of a history, nor of an empiricism, but of a mythological problem exuding from the essence of an immigrant experience.

Striking a similar note, one scholar of migration says: "It will be appreciated that such a transfer en masse [a cultural migration] to a different geographical environment is always very difficult."[8] He is right. The intensity of migration is responsible for a cultural despair we may never understand,[9] but the difficulty lies in problems of the spirit, not in problems of chronology. Problems of migration are so incredibly difficult because, like major alterations in the *individual* human spirit, they require mythologizing and transforming—perhaps the creation of a new crowd symbol,[10] but certainly not an assumption of historicity.

Several years ago I "conducted research" among a cultural cross-section of Utah Mormons concerning what I came eventually to call their migration myth.[11] As I glance through the modest publication which issued from that study, I find that in spite of the fact that I used terms like *myth* and *folklore*, I was really writing as a historian, as one who saw in the western migration of persecuted Mormons a chronological rather than a mythological event. I was mistaken. My method was to compare the facts of history with the illusions of mythos, when I should have weighed the manifest fictions of history against the verities of the myth.

One of the most widely shared cultural verities among Utah Mormons (and perhaps others world-wide) revolves about the coming of the first group of Latter-day Saint pioneers to the valley of the Great Salt Lake. Mormons believe that Brigham Young, prophet and leader of the first party to enter the valley, uttered the words "This is the place," upon first seeing the valley unfold from his vantage point on the mountain. At the mouth of Emigration Canyon, just east of Salt Lake City, through which the group passed late in July 1847, stands a shrine called "'This Is the Place' Monument," commemorating the prophetic utterance.

Besides the murder of Joseph Smith, the entry into a valley of vision and prophecy is likely the major mythological event in Mormonism. Despite literal icons of the historical, which persist in journals and official church documents, it is the mythology of world-view, the establishment of a new *axis mundi*, of a new Zion, which persists in the narratives of Mormons about the event. A rather widely lauded economist–geographer–sociologist, George Kingsley Zipf, proposed a theory which was assumed to account for human migrations. According to Zipf, "Every individual's movement, of whatever sort, will always be over paths and will always tend to be governed by one single primary principle which, for want of a better term, we shall call the *Principle of Least Effort*."[12] It is true that in human and animal nature, in times of peace and even in times of certain crises, well-worn paths of flight or concealment are taken, but in times of duress, times which lead, perhaps, to the major migrations among humans, the principle of least effort, arrived at by the empirical systems of a mathematical culture, is false.

Mythical migration, as with the Utah Mormons, the American Puritans, the Children of Israel, involved the principle of supreme effort: the re-establishment of a new identity in a new land, problems which can only be overcome through systems of mythical perceptions. The abandonment of familiar habitat and familiar trails involves a sacrifice incalculable in terms of dollars or miles traveled; the loss of the familiar produces a death of spirit; that death of spirit can only be overcome through the revivification of mythos, the re-establishment of a cultural identity which completely transcends history and economics.

It is not surprising, then, that the myths (or legends: images established in time) revolving about cultural migrations are the most sturdy and revered of any a culture holds dear. And from the vantage point of mythos, there are striking similarities between and among the migration narratives of various cultures.

Mythological migration is certainly "the main mechanism of adjustment"[13] to the terrors of new places (the Desert West, for example) and new ways (the necessity, perhaps, of irrigating crops). But an important element, mytheme,[14] in cultural migration is the non-denial of the place left—what may be usefully described as the longing for the womb, for the place of sustenance which has been left behind and which can never be wholly regained.[15] For American Puritans the womb was England; for Utah Mormons it was Jackson County, Missouri. Among certain West Indians who have migrated from the womb, a belief persists that "they will return home some day and this belief determines their relations with those remaining behind" and thus affects the whole community.[16]

The longing of Mormons for a mythical Jackson County, Missouri (where they suffered severe persecutions), in which they will reign supreme, and in which they will etablish a New Jerusalem, is a crucial mytheme, cohesive unit, in the overall mythos of the migratory experience. The infamous Mountain Meadows Massacre, in which Utah Mormons massacred a wagon train of Missouri immigrants en route to California,[17] and which historians have been rather unsuccessfully trying to reconstruct and understand for decades, is a violent manifestation of one mytheme: the desire to return to a womb-space, and to there regain eternal communion. If the mytheme involves a vision of Mormons as the sole inhabitants of part of Missouri, then the elimination of not only the persecutors, but the soon-to-be-displaced, seems a natural, forceful, fleshly-real implication of the myth. The call to Zion, both into the West in the literal migration as well as the projected movement backward into the womb, is responsible for one of the most spiritually intense migrations of relatively recent times. But, again, this movement becomes lucid when viewed from a perspective of mythos; it becomes opaque when glimpsed through the mists of historical reductionism. Perhaps such a view of forward and backward, of literal and spiritual migration operating in counterpoint, can be created and sustained, held in eternal and meaningful balance, only "by a tradition of unhindered migration."[18]

There are other crucial mythemes which pervade mythological migrations. In an insightful book published in 1884, Albert S. Gatschet wrote
explicitly and perceptively about mythological thinking among the various
groups of the Creek Indians. According to Gatschet, the Creeks possessed
what he calls pictorial or ideographic writing on tanned skins to perpet-
uate the memory of "historical facts" such as epidemics, tribal wars,
migrations. Although Gatschet obviously viewed past events in Creek
culture as essentially historical (a view very difficult to avoid, since
modern culture dictates a worship of history), he nevertheless provided
some of the most essential material in print about the nature of mythic
migration. Evidently, the Creeks transmitted certain "facts" to their
posterity through the identification and manipulation of certain beads
arranged on a string. "Only the principal events," writes Gatschet, "were
recorded by these beads, and without any historic detail; hence, a
single string often sufficed to recall the history of twenty or twenty-five
years."[19] Gatschet refers later to the beads as "national archives."

Meaning of a mythic event among the Creeks was not assumed by
a careful recounting of specific "historical" detail, but by a symbol of
the past, a mythemic icon, one which could retrieve the events of the
past, making them re-liveable. One record kept by the beads was that
of the emigration of the Creeks from their ancient cave homes along the
Red River. Belief in the veracity of the beads, in their ability to call or
recall an image from the past, was so strong and omnipresent among the
Creeks that an ethnologist, Milfort, "at the head of two hundred Creek
men, undertook an expedition to that renowned spot, to gratify himself
and his companions with the sight of the place itself from which the
nation had sprung forth, and all this solely on the strength of the belief
which these bead-strings had inspired in his companions."[20]

This belief of origins among the Creeks, of what the beads assumed,
portrayed, and could recall, seems a precise analog of the persistent
Mormon belief in "This is the Place." The national archive among
Mormons, the mythological repository of significant cultural events,
impervious to the manifestations and inroads of history, expresses itself
in the utterance: "This is the Place." Like the string of beads of the
Creeks, this utterance, this word, establishes the *axis mundi* of the culture, the place of beginning, the site of cultural validity. The event is
not historical, but mythological.

Because cultural migrations are mythological rather than historical events, they remain indelible in the folk memory.[21] If the event is expressed through the form of legend, it becomes an image established in time—one absolutely unaffected by changes in the *historical* milieu. If the event is verbalized as myth, the place between the ordering codes and reflections upon order itself, it becomes a cultural verity which will last until the culture is destroyed. These predicaments of human movement are as difficult to understand, rationally, as the circular journey of the mythic hero. The *lived providence* of the Mormon migration west, the movement of belief across a landscape of non-meaning, requires the keys[22] of mythos, not the tools of history, to be understood.

"There are peoples and individuals who will not give credence to a legend which does not contain miracles."[23] This is true both of the savage mind of the Southern Creeks and the mainstream-American, modern mind of educated Mormons. Mythology, clearly, is no respecter of persons. To Mormons, the migratory event is a moment of revelation, not a problem of history, and attempts to understand and come to terms with that movement through historical antecedents are impossible. The "national archive" of the folk is not based on orderly systems of cataloguing and retrieval, nor on the completeness of the visible archive; it is based on the fluidity of mythic perceptions and convictions, convictions growing from the verisimilitude of a landscape which in every particular reinforces the movement of belief.

Perhaps the single most important event which has kept Mormons and Mormonism from being totally engulfed, obliterated, by the status quo is explicit belief in the veracity, the spiritual veracity, of the Migration Myth. The myth itself establishes a tangible but fluctuating area of liminality, a horizon into which the people move, and which moves with the people, a place totally removed from the historical and the empirical, a mythical island in a sea of rationality which, boundless and limitless, accommodates a world-view and a perception of the past totally rejected even by documents of sacrality held dear by the group itself.[24] In its non-respect for power and chronology, the movement of mythos is a prime validator of cultural identity, a fixer of the cultural landscape.

Chapter Ten

Manifest Destiny:
The Landscape as Text

The past defines the present because mankind has not
yet mastered its own history.
Herbert Marcuse
Eros and Civilization

In the United States, there is more room where
nobody is than where anybody is.
Gertrude Stein

Is it Ulysses that approaches from the east
The interminable adventurer?
Wallace Stevens
"The World as Meditation"

What a landscape becomes is what a country is. And a country is a
slough of ideologies. This is nowhere clearer than in the ideology of manifest destiny, which defined (and defines) a nation and its -isms, the
thrust of meaning. Looking for roots, for *the* roots of the chilling term
manifest destiny, is a search of some confusion. If one reasons, with
Vladimir Propp, that origins are confused, even nonexistent, without a
morphology,[1] the shape of meaning, then one will not expect to find
comfortable antecedents before one discovers meaning, or a set of possible meanings. But the search for origins continues unhindered. We are
engulfed in a circumstance which allows no view either forward *or* backward, because origins are, perhaps, existent only and important only
within the context of historicity.

In an article on the origins of manifest destiny, Julius W. Pratt concludes, or at least the evidence he presents concludes, that the origin of the term is unknown. Pratt says the phrase passed from journalist John O'Sullivan into "the permanent national vocabulary,"[2] but evidence about beginnings is obscure. This article exudes the inability of the historical method to illuminate origins of meaning. Therefore, historians date the term to the 1840's, because of a rash of editorial frenzy, which, about that time, attempted to create a national mood of expansionism,[3] a mood which the popular press had striven to transform to a national conscience decades earlier. "It belongs *of right* to the United States," wrote the mood-creators, "to regulate the future destiny of *North America*."[4] Manifest destiny, or one of its most visible components, religious nationalism, lives here, although it is not called by name. But history finds the birth of manifest destiny in O'Sullivan's editorial in the *New York Morning News*, December 27, 1845.[5]

The problem with manifest destiny is that it won't stand still. It won't stand still because it is a motion, a direction. It is not a *thing* existing in time, but a projection into spaces which are clearly transcendent; by its own nature, it resists being frozen in time, which is why it is so difficult to approach historically. The projection of a manifest destiny is given voice: "With the valleys of the Rocky Mountains converted into pastures and sheep-folds, we may with propriety turn to the world and ask, whom have we injured?"[6]

Attempts to reduce manifest destiny to supposed component parts, to a "vague, uneasy sense . . . of an insufficiency of good land,"[7] or an upsurge caused by economic distress,[8] simply further the reductionism of stuffy historicism, of assumptions which claim that the whole of existence is reducible to a set of verities, when in actuality, although we sense the importance of, the crucial meaning of, manifest destiny, "effective methods of analysis and tools of inquiry for dealing with it have not been adequately developed."[9]

The development is slow in coming because we continue to circulate and recirculate old ideas and old methodologies. Frederick Merk, in a work which seems to have the final historical word on manifest destiny, claims that the problem can be explained through recourse to history. Early in his work he quotes Santayana from his *Life of Reason*: "Those who cannot remember the past are condemned to repeat it."[10] But one yearns to ask: What does "remember the past" mean? Do we remember all of the past, or those parts which best serve us? Do we remember the past as it affects us directly, as it bites our very flesh, or the past removed and abstracted to other times and places? Or do we remember the official past of the status quo, the past of libraries and museums—the past of the sarcophagus? Santayana was wrong. The past, the historical past, holds no pieces to the puzzle, at least not the puzzle of actualities and living human problems. Dwelling in the historicity of past experiences blinds us to the verisimilitude of the moment and to the great uncertainty, not the mathematical surety, of the future.

Or when the historian with his discourse enters the manifest destiny of his colleagues, he becomes like the nationalistic journalists of the nineteenth century: his language betrays him, shows that in remembering the past he is doomed to eternally relive it through the rhetoric of the status quo: "[Manifest destiny] is still the beacon lighting the way to political and individual freedoms—to equality of right . . . of economic opportunity, and equality of all races. . . . [It is] the torch held aloft by the nation at its gate."[11] Here the past is a rhetoric, in which the historian resides. When he defines the language of manifest destiny as that of "dedication to the enduring values of American civilization,"[12] he assumes the role of politician. And what are we asked to make of all this? What are we expected to believe of the gospel of manifest destiny? And what is it we will be doomed to relive if we do not remember this rhetoric? I try to remember this language, this voice, and still manifest destiny eludes me. It is a projection whose presence shrinks as I search for it in the reduction of historicity, in the promise of origins where origins disappear into a surety of a chronology.

Merk writes that "the manufacture and dissemination of propaganda has been a major industry throughout history."[13] But it is, perhaps, only within the context of a history, the past *for*, not *of*, a group, that propagandizing is possible, that nationalism, politics, desacralized religion, and technology determine the thrust and meaning of past events. That is the destiny "found written in every page of our history";[14] *that* is essentially our history, be it writ about destiny that is manifest or otherwise. Or consider discussion of the manifest destiny that sees "the virtual disappearance of continentalism from American *thought* after 1848."[15] We are, however, not concerned with a problem of American thought when we approach the vastness of manifest destiny, but with American non-thought, with a cultural force which cannot be quantified and analyzed by traditional means, especially the means supplied by historicity, the perversion of cultural events (be they delightful or terrifying) into a Sickness unto Death, a process which imposes nationalism and politics onto the fluid movements of a culture, movements which defy historical analysis. Manifest destiny only becomes American history upon our insistence.

If, as Sacvan Bercovitch and others have suggested, the American Puritans are responsible for manifest destiny, then religion, the European fundamentalism (fundament: ME. *fuundement*: a base or foundation; the buttocks; the anus) imposed upon a landscape forced to speak of God and of the Devil, was nationalism, and Cotton Mather's invective against Satan, his claim that the landscape was to be sacralized with nails, boards, knives, and grains of salt,[16] amounted precisely to the transformation of landscape into a problem of manufacture, a problem of nationalism. But manifest destiny lies beyond the blatant nationalism of desacralized religion; as a cultural force, it has escaped the Sickness unto Death, the transformation of a cultural event into a historical problem. Religion has become history, and cannot be trusted, in its coupling with technology and economics, to unravel the problem of cultural thrust. Only the superficialities of expansionism, or of manifest destiny, are associated with crusading ideologies.[17] The essence of a mythological problem is impervious to nationalism. When propagandists viewed the wrenching of Texas from Mexico as a resonant part of a grand "plan, favored by God, for North America,"[18] they simply resorted to the tricks of god-finding, not to the deep meanings of culture. Manifest destiny is not a product of nationalism, but when viewed from a historical perspective it becomes nothing else.[19]

And views of manifest destiny which force it to a crusading image of "the elevation of neighboring peoples to equal statehood and to all the rights and privileges which that guaranteed"[20] show clearly the simultaneity of history and nationalism. And religion, history, politics, and nationalism become one in statements of manifest destiny as essentially "the *doctrine* that one nation has a preeminent social worth, a distinctively lofty mission, and consequently unique rights in the application of moral principles."[21] Again, the rhetoric. And we must remember that the intensity of religious fervor may have nothing to do with mythos. That is, pronouncements about God and mother-country are vestments of the history *for*, not the history *of*. National idealism,[22] despite protestations to the contrary, is in fact economic, social, and political. Cultural idealism may be none of these. And terms like *natural right*[23] are so blatantly self-conscious as to obviate all cultural meanings. Cultures do not perceive natural rights, they strive simply for that which in their mythological context is natural, is unself-conscious, is equilibrium in its essence. Nationalistic theology[24] is just that: politicized (and therefore desacralized) religion. Expansion was only rationalized[25] insofar as it became a historical, not a cultural, problem. Only when viewed as a historico–nationalistic "entity" does manifest destiny suggest that "the American people were destined to extend their democratic principles over the North American continent."[26] Even Ralph Waldo Emerson was afflicted by the disease of nationalism when he wrote: "We are sent to a feudal school to learn democracy," or "There is a sublime and friendly Destiny by which the human race is guided."[27] The friendly destiny, although unstated, was the expansion of Americanism.

When traced as historical phenomenon, manifest destiny manifests other symptoms of the disease. In the strict (and historicized) context of a working place, it may simply equal racism.[28] Or when viewed from a pinnacle of exuberant technology, manifest destiny is literally elevated to the prophetic. Technology is the whore of "modern" nationalism. And thus: "Of major importance in the growth of Manifest Destiny were technological changes, including those that transformed transportation and communication."[29] In a sense, then, the machine did not *enter* the garden,[30] the machine *made* the garden of nationalism.

Technology's illusions were manifold, and were the most concrete expressions of the national sickness. "The success of Morse's magnetic telegraph," writes one historian, "fired the public imagination. It drew from President Tyler the awed exclamation: 'What hath God wrought!'"[31] Tyler's rhetoric of transformation was certainly to the point. What God, of course, had wrought was history, nationalism, politics, religion, and technology. Tyler's statement better than any shows that a sense of historical destiny was, in every particular, a sense of illusion—illusion of the sweep of landscape, and of culture clinging to the face of that land. The Sickness unto Death embodies a refusal, a denial, of the cultural problem, a denial of interpretations of the past which find a sense of that past in the rhythms of mythos. It may, therefore, be that the *program* of manifest destiny was never consummated, since the supposed program was a shout of nationalism. The program was not consummated in the flesh: the United States did not engulf and become engorged upon all lands within its reach. But manifest destiny as projection, as *the myth*, was and is being consummated in the spirit.

This sense of projection, the essence and lasting face of manifest destiny, is manifest in several ways and in several places. If the New World was seen by religionists or others as "a new earth for building a new heaven,"[32] the landscape is obviously being transformed in an image of newness. This projection of newness, of heaven and earth, into a wilderness seems meaningfully different from the rank politicization of God by Mather's economic pronouncements. It is this expression, this projection of newness into a landscape, that kept America facing westward, despite the fact that "the Goddess of Liberty faced eastward."[33] Ironically, the East remained the hope of morning, the place of beginnings, while the West bore the projection of the mythos of manifest destiny, a destiny consumed by an unending movement, motion, a motion historians may trace as "periodic peaks of enthusiasm,"[34] but which persisted in its flow from east to west. Perhaps this projection was a continued movement to unite disparate elements, not to engulf them— as, perhaps, the original colonies were once united for, at least we may believe, a mutual commiseration. If so, a national problem like the Civil War was not a war of economics, manufactures, nor of slavery, but a conflict of manifest destiny, a destiny, which if abandoned, would destroy the cultural exuberance of the projection. It is true that the united colonies had a common language, and that manifest destiny spoke English, but the projection of motion onto the landscape was a dialect of meaning thoroughly mythological—a new tongue for a new land, not a land of literal politics and technology, but a land accommodating the motion of projection inherent in manifest destiny.

Take, for example, the enigma of the magicians: Lewis and Clark. Their movement *up* the Missouri River, into the West-of-promise, was not a historical but a mythological event—at least in its importance to a cohesion of motion. Neither Lewis nor Clark, as their journals attest, was more intelligent, benevolent, farsighted, or enthusiastic than other explorers. But they were seen as the first, as the projectors of a mythology onto a landscape that existed long before O'Sullivan. Lewis and Clark were magicians, not explorers, because they were at the liminal point of the transformation. No perception of or by the historical can account for the impact they had on the landscape of manifest destiny, because they were living emissaries of the motion of projection. Their journey and return "completed" a mythological round as real and as meaningful as the hero journey discussed by Campbell.[35] The elixir they brought back to the culture that sent them was, simply, proof of the efficacy of motion, not the riches of a technological–economic world.

There were no limitations to the possibilities of motion called manifest destiny, and views which attempted to limit them in a geography[36] were simple politicizations of the mythological, by those who were blinded to the cultural possibilities of landscape by the actualities of a world thoroughly historicized—the Sickness unto Death. People were so thoroughly transformed by the novels of Cooper, by their projections, because he wrought a cultural transformation similar to Lewis and Clark's: he reaffirmed the boundlessness of the motion. Landscape became, was becoming, not mere commodity, but a passage to a mythological world. We were all overwhelmed (Thoreau, Twain, Emerson, others) by the boundlessness of unending motion, and we could only give it speech through the eyes of historicism, from the vantage point of the icons of a desacralized universe in which we had grown accustomed to the absolute limitations of all events. We imposed a death-experience on the terrors and the joys of the boundless, not totally unlike the death-experience imposed upon Jews by operators of the crematoria. Jews refused to accept a world of narrow cultural boundaries.

One German writes that a doctrine is essential to every people as their *Daseinsberechtigung*—the doctrine of a national mission.[37] He is right. But there is profound difference between the rapaciousness of nationalism and the projections of mythology. Not that mythos is not a destroyer. It is. It is as it works its ethnocentricity. But the elixir does not fatten bank accounts; it enriches the consciousness of a people. The movement west (west being not so much a place as an illusion) was and is a national mythology. The movement was not land hunger[38] (although that seemed one of its manifestations); it was a hunger of spirit, a hunger which persists after the land, after the possibility of land, has disappeared. Myth, the sentiment for humanity, persists. It persists in the form or formlessness of manifest destiny, and it defies historicizing.

Notions that American expansionism disappeared after such and such a date may carry shards of truth,[39] but those notions invariably talk of manifest destiny and the death of manifest destiny in the same breath. Ultimately, manifest destiny is the motion of projection, not the nationalism of expansion. Manifest destiny is a living verity even after the land as literal form has disappeared, because it is thoroughly imbued in and with the unself-consciousness of culture, and will disappear only with that culture's death. Native Americans had no manifest destiny because their projections of motion were profoundly different from the projections of those who destroyed them. The madness of Emerson and others for supposed expansionism seems so out of place, so radically different from other soft and careful statements, because we have misread them. They were not revelling in politics, but in the possibilities of a mythology. "The harmony of nature," wrote Emerson, "required a great tract of land in the Western hemisphere."[40] In his madness, he spoke of projections, not of economics. The morphology of manifest destiny sings that the thrust was ineffable, the journey replete with heroes, its origins beyond historicity.

In an expanse of movement voiced by manifest destiny is a vision of unity and totality exactly mythic. "It reminds us," says Bercovitch, "of the power of rhetoric (in the service of ideology) to shape our view of history, and by extension to shape history itself. It reminds us, too, of the way a culture can use myth to circumvent the most obvious contradictions."[41] Bercovitch has no feeling for the actuality of mythos, but he is right in suggesting that myth, mistakenly called history, has shaped views of what America is and what it will become, just as other myths have shaped and will shape cultural perceptions. Eliade writes, for example, of Marx incorporating into his philosophy, and his philosophy of history, "one of the great eschatological myths of the Asianico–Mediterranean world: the redeeming role of Just Man (in our day, the proletariat), whose sufferings are destined to change the ontological status of the world."[42] The world is transformed through the movements of mythologies, not by literal perceptions of the historical.

So we must finally turn to the problems of transformation, in which the landscape becomes a living text of cultural events. Writers speak often of the destiny manifest in America's geography,[43] that manifest destiny equaled geographical predestination and "alone seemed sufficient to assure the sweep of the nation to the Pacific."[44] Or that the love of liberty and independence was natural to the American continent.[45] Such statements are easy to dismiss as the rabid politics of expansionism, but they seem something more: an expression of the myth motivating manifest destiny. The geography of the western country was not responsible for manifest destiny.[46] If it had been, the Native American would also have been motivated by the same projection. He wasn't. Instead, the projection of manifest destiny transformed the landscape into its own image. Manifest destiny is a vision of transformation, in which the landscape becomes a text of projection, an assurance of the verisimilitude of motion, of the language of movement. "How much better," said Emerson, "when the whole land is a garden."[47] He provided a right-reading of the text.

And the landscape was coaxed to speak the language of manifest destiny. "The Puritans discovered America in scripture," writes Bercovitch, "precisely as a biblical scholar discovers the meaning of some hitherto obscure text."[48] Something akin to this bestowal of language took place not merely in the rhetoric of manifest destiny, but in the language of the landscape it transformed. The language is one of madness in that it is not grounded in the rational, in the coherent and predictable flow of events; but it was the text of landscape. It is this language Thoreau spoke, and this text of manifest destiny he read when he wrote: "Eastward I go only by force; but westward I go free. . . . and I may say that mankind progress from east to west."[49]

This is the language of manifest destiny. The rhetoric of expansion, of politics, nationalism, desacralized religion, technology—was a superficial dialect of the booster club, of the stasis of Americanism. But this langage of manifest destiny was a literal reading of a text, of a text the landscape was made to speak, of a mythos that transformed wilderness into a moving projection of cultural truth, of the entire east-west progression of Western civilization.[50]

Chapter Eleven

The Donner Party:
History, Mythology,
and the Existential Voice

never take no cutofs
    Virginia E. B. Reed

My own emotions will not permit me to attempt a
description which language, indeed, has not power
to delineate.
    W. H. Eddy

so he cannot
move on nor come
deep into the place.
    George Keithley
    The Donner Party

By what freak chance does the skin of illusion ever
split, and reveal to us the real?
    Annie Dillard
    Holy the Firm

Even among the auspiciousness and totality of historicity, there are
things, moments, even institutions, about which we have no history.
Michel Foucault speaks boldly of such apparently unmoving histories:
"the history of sea routes, the history of corn or of gold mining, the
history of drought and of irrigation, the history of crop rotation, the history of the balance . . . between hunger and abundance."[1] We have,
also, no history of human suffering, or of the matter of suffering at all.

We have no sense of history of such matters, not because history has been slow to incorporate them, but because such matters lie beyond the grasp of history.[2]

So, a question: Is the Donner Party, that group of people engulfed by blizzards on the east slopes of the Sierras in 1846, reduced to starvation, to cannibalism—is the Donner Party and its misfortunes a history? And if so, to what extent?

We have, during the passage of many years, been thoroughly taught that the misfortunes of the Donner Party are indeed the property of historians, and although terms like *terror*, *drama*, *tragic*, *suffering* have been attached to the group, those terms have been used as terms of history, as terms which recover a chronology. Or they have been rather easily transposed to a "literature" of the group: largely novels which, through an assumed historicity (dealing with places, times, events, supplied by historians), have attempted to clothe historical events with the drama of human predicament. Interpretation, however, is no respecter of persons, and the tools and language of history, at this moment, need a re-evaluation and an establishment of worth.

In his book *The Parasite*, Michel Serres includes an interlude he calls "Noises," and within this interlude he says: "No one listens to anyone else. Everyone speaks; no one hears. . . . they all play their favorite instrument, whose name is their own. . . . History is programmed; everyone has a score."[3] With this common text, which everyone plays, and which everyone finds harmonious, comes a discordance, a noise, a reality beyond suppositions of careful order. The noise of history (its discourse, if you will) assumes a symphonic order—but only because everyone has the same score. The image of the score, its sense of totality and its sense of truth, has meaning in the consensus; but outside itself, beyond the careful limitations of the score, of the *music* itself, history is a noise devoid of human meaning, an illusion of illusions. And in such a context human meaning is neither approachable nor recoverable.

For example, in an "early" history of California, Eliza W. Farnham included a section on the Donner Party. Her purpose in discussing the group, one discovers, was to forcefully illustrate the natural superiority of women. As other interpreters noted, the women of the party did withstand the rigors of starvation and exposure better than the men,[4] but Farnham went beyond observation (as does *all* history) to champion the "sublime endurance . . . by females."[5] Whether these perceptions become historical, or anti-mythical (against the holiness of the Patri-archy), one wonders to what extent the whole of human utterance is political perversion—noise.

Mrs. Farnham was certainly not alone in the dissemination of noise. The noise of history pervades all historical documents attempting to enclose the Donner experience. In a scholarly article J. Roderick Korns reifies the Donner lives through the noise of historical discourse. Describing the party, he uses terms like *celebrated*, *horror*, *drama*, *heroic*, *grisly*, *spiritual and physical stresses*, *grim expedient*, *ordeal*, *classic episodes*.[6] It is this reifying noise which transforms an inaccessible (to the historical method) human problem into an illusion of historical order, an order which transforms the chaos of human actuality into stereotypes of Greek tragedy, the artifice of the drawing room—or of the landscape itself transformed. "Our concern with them," writes Korns, "in their experiences upon the Hastings Cutoff is constantly attended by our painful consciousness of their eventual fate."[7] This, in actuality, is probably true, but it is the historical method which has created this painful consciousness, this illusion of fate. Without hindsight there is no such thing as fate. And Korns later remarks that discovery of Reed's journal, itself a kind of history, has made it possible to deal definitely with the Donner Party on the Hastings Cutoff; "the daily record that would fix their experiences in a chronology has been lacking."[8] That, of course, is precisely the main goal of historiography: to fix experience in a chronology, to create a stasis of events within the borders of a time. Only hindsight can provide such actualities. The ordering of detritus persists.

Spring 1847, a California paper printed a "remarkable" poem by John Denton, one of the party who died. The poem was supposedly taken from his journal, and was written as he lay dying in the snow. The journal was evidently, or conveniently, lost, but supposedly contained "a graphic description of the sufferings of the unfortunate party."[9] And yet *nothing* of this sort, except from the clever hindsight of historicity, exists or should be thought to exist.

Major interpreters of the Donner experience have attempted to mirror this reification. George R. Stewart, in his "Classic Story of the Donner Party," establishes not a human event, but a drama. He opens: "Tamsen Donner was gloomy and dispirited as the wagons pulled aside,"[10] attributing this reading of humanity to Thornton's journal. He continues, and continues, and constructs, as *all* others have done, the horrors of starvation and cannibalism, lodged, of course, within a chronology, which is the only place their horrors can be read. "Around them," he says, "lay a scene of *filth* and *mutilated* corpses. . . . The seven men stood *speechless* and *awe-struck*, and as the intense silence of the forest seemed to sweep in upon them, even Fallon, the mountain-man, felt the *creeping horror*."[11] Such "information" is neither retrievable nor existent. We have no perception of these supposed horrors; Stewart transforms the landscape into a sweeping presence, and the mountain man (a term, after all, for an occupation) into one who was usually impervious to terror and suffering. That is our history.

Although Bernard De Voto's discussion of the Donner Party is, in some ways, more complex than Stewart's, his historicism is synonymous. Under the heading of "Atomization," meaning disintegration of the group to individuals, De Voto writes: "It has been a favorite story of historians and novelists because it is *concentrated*, because the *horror* composes a *drama*."[12] More noise. Events do not compose themselves; composition is imposed upon them by the historian (and in the case of the Donner Party, also the novelist). The concentration (whatever that may mean), and the horror are also impositions of hindsight—attempts to reify and codify, and therefore make palatable, a virtually inaccessible experience. Speaking later of the Great Salt Desert and those crossing it, De Voto describes a grave dug in the salt mud, saying, "The Land of Canaan had claimed its second life from the emigration of '46."[13] This obvious transformation of the landscape to an illusion of Biblical Landscape may be viewed by many as vital, moving history, but such details, as they accumulate, re-create the problems of the party in the image of other predicaments, so that the Donner Party is no longer the Donner Party, but a collage of other times and other faces, a shattered image of discordant events, a cacophony of cultural illusions.

Nothing I know of, even the horrors of the crematoria, suggests, as De Voto does, that men and women carry "death in their hearts."[14] They only do so in the pages of history. We may never know what they carry in their hearts in the face of extremity. Certainly it is something we may not recognize and therefore have no language for, since we have been taught to transform whatever may be there into a chronological capsule, a horror, a drama—the easy excesses of hind-sight.

Such transformations are everywhere. One interpreter claims that his text is "an attempt to simplify the Donner Story."[15] Simplify from what to what? And he calls the Donner Story "the great epic of emigrating America."[16] To die in caves of snow is epic? To eat hides is epic? To preserve one's children is epic? These acts or circumstances are biological, and there is no such thing as an epic biology. Or, says another, "The delirium preceding death by starvation, is full of strange phantasies."[17] More noise. More hindsight. Perhaps the moment preceding death by starvation is the absolute moment of lucidity. At least, it seems a voice we do not hear; about the starvation-death of William Hook, William G. Murphy wrote: "He did not die in great agony, as is usually alleged. No groan, nor signs of dying, were manifested to us."[18] Our supposi-tions about human events and their meanings are grown and nurtured by a historicity, by the noise of the chronological transformations and their associates.

History is a divinity. It becomes a divinity, a dogma, as we speak of those who died before the snow, that "could those who performed the last sad rites have caught a vision of the horrors awaiting the party, they would have known how good was the God who in mercy took her to Himself."[19] Therefore, concludes this dogma, "under such protracted suffering, the animal outgrows the spiritual in frightful disproportion."[20] And through the historical transformation and subsequent discovery of a god and his dogma come the awards, the official recognition, "the one unmistakable symptom that salvation [or illumination, the non-transformation] is beaten again."[21] The award: What was an accident, like being wounded in battle, becomes an emulation: "The Donner Party has been selected by us [Native Sons of the Golden West] as the most typical and as the most *varied* and *comprehensive* in its experiences of all the trains that made these *wonderful journeys* of thousands of miles, so unique in their *daring*, so *brave*, so *worthy of the admiration* of man."[22] At times the noise becomes unbearable; or it becomes most pleasing for those who hear it as harmonious.

The most antithetical moments of noise are those issuing from entry of the historian–narrator into the "characters" of the Donner event. "I have heard it said," writes Hoffman Birney, the mouth and mind of

William Eddy, "that the human memory fails to record the incidents of periods of tremendous mental anguish or physical stress"—but "I can recall every detail."[23] This narrative is an absolute dramatization of the unknown, the unspoken, and perhaps the unperceived, the unfelt. Even the god-finders, the dogmatists, do not enter such extremities in their efforts to transform the event into the drama. The absolute madness, cacophony, of such a view is expressed in a judgment of Tamsen Donner. Because "the heroic Tamsen was an educated woman, sensitive and sympathetic," her lost journal would have provided a clear and detailed witness of suffering, distress, and death, while the uneducated Breen's journal is simply a preserved scrawl.[24] The natural course of all historical dogma leads to elitism, to the subordination of events to provide a shining history *for*, for those who know and understand the meaning of human suffering.

Even the Reed journal, unlike the scrawl of Breen, is an attempt at a historicity. Reed's journal ends when his troubles begin (a fight, a death—banishment). Breen's begins with his troubles in the snow. The details of the Reed journal are only technical, bare detritus, the dead language of instruction. The Reed journal is a history with a purpose, and it expresses various transformations: "neat little valley, fine water . . . good grass";[25] "burried him at the uper wells at the forks of the road in a *beautiful* place."[26] Landscape is beatific.

Even the most rigorous historical delineation involves a series of transformations. In his defense of Lansford W. Hastings, Thomas F. Andrews says Hastings, in his enthusiasm to promote a new route to California, was only doing what others, like John Charles Frémont, had done. But at the point of the human event, of the suffering of the Donner Party, what do Hastings' motivations mean? History (and mythos) invariably yearn for a scapegoat, and history in its particular transformations assures that one will be provided, that the chaos of circumstances will always have an empirical meaning. And after this defense of Hastings, Andrews turns to the Donner Party, writing: "The stage was set for the *unfolding* of one of the most *stirring dramas* recorded in the *annals of the West*."[27] The West has annals only as it is provided with them, and these annals, these dramas, are only assured by the noise of history, and by the literature inspired by that history. In their attempt to create verisimilitude through characterization, novelists invariably transform those of the

Donner Party and the events they suffered to an image of themselves. And these novels then become works of history, or a literary history, which is the most destructive of literatures, since it assumes a historical moment (the already-transformed), and transforms it again. The noise of literature can be more devastating than the noise of history, its sedimentation more neatly choking the human event—in the name of art: a simple dressing of history, a perversion of the deep meanings of the journal, the clever, the smooth—a misreading of human actuality. So Patrick Breen's voice becomes squeaky; Keseberg's sleep is shallow and restless.[28] Their sleep and voices portray an essence, a misreading, which history has provided them; the voice and the sleep act out the historical drama. And in the snow, among the dead, everyone, like the historians, "knew it was only a matter of time."[29] There is nothing in the journals to suggest the sufferers felt or thought of an imminent death. And in the novels the snowshoers weep as they skewer human flesh over a fire; their tears are the tears of history. And "their horror over the unrecognizable things [butchered corpses] left in the snow could not be blunted."[30] History teaches this; the journals do not. The perversion of human nature here outstrips the historical in its reification, its claim to the actuality of human emotion.

Which raises another problem of historicity. Certain interpreters of the Donner experience have assumed that they can somehow approach, enter, the pathos of the group by immersing themselves in, or by traveling over, the landscape the party traveled. Homer Croy, for example, wrote that "to understand the story better, I went over the trail from the Donner Farm, Sangamon County, Illinois, to Sacramento, California."[31] And he appropriately adds that "when I saw the museums [housing artifacts from and of the Donner party], the relics made the story moving."[32] Actually, these two statements by Croy are synonymous in view and intent. The landscape itself holds no meaning of or for the Donner Party; it was, as we shall see, impervious to their experience. What Croy then attempts is a transformation, both of the landscape and of the artifact, into a vision of human suffering. Nature becomes, therefore, an artifact which is made to speak the drama, the horror, as do the dead artifacts in the museum. They become thoroughly historicized to reflect and speak a chronology, or an attitude. But the landscape of death is impenetrable, or does not exist.

George Keithley, the poet, made assumptions similar to Croy's. He writes: "I wanted to be as familiar with the material of the story as I could."[33] So to see and feel the life of these people, Keithley made the illusory trek—beginning in Illinois, then west through an iconography of nature: the trails, the monuments; through the Salt Desert; even working in the snow of the pass: the cabin sites, the lake. I am not suggesting that one cannot, does not, learn and experience through proximity with landscape. But a human experience of the past cannot be re-created by well-fed hindsight, by simply traveling over a land that for decades, centuries in fact, has been forced to speak a language of honor and of nationalism. The landscape of death, I repeat, is impenetrable, and can perhaps be experienced only by those who, not devoid of hope, but facing a vastness incomprehensible to moderns, to the historization of experience, are cold and dying in the snow, who have perhaps become integers of the landscape itself. Such problems are totally beyond and impervious to a chronology, the noise of history.

The mythological event, however, does have a language rather than a cacophony. And expressions of this language are seen in the Donner experience, and perhaps account for what seems the national preoccupation with the Donner Party. This language is not devoid of transformations, but rather than transforming the event into a chronology, it transforms the event into a cultural image. Therefore, one transformation involves the projection of manifest destiny, the movement of cultural validity. And this voice can occasionally be heard from between the details of history. De Voto, for example, notes that "the party itself had been unable to keep an accurate account of time."[34] This is crucial. From within the group itself, time was lost, at least the meticulous time of technology and historicity. And it is within this timelessness, which lies between, under, and apart from the historical, that the language of mythos is faintly heard. Manifest destiny, the projection, is not a problem of time, but a problem of consciousness, of the resuscitation of motion. And whether we interpret the motion as pleasure or tragedy is not important; what is important is the motion itself, and *cultural* perceptions of that motion. The motion (whether hindered or unhindered) is tantalizing and unforgettable—it is cultural lifeblood. But there seems more to this problem, from a mythical perspective, than the projection alone, although the importance of the projection must not be minimized. Another possibility is the language of survival.

In a piece on the retreat of the British army from Kabul to Jalalabad in 1842, Louis Dupree discovers that the perceptions of survivors, their language and their "facts," reflect the views and wishes of their culture. So, from the British point of view, the British are victorious, they survive, and are to be honored.[35] Both sides claim victory in warfare, not necessarily because of perversion of data, but for cultural validation, and the survivor speaks the language of validation. This was certainly true among those of the Donner Party who survived the snow, and who spoke about it. Since culture exists on several levels, it is given several voices.

Virginia E. B. Reed, for example, in a letter written spring 1847, went to some length to absolve her family of cannibalism. "When pa went to the Cabins," she wrote, "some of the compana was eating those that Died but Thomas & Martha had not ate any."[36] And also: "but thank god we have all got throw and the onely family that did not eat human flesh." Here the survivor becomes a kind of historian, working from hindsight, and transforming the culture to the level of the acceptable, of the have-not-sinned; this transformation is not firmly grounded in a chronology. But later, survivor Virginia Reed Murphy deals in the noise of history despite her experience. "The *misery*," she writes, "endured during those four months at Donner Lake in our little dark cabins under the snow would fill pages and make the *coldest heart ache*."[37] Or she speaks of "the moan of the pine trees, which seemed to sympathize with our loneliness,"[38] and the soft, "pure white snow."[39] The noise here is unbearable, the cacophony has obscured any legitimate voice of survival and replaced it with a transformation and a chronology, the neatness of details, the encapsulation of nature: the real story with a thoroughly predictable noise. Snow is pure; a moan of trees sympathetic.

Interpretation is no respecter of persons, and here the language of survival, the mythical voice, seems easily accommodated by the historical. So that a major question looms: What does the survivor know? What is the survivor able to tell? Eliza P. Donner Houghton asks: "Who better than survivors knew the heart-rending circumstances of life and death in those mountain camps?"[40] Who indeed? What the survivor knows is seldom told (the voice may not be legitimate), and what the survivor does tell, beyond the immediate re-establishment of culture, is a history. The lone survivor syndrome is of a fleeting mythology on the one hand, and a thoroughly taught historicity on the other: the transformations become blurred, not easily distinguishable. So Eliza P. Donner Houghton will tell the real story, adorning all involved (like the Native Sons of the Golden West) with the honor they so richly deserve.[41] In this case, the survivor knows only what she has been taught by those non-survivors who were never there. "I would tell the story of my party so clearly," she writes, "that no one could doubt its truth!"[42] The chaos is rendered absolutely intelligible; the survivor is historian. What this experience means is precisely, in our clarity, what we want it to mean: the divinity, the dogma, the transformation.

C. F. McGlashan rather ironically writes that "the scenes of horror and despair need no exaggeration, no embellishment."[43] Yet embellish he does through the dramatic noise of *horror* and *despair*. We have seen no language for the elemental experience in the snow, only an omnipresent noise of its transformations.

But the quiet language of suffering distorts history. And De Voto, with a ray of insight, says that the starvation, the cannibalism, as occurrences are commonplace, but that "it is as the commonplace or typical just distorted that the Donners must be seen."[44] In the distortion is the quiet language, a religion of the dead, which more than any other problem or manifestation associated with the Donner Party has captivated a nation eagerly watching the projection, the movement. "No-one," says Elias Canetti, "who studies the original documents of any religion can fail to be amazed at the power of the dead."[45] On one level, this is the fascination with the Donner Party, and the noise of history is the failure of modern men to give the power of the dead a language, to clothe the death-experience with a forgotten dialect. Fear of the dead is universal; and "it is the jealousy of the dead that the living fear most."[46] If history can revitalize the dead through its various transformations, then the fear and the jealousy are at least sedimented. But through the language of mythology, the dead are not revivified, and they remain, beyond time, within the national consciousness. Often (as here) yearnings of mythology are denied by the sharp details of a historical present.

There are voices besides the noise of history and the language of mythos—voices speaking from the snow. There is also the not-said. John Breen, survivor, wrote nothing of the months in snow, but praised John

Stark, a man perfect in body and mind.[47] But the horrors, *they* remain unsaid; they have no voice—not within the transforming noise of history, or the culture-validating language of myth: the syndrome of survivors; the jealousy and fear of the dead; the obsession with the projection. But there are other voices: nameless, faceless, non-transforming—the voices of existence, of the individual essence. We hear these voices in small notes, if we hear them at all, in forgotten and undisfigured pieces. We hear the voice in what is remembered, not what is taught. "Just one happy play is impressed upon my mind"—a sunbeam came down the snow steps and made a bright spot on the floor.[48] This is the voice of a new world, one basically untransformed, and therefore unintelligible. It is the bridge Wright Morris crossed as a child, the image of the bridge, the black water beneath it, and a barn beyond that. "Nothing special. Just something I would never forget."[49] Unimportant because it has no place in the hierarchy of history or literature, in the subordination of events. This is the elemental voice, the voice of feeling and the voice of experience: the essence of human suffering, in which there is no drama, no tragedy, no transformation—an experience beyond traditional methods of interpretation.

Amidst the blatant transformations of Virginia Reed Murphy, this voice whispers. Of her sister Patty's doll, carried throughout the experience, she writes: "Sitting before a nice, bright fire at Woodworth's Camp, she took dolly out to have a talk, and told her of all her new happiness."[50] This memory is like the sunbeam and the black water under the bridge: crucial, elemental, untransformed, somehow a voice of the suffering, an indication of the voice of existence, totally devoid of any values we might impose.

There is another voice, more sustained and continuous, because we view it as narrative, as the (a) story of the Donner Party, which is precisely what it is not. It is a voice from and in the chaos of experience, the elemental. Patrick Breen's journal is such a voice: it does not instruct; it does not transform; but it does portray the perceived, the voiced, within the context of human suffering.

Friday, November 20, 1846 (these are not "normal" dates, but markers to distinguish one sunrise from the next), Breen writes: "we now have killed most part of our cattle having to stay here untill next spring and live on poor beef without bread or salt."[51] There is projection here into the future, but the future is always an unknown: the chaotic object of a hope, or fear. Within this isolated passage lurks, again, the voice of human predicament, totally ahistorical, totally beyond the curse or the blessing of hindsight. That is partly, at least, the nature of the journal in its unself-conscious essence: the search for a voice in spite of a language. Breen seems obsessed with several things (they become images, unsubordinate, in the journal): wood, wind, snow, clouds, sun: those things which are not and which cannot be the subject of a history, or of most of that which we call literature, because they are insignificant and untransformed. These enumerations of wood, wind, snow, clouds, sun comprise most of the journal. We are in the bowels of landscape without hope of transformation:

> Sunday, November 29, 1846: "hard to get wood"
>
> Monday, November 30, 1846: "no liveing thing without wings can get about"
>
> Tuesday, December 8, 1846: "hard work to [get] wood sufficient to keep us warm & cook our beef"
>
> Thursday, December 10, 1846: "snow 8 feet deep on the level dull"
>
> Sunday, December 27, 1846: "scarce of wood to day chopt a tree dow[n] it sinks in the snow & is hard to be got."
>
> Monday, January 11, 1847: "wood scarce difficult to get any more"
>
> Wednesday, January 13, 1847: "snowing fast wind N.W snow higher than the shanty must be 13 feet deep dont know how to get wood this morning it is dredful to look at"

There is only incidental mention here of the *dramatic* and *captivating* ordeals of cannibalism and starvation. Why? Because they could not be recorded? Because Breen was a Catholic? Because he had something, everything, to hide? Or because, when compared with the enclosing presence of wind and snow, these historical, these mythological events were meaningless? Then:

> Saturday, January 16, 1847: "no telling what the weather will do"

and

> Friday, February 12, 1847: "we hope with the assistance of Almighty God to be able to live to see the bare surface of the earth once more."

The weather is beyond meaning, beyond transformation. The snow, and the snow, is beyond meaning, and beyond transformation. Yet both are given a voice here, and the voice that expresses them is the voice of suffering. This journal is a text. We know this world, we hear this world, from the text, from the voice of suffering, not the noise of history (to which this voice is invisible) nor the language of mythos, which must also transform.

The journal ends, the voice stills, as abruptly as it begins:

> Monday, March 1, 1847: "there is some amongst them some old they
> say the snow will be here untill June."

The snow has thinned; the hunger abates; the voice disappears. The snow remains; the voice leaves. This is the exact antithesis of well-fed historicity, the exact reversal. As the event blurs, the noise of history increases, and it belabors itself for itself. But the essence of human suffering, the scarcely perceived is quiet when the possibility for transformation returns. What we know, or what we hope to know, is that suffering, the voice, portrays a certain set of images, which are really not a set at all, but which are permanently fixed in the *is* of human events. The voice is completely beyond the politics of history because it is untransformed and untransformable. It is simply that which is and that which will be: the image, without a name and without a face.

What De Voto calls atomization of the group to individuals[52] did happen, but what he could not recognize was that it produced, or made possible, the voice of existence, the voice quitted by the group and its transformations. "The language of the absolutely lonely man is lyrical,"[53] wrote Georg Lukacs. He was wrong. The voice of the absolutely lonely man is an untransformed image of that which we have never understood. It is not the lyrical; it is the existential.

And the poets too would speak of this: "Nothing in nature was what it might seem!"[54] That is the voice of the absolutely lonely man. But we go too far when we affirm "the slow intelligence of the snow,"[55] or "the rich enduring sound of human speech."[56] These are transformations, not images. These are the illusions which quiet the voice of essence and make possible the drama of history and of the thing we call literature.

So we finally ask, demand: what do we really know? We know, with Vardis Fisher, that "Tamsen Donner was dead."[57] And we assume we know that these events of the past have a meaning which grips us, which wrenches from us and yet validates our transformations. Do we know that "the only permanence is in our past"?[58] And if that is what we know, how do we account for the disappearance of the voice? It is never permanent, seldom retrievable, always surprising: an image of endurance. But in and of the past? Do we know?

Perhaps the past is a problem of victimage, that we "really need more victims to remind us that we're all victims."[59] Perhaps the past is simply that freak chance which makes possible the splitting of the skin of illusion, the revelation of the real: of the voice of existence, the revelator, the one untransformed and untransformable.

Chapter Twelve

The Fracture of Mormonism: Science as Religion, or Religion as Science

In fact history does not belong to us, but we belong to it.
> Hans-Georg Gadamer
> *Truth and Method*

The proponents of competing paradigms practice their trades in different worlds.
> Thomas S. Kuhn
> *The Structure of Scientific Revolutions*

God has no allergies.
> Jacques Derrida
> *Dissemination*

Ye cannot serve God and Mammon.
> Jesus Christ

After Mormonism was firmly established in the vastness of western deserts, it reached outward for verification of its dogmas. It plead to the world for sustenance and succor. This outward-reach cannot, I think, necessarily be isolated in a classical or celebrated movement, but it can be understood (though not incorporated) within a particular moment in time. The time, asserted by history: summer 1873. The moment, we can neither arrest nor calculate, for, like persistent images of the Donner Party, it reflects the attitude of an entire generation, and of generations to come.

Othniel C. Marsh, Yale professor and eminent paleontologist, visited Salt Lake City in the summer of 1873 after one of his fruitful "digs" in Wyoming. Marsh was evidently surprised by a warm and cordial welcome he received from Brigham Young and other prominent leaders of the Mormon church. This warm welcome, Marsh learned, was due to his discovery of *Orohippus*, a very small Eocene horse, as well as other fossils. Young questioned Marsh pointedly about the discoveries and finally explained that people had doubted the authenticity of the Book of Mormon because it claimed horses had existed in America around 600 B.C. No evidence of horses in America had been discovered before Marsh's finds in Wyoming. "So it seems that while most theologians are regarding the developments of the natural sciences with fear and trembling, the chiefs of the Mormon religion are prepared to hail the discoveries of paleontology as an aid in establishing their peculiar beliefs. . . . And thus Prof. Marsh . . . is raised to the rank of a defender of the faith."[1]

Although this confrontation between and eventual marriage of science and religion may not have reached the level of a widely celebrated historical movement, it is a crucial moment in time: a manifestation of fracture, a cross-over, a reasoned change in world-view. Brigham Young had for some time viewed science as a buttress for true religion, stating that "the religious teachers of the people advance many ideas and notions for truth which are in opposition to and contradict facts demonstrated by science."[2] Therefore, false religion can also be exposed by weighing it against the verities of science.

It is rather well known that Brigham Young was contemptuous of the physicians of his day; he was not reacting against the kind of science he welcomed in the discoveries of O. C. Marsh, but against the "heroic" school of medicine, which dealt in quackery and brutality,[3] at least from certain interpretive vantage points. "Brigham Young called the regular medicine of his day 'the most imperfect of any science in existence.'"[4] So, as there was good and bad religion, there was also good and bad science. The task then, in a pursuit of truth, was to bring good science and good religion together to create a spiritual harmony.

Young's espousal of true science, however, differed rather remarkably from the views of Joseph Smith. Like Young, Smith abhorred the medical heroics of his day. The Smith family had experienced the horrors of

"American orthodox medicine" on several fronts. Joseph was given a permanent limp from his brutal osteomyelitis surgery, and in 1823 his oldest brother, Alvin, died apparently from complications caused by a dose of calomel.[5] Unlike Young, however, the Smiths displayed a warm affinity for herbal remedies,[6] probably as a reaction against orthodox medical practices[7]—the popular science of the day.

This affection for herbal remedies was clearly dogmatized by Joseph Smith. In what was destined to become Mormon scripture, Smith wrote: "And whosoever among you are sick, and have not faith to be healed, but believe, shall be nourished with all tenderness, with herbs and mild food."[8] He also said, "And again, verily I say unto you, all wholesome herbs God hath ordained for the constitution, nature, and use of man."[9] Scripturally, then, Mormonism was destined to be a religion clearly espousing the use of folk remedies. Such affinities are still evident in the Mormon herbal underground.[10] Recent "research" has shown that Mormons espousing non-scientific cancer cures have a strong religious background, strongly influenced by early Mormon teachings and beliefs.[11]

One might conclude, then, that Joseph Smith, for whatever reason, rejected the science of his day, while Brigham Young, for whatever the reason, espoused and defended the science of his. And at this point, between the agitations of two separate discourses, one asks: What is truth? Is it a behavioral, verifiable icon waiting to be discovered? Does it change from generation to generation? That is, does it change in essence, or only in its disguise? Truth is our own image reflected everywhere. And even then, in such a predictable, such a familiar form, it is never what we think it is. We are confounded by our own warm illusions, the exact reflection of our faces, bodies, loves, lives. "We all know that the naked truth is found at the bottom of a well."[12] And in the well we discover expectations, which are shattered by disturbances in the pool. Pure unvarnished truth fluctuates, oscillates.[13] And when it settles it continues to reflect the image we love: the image of ourselves in plenitude and contentment. Truth is the unending reflection of an image. Problems of truth, then, are assumptions about the world, a world in transformation. "Truth," wrote Francis Bacon, "will sooner come out from error than from confusion."[14] But both error and confusion allow the emergence of truth. The *error*, or the *confusion*, is the emergence of an image, our image, reflected everywhere. But even amid such contentment, there is something unbearable about truth.[15] Perhaps a gnawing fear reminds that there may be images somewhere, beyond our grasp, which do not reflect the perfection of our own faces. Certainly, this problem is crucial in the space of the fracture: What is truth?: I must insist on my own reflection.

And what is science? Is it the discovery and advertisement of the proper image, the one therefore reflected everywhere? Science is a system of measured prejudices. It is science and only science which discovers the proportions, the exact size of the everywhere-reflected image. Science measures the image. It will give us the image in several sizes. For Hans-Georg Gadamer, literary and historical studies, the methods of human sciences, communicate the idea of the sensus communis.[16] This is a warm and pleasing idea. Communities and senses of communities, despite our warmth, are invariably exclusive. They exclude everything that does not reflect the proper image. So that within the sense of community (that which "mediates a unique, positive knowledge")[17] truth and science are loved and given proportion, and in return for this love, they both give a proportion: a reflection, and a measurement, of the image. Science and truth are eminently compatible, as are science and religion; they function synonymously to suppress human essences by measuring and transforming them into the proper images: a pleasing discourse of repression, of similarity.

In the opening section of Michel Foucault's *Discipline and Punish*, in the section titled "The Body of the Condemned," the interplay of truth and religion is harmonious. The execution of Damiens, the regicide, is presided over by the truth of the Kingdom and the truth of the Church. The spectacle begins before the main door of the Church of Paris,[18] and when Damiens has been drawn and quartered, he is examined by the parish priest.[19] Truth is a grand circle which encompasses everything, a *sensus communis*, an image everywhere reflected, an illuminating synthesis. And history is also there; it also gives the sense of community. Said Nietzsche, "It is the sure sign of the death of a religion when its mythic presuppositions become systematized, under the severe, rational eyes of an orthodox dogmatism, into a ready sum of historical events."[20] This is the sense of community, the synthesis. The voice of synthesis is a pervasive voice; it is the discourse of harmony in which science equals history equals religion. "What the world is crying for," writes one Mormon scientist, "is synthesis."[21] This is the voice of the fracture, the voice of community. (Such a voice is no ultimate respecter of persons.) It is the same voice Brigham Young used when espousing the discoveries of Marsh: true science and true religion together form a community. The sense of community is everywhere in the discourse of harmony, the discourse of belief (the actual discourse—noise—of the fracture). Priest and apologist, eminent scientist: all play the same harmony within the fold of belief.

So that: "Latter-day Saints may have a unique contribution to make to a humanistic synthesis of science and religion. . . . The modern explosion of scientific and technologic knowledge is . . . evidence of God's grace."[22] The everywhere-reflected image here is one of the gospel of wealth: God blesses those who synthesize. And the synthesis is a transformation. "Mormons see God as the ultimate scientist."[23]

Here, God is a symbiosis. The community is symbiotic. One institution feeds its counterpart, and therefore both speak a discourse of harmony. God's face is the face of the image: a perfect reflection of a parasitic (symbiotic) relationship. The question (symbiosis) is not one of benefit; it is one of community, of the symbiotic and synergistic relationship of science and religion.[24] And on the symbiosis turns our salvation or our damnation.[25] Science is the transformer. When religion is enfolded by an aura of science, we are saved. The gospel of the transformation is now provable (it can be measured), and within the measurement of truth lies salvation. The empiricity of an "I know" freezes the image perfectly; the testimony of divinity is the ultimate symbiosis. The measurement is exact, and it is perfect. The "subjective aspect of science makes it not only possible but in fact desirable for the religious and scientific communities to be allies."[26] And more profoundly, "the origins of modern science [as it has been historicized] may be traced to the disappearance of those extrasensory links to the world of nature."[27] Therefore, nature is reduced to the image of science, the sense of community. And when coupled with religion, God is transformed to a chemist.

And of course, to enter this community, to be a part of the reflected image, one must, like Damiens, display "intellectual humility and submissiveness coupled with a childlike and faithful curiosity."[28] A faithful curiosity is not a curiosity at all, but a sense of communion, a part of the image.

These views are crucial. Normal science[29] has normalized revolutionary religion. It has created a status quo which must be defended at all cost. Mormonism is thoroughly infused with a normal empiricity. Even the payment of a tithe must equal the exactment of a blessing. The status quo picks and chooses. The status quo of normal science serves the religion (in their symbiosis) and therefore disturbances in the empiricity of the status quo (as with the *problem* of evolution—a ripple in the continuity of community) must be rejected as the testimony of deity is simultaneously empiricized. Mythos is a totality; community is a fragment. Mythos seeks new meaning in the symbol of the horse; community transforms the horse to a historical and empirical problem. God is forever implicated in the symbiosis.[30]

Therefore, "science dominated by the spirit of religion is the key [to] progress and the hope of the future."[31] The discourse, we see, becomes omnipresent. And we may trace in the historicity of the empiricization of Mormonism certain flaws in the glass: the antagonistic diatribe of Joseph Fielding Smith.[32] But such renunciations were only flaws, because by then it was too late. Even prophecy cannot dissolve a sense of community. The culture had, to its core, been empirically determined. Now, there is only a question of false science or of true science—false science being that which is not compatible with the image. "God is a God of law, of order, of rational behavior, rather than a deity of mystery, of transcendent and capricious whims."[33] God is a scientist.

And as statements on Mormonism's new-found science proliferate, become effusive, the discourse of harmony persists. It is everywhere. Orson Pratt's *Key to the Universe* is for sale at the Church Historian's Office;[34] the symbiosis is manifest. And the epigram to the book: "Planetary and Stellar Worlds 'roll upon their wings in their glory, in the midst of the power of God.' " In this curious mathematical work, the not-said outweighs the force of *obvious* measurement. The not-said: the symbiosis, the testimony that science equals history equals religion.

And so the task continues: the reconciliation of "the principles of true science with the principles of true religion."[35] This becomes the entire force and the entire discourse of the movement of Mormonism. God "allowed man, on October 4, 1957, to successfully test an engine potentially capable of taking man to any part of the universe."[36] Visible Mormon scientists become spokesmen for God and for his mysteries, which are not mysteries at all, but a pleasing discourse of symbiosis. Therefore, "October 4, 1957, will come to be recognized as one of the great dates in human history."[37] The symbiosis now becomes a chronology of great importance, the repetition of the sentence (or of its intellectual fragment): Science equals history equals religion. This harmonious symbiosis,[38] this celestial chronology, becomes the discourse of belief. And the discourse persists: "Science and religion are two great avenues of truth which men should explore with humility."[39] "There can be no conflict between true religion and correct science."[40] "The gospel and science have the same objective—the discovery and possession of truth—all truth."[41]

This discourse of symbiosis persists from great to small, from the rigorous to the flaccid[42]—it is the noise of belief, of harmony, of synthesis—of the measured prejudice. This is not the blurring of genres, the re-examination of a world fragmented by the institutions of men; it is a transformation of the chaos evident in non-truth into the peace and harmony of the parasitic relationship; it is the voice of the fracture, of the normalization of revolutionary religion. Mormonism now becomes a tissue of manifest cause/effect problems, problems (situations, circumstances, symbioses) which through their apparent dogmas become revelation: the will and the mind of God: the image of the status quo.

The voice cannot be stilled; it perpetuates itself: "Science supports religion."[43] It must, of course. Or an image wavers, no longer reflecting the face of its owner. Dissonance is introduced, harmony denied. Or the everywhere-reflected image is re-harmonized: "In any event, at least on the basis of scriptural evidence, *'religion' cannot disagree with science on the matter of the method of creation*!"[44] God can and should be discovered both in the laboratory and the field.[45] "The doctrine that tea and coffee is injurious to man is scientific."[46] And finally, the apotheosis, the continued affirmation of the symbiosis: "Every scientific discovery may be incorporated into the gospel,"[47] the priest and the physician (as well as the prophet) being one and the same.[48]

Within the apparent healing airs of symbiosis, of prophet, apologist, scientist, historian displaying the same manifest discourse, a rift appears, a fracture yawns. "To 'demythologize' any part of the Bible," says Frye, "would be the same thing as to obliterate it."[49] The rift is widest when it seems most clearly soothed and healed—harmonized.

And so a world demythologized cries for synthesis.[50] It was the blessed rage for synthesis which coaxed Alfonso X, in the thirteenth century, to proclaim that "if God had consulted him when creating the universe, he would have received good advice."[51] It is at this point that "poison, under the eyes of the king, appears as the truth of the remedy."[52] It is at this point that synthesis and symbiosis become precisely synonymous, and this synonymity leads to the historization and empiricism of mythos.

There is little doubt that this sought-for symbiosis was responsible for plunging Mormonism into the mainstream of American life, into the technological rage of the West, into the gospel of wealth. And we do have a survivor. But what is the shape of this survivor, this symbiosis? It is, of course, the shape of truth. And "truth is the desired objective of all rational human action."[53] And that again is exactly the point. The fracture of symbiosis, the renunciation of mythos, does produce the truth of rational human action. And truth is *our* image reflected everywhere— in this case, within the context of a system of measured prejudices, a harmony of synthesis.

Chapter Thirteen

The Transforming Image: Landscape as Culture

A transformation of consciousness and a transformation
of language can never be separated.
Northrop Frye
The Great Code

They dance fire itself; they become fire; their move-
ments are those of flames.
Elias Canetti
Crowds and Power

Human life, rational life, is a system of transformation. The various
transformations themselves have been transformed to a system, as with a
union of religion and science. Chaos, like truth, is unbearable. So we
take comfort within the transformation, and within a system of transformations. And this sense of comfort (weighed somewhat tentatively
against the rumblings of a hidden chaos) is continually expressed, as is
its system.

A religious leader speaks: We know from the writings of John
Charles Frémont that the West was a place of great hostility, that the
frost dates (the latest in spring, and the first in fall) were so close that
there was no growing season—at least not for corn, even barley, and
other human-sustaining crops. It was only when God's people claimed
these wilderness valleys that the growing season became a growing season,
that an agricultural people could sustain themselves. For the desert to
blossom like a rose, the first requirement was that God change the frost
dates.[1] This image of landscape as a map of God's will, as a text of

providence, points to the astounding pervasiveness of what may well be man's most indigenous institution. Man is the animal that transforms. And the transformation is an institution of power. Elias Canetti has written that "the talent for transformation which has given man so much power over all other creatures has as yet scarcely been considered or begun to be understood."[2]

Man can rarely explain the institutions he holds most dear; they lie hidden beneath a subterfuge of forms: nationalism, history, the various shapes of illusions. Man is the animal that transforms, and these transformations (perhaps even reifications, metamorphoses) occur on several levels, or they can be seen from several points of view.

There are transformations in nature from which man might take his cue, but these transformations are difficult and virtually invisible. Elemental nature is transformed, and biological and chemical nature are transformed. The close and careful work of atoms is seen not in the numbered orbits of electrons, but in an array of substances in which compounds are changed and conceived. Nature is transformable, but it also transforms. Asparagus, for example, will readily change sex if it (he? she?) receives too much water, and naturalists have observed a transformation of sex in range plants suffering (or enjoying?) extreme cold. Only in its most visible forms is nature predictable, and Western man, at least, seems blind to the subtleties of nature.

Perhaps it is this blindness which is responsible for certain levels of transformations, for nature in its infinite variety is not predictable; and to transform, one must be able to predict. One way Claude Lévi-Strauss put Brazil into words was by discussing, projecting, the steady, humid heat "which freed my body of its usual weight of wool, and abolished the contrast between house and street."[3] So nature here is a transformer, and the transformation involves stripping a European of certain perceptions about landscape. But these perceptions are replaced with an abolition, in which a familiar contrast disappears. Here, nature strips the philosopher[4] of illusions; usually, quite the opposite is true; that is, man endows nature with the face of his institutions. And so blind to the subtleties of nature, the chaotic inner-face, man transforms nature into a predictable image. Franz Kafka captured an essence of transformations in his vision of Prometheus:

There are four legends concerning Prometheus:

According to the first he was clamped to a rock in the Caucasus for betraying the secrets of the gods to men, and the gods sent eagles to feed on his liver, which was perpetually renewed.

According to the second Prometheus, goaded by the pain of the tearing beaks, pressed himself deeper and deeper into the rock until he became one with it.

According to the third his treachery was forgotten in the course of thousands of years, forgotten by the gods, the eagles, forgotten by himself.

According to the fourth everyone grew weary of the meaningless affair. The gods grew weary, the eagles grew weary, the wound closed wearily.

There remained the inexplicable mass of rock. The legend tried to explain the inexplicable. As it came out of a substratum of truth it had in turn to end in the inexplicable.[5]

What we are left with is an inexplicable essence, which is faceless, and which is also unbearable without the various vestments of the transformations. So transformations make the unbearable bearable (even pleasing) by making it predictable. And predictability, of course, forms the core of human institutions. But this predictability from the point of view of the transforming culture does not reflect the face of the culture, but the face of deity. Therefore, "the basic 'recipe' for the reification of institutions is to bestow on them an ontological status independent of human activity and signification."[6] Marriage may be reified, for example, as a god-centered, god-authored institution, rather than a biological, or human-centered structure. The faces of the transformations are ineffable—because the energies of the transforming process are directed toward the construction and subsequent worship of a monument. As Northrop Frye says, "The genuine work which is founded on the human need for food and shelter moves in the direction of transforming nature into a world with a human shape, meaning, and function."[7] And the human shape is actually the form of deity. Chaos is endowed with stasis by clothing it, like the rock of Prometheus, with the ineffable form of deity, and therefore the transformation is unquestioned and unquestionable. The transformation is an image of nature seen through the eyes of God.

When Michel Serres writes that "the secret of the fable is metamorphosis in the fable,"[8] he captures not only the essence, but the latent power of a narrative form. The fable's core is transformation, because transformation itself makes the culture, the purveyor of the narrative, essentially magical. And the magical is the ineffable, because unlike science, magic can never be doubted.[9] The subject of the transformation, as it "experiences" nature, becomes the real, and "dissolves the whole outside world in mood, and itself becomes mood by virtue of [its] inexorable . . . essence."[10] Mood is not transitive. In its fuzziness it becomes most clear: a feeling undeniably true, a face of culture. This clarity is apparent in certain transformations associated with Luvale initiation. Lévi-Strauss writes that a Luvale boy may urinate only against certain clearly specified trees during the time of his initiation. All of these trees are hardwoods, "symbolizing the penis in erection."[11] Such transformations give nature a feeling undeniably true; they establish a mood which explicitly determines human action and activity. The magic here is sympathetic, but sympathetic magic is a transformation of nature into a mood essentially human. Through the attainment of such a mood, man has incorporated *into himself* all of nature—all of nature, at least, which was visible to man in a certain time and place, within a certain space. "It was through the development of transformation that he really became man; it was his specific gift and pleasure."[12] The pleasure is derived from the establishment of mood, from the projection of a transforming magic.

This magic is pervasive, and as we should expect, is present in man's perception of his sexuality. "The concept of transformation through copulation is very old indeed."[13] And in these projections of magic, a biological verity is transformed into a cultural prohibition. Transformations are means of control, ways of establishing and exercising power, thus dressing the chaos in predictable clothing. But the status quo approached and established here is not historical; it is a validator of culture. So nature becomes an array of transformations. "There is scarcely a rock," says Canetti, "which does not signify that some particular creature once lived and did great deeds there."[14] The stone is the tangible manifestation of the legend. The thing transformed wears, by new definition, another face. That is why a verdict on the beauty of a landscape depends on the "artistic taste of the time."[15] The artistic tastes of the time are faces of transformations, and if a landscape wears the proper face (which may mean a certain density of granite) it speaks a predictable dialect; it approaches a conception of mood.

"Nature is not in itself contradictory. It can become so only in terms of some specific human activity which takes part in it."[16] If transformations introduce certain contradictions, it is because the mood projected from the transformations becomes many moods because of the perspectives of many cultures. In, or through, the transformations of nature man establishes not only a cultural mood—he also transforms himself. Man may "complete nature through writing";[17] and in such a completion (although nature alone can complete itself, since nature is *all*), a style and a mood are expressed—a style and mood which are authorial, both of which are transformations. Despite the *fact* that "nature takes place; it can't be added to,"[18] both man and culture view nature as fragmented because so much of it remains invisible. If a culture sees only what it eats, or what it considers beautiful, the other part of nature, the symbol without meaning,[19] is invisible, and beyond possibility of transformation.

Man must continually transform himself, or his experiences. Style is a transformation. "Everything that happens may be meaningless, fragmentary and sad, but it is always irradiated by hope or memory."[20] The mind subordinates on its own, and in such subordination thrives the transformation. What is sad becomes hopeful; the self transforms itself into an image of itself. Beyond the cultural transformations visible in totemic systems, "many people observe food prohibitions because they believe themselves to be an animal or fruit which their mother found or noticed while she was pregnant."[21] Such perceptions may be culturally determined in that the animal or the fruit may only have certain associational possibilities, but the self has incorporated the belief in himself, and thereby the world is transformed. "The relation between the person and the object is so close that the person possesses the characteristics of the object with which he is identified."[22] This may be called *style*, or *vision*, but its manifestations are transformations of the self. Within the totemic system the individual is also affirmed through his transformations.

These relations between culture and self, these transformations, are very complex. The individual is his culture, but not entirely. It is through the interrelationships of transformations that "the Holy Ghost speaks every tongue, and everyone hears him in his own."[23] Cultural transformations may reify experience into deity, but the voice the individual assumes can be found only through his own transformations. Voice, style, is difficult to attain, or to develop, or to realize within a transformation. The voice is often confused with "spaces of transformation only, singular spots or slack varieties."[24] The individual transformation is an affirmation of the individual voice.

Such a voice may be discovered in rites of initiation, despite the fact that these rites seem instituted by the culture. Rites of initiation are rites of magic, and among certain Australian tribes, "the medicine men cause their magical influence to enter the novices, thus making them pleasing to Daramulun [the Supreme Being]."[25] At a point in the initiation, an incisor is removed from the initiate,[26] and this absence of tooth, this space, is proof that the deity has swallowed the boy and disgorged him as man. At this point, after the transformation of culture, of boy to man, the initiated is responsible for his own transformation. What he makes, in his existence, of the space is up to him. One has visions for oneself. And one's visions transform one's being to an essence beyond definitions of culture. From the view and situation of the individual, nature cannot be transformed until the individual is transformed. From this point, and only this point, do the ancestors become "nothing but the products of transformation."[27] Without the individual transformation, the cultural transformation of the ancestors is without force, since the cultural transformation must be lived in the individual to become meaningful. Cultural transformations are movements of power; individual transformations are movements of identity. Silence, despite Canetti's claim,[28] makes possible the self-transformation. Speech facilitates the cultural transformation. Problems of silence, of self-renewal, cause the hunter to compose "a new manner of hunting to match the change in his quarry; he has to transform himself."[29] The voice is barely audible: silent. It accounts for subtle changes in the status quo through transforming and re-transforming the individual.

The mask also transforms the individual, and the mask is silent. The mask, through its silence, allows one to enter another existence, to be transformed. This occurs within the context of culture, but not because of it. It may be, momentarily, that "a man who is disguised does not want to be recognised, but instead to appear as someone else and be taken for him."[30] But a man disguised is not a man hiding, but a man transformed. Mask silence does not hide or cover, it opens a new world in which acts and activities are transformed to match its newness. A person who plays such games does not deny continuity with himself,[31] he becomes continuous with himself, and with his culture, through a transformation; he exists for himself and by himself within a context of culture. His identity is not lost, but regained, which is why masks are so essential in religious activities. Without possibility of transformation, the mask is only a lie. Thus, originally, the mask did not obscure, it illuminated, and illumination is an essence, a combination, of result and process.

Transformation leads, through its combinations, to an image, a transforming image. If a man identifies himself with the unit of his money,[32] this identification becomes the transforming image, and the image is without or beyond history. From the point of view of history, narratives of the image, of the self and of the place transformed, are inevitably fictitious.[33] Tradition, in which the landscape and its vestments have been transformed to a cultural image, may associate "local features with people who lived long after their construction."[34] Without the possibility of transformation, which the thrust of history tends to arrest, the mask is only a lie. When the mask illuminates, the landscape speaks an image of culture, and the individual transformation may also occur. The transforming image is reality;[35] and embodies the only possibility for reality, since nature by itself is sufficient in and of itself. Transformation is a "deformation of information,"[36] and the image, like all images, is an illusion. The real, like truth, is reflected in the image. "Metamorphosis is omnipotence,"[37] because it clearly fixes the transforming image; time and space merge in an image of transformation.

So what we possess is a landscape with two faces, one more apparent than the other: the face of the culture, and the face of the self. "The transformation is a transformation into the true."[38] But truth, the true, is the self-image reflected everywhere. Nature is sufficient in and of itself. The transformation is true to itself: it reflects image unflinchingly. It is not simply that "the being of representation is superior to the being of the material represented";[39] the point is that the image is the true; it is the representation, the transformation, which creates and validates simultaneously. And such an image is an ethnocentrism which sees truth in the material represented. The rock invariably bears the shape of the culture, and the shape of the individual transforming image. According to Lévi-Strauss, "Completely virgin landscapes have a monotony which deprives their wildness of any significant value. They withhold themselves from man; instead of challenging him, they disintegrate under his gaze."[40] The crucial word here is *virgin*, if virgin means untouched by man, untouched by his hands, and by his mind. Untouched by hands, a landscape can appear serene; untouched by minds, the landscape is monotonous because it reflects no culturally coherent image; an image of the-thing-itself can never be an image of truth. A burden of truth, of an omnipresent image, is easier to bear than a vision of chaos, which cultures seldom experience because of the omnipresence of image. The increase of a culture cannot be separated from its transformations.[41] Without the transforming image, a culture has no increase; it will rot in monotony. Perhaps this is why, knowing we are killing nature, we continue unabated. We may drown in our images of ourselves, but we have no other cultural solution, no alternative to the monotony of the untransformed. We cannot bear to think of nature without us. The hunter transforms himself and his prey to fit an image, to conform to an increase. What the Bushman feels, thinking of a distant ostrich or springbok, is himself.[42] And his transformations of the animal correspond precisely to the transformations of his own body. All transformation is therefore a kind of cannibalism, an alliance in which nature is consumed by the transforming image,[43] and re-formed in the image of the culture. Nature, when viewed by the image, cannot exist by itself. A landscape is only meaningful as it is incorporated by image, as it is given the language of the transforming culture. All human activity bears a degree of ethnocentrism; the absolutely non-ethnocentric is the absolutely untransformed. To change a culture, one must change its transformations: a task no revolution has ever accomplished.

So the transformed landscape wears the face of the self within the face of the culture. The religious leader who spoke of the landscape being transformed into an agricultural haven by the presence of God's chosen was expressing the image in its totality. In fact, he, of all people, spoke most rightfully and most self-assuredly, because "the man who is himself denied all transformation [his own voice is stilled by his figuration of power] can transform others as he pleases."[44] And others *are* transformed; their voice is a voice in unison: the power of an image.

The landscape is *its* transformation, is the cultural legacy it has been coaxed to wear. Is a human space, both of culture and of the individual: a coalescing image of truth and meaning.

Chapter Fourteen

Human Spaces: The Fields of Symbol

Anything that couldn't be reduced to a formula did not exist.

Elias Canetti
The Torch in My Ear

We are doomed historically to history, to the patient construction of discourses about discourses, and to the task of hearing what has already been said.

Michel Foucault
The Birth of the Clinic

Human life is a tissue of spaces. These spaces join one another, they intrude upon one another, and they occasionally melt together, becoming one space, or no space at all. I have on both my hands a field of spaces, a field of white spaces. These spaces are scars, and these spaces provide *me* absolute access to the past, a past irretrievable and unknowable through history, but a past vivified by the space of the scar. These spaces have a textuality: through them I read pains of the past, and the vastness of circumstances surrounding those pains. A ragged scar, a white field, from the thrusting point of a knife; in it, or through it, I read a squash harvest, a black widow spider, a blade mistakenly running home in the flesh of a finger. And I read much more through this living text, this white space. The spaces we are, we inhabit, we create, are manifestations of a past, of a time-of-times, of circumstances that are, perhaps, beyond codification: they begin without cue, and they end without chronological limitation.

Because we have been taught not to look to these spaces for past-meaning (but instead to the rigidity of the historical text, or the ethno-centrism of the genealogy), their meaning seems difficult, or we allow for no meaning at all in these spaces, these symbols of the intensity of life, "created in the shock of trifles."[1] These spaces do have a word, perhaps a *last* word, but only if they can be read, or only if they can be read for what they are (their field, their whiteness) and what they represent (a past so immediate, so crucial, that it may have become invisible). "Bareness and space (and spacing)," wrote Agee, "are so difficult and seem to me of such greatness that I shall not even try to write seriously or fully of them."[2] They are momentous because they reveal a lived past, and they are difficult because we ignore or subvert them. The noise of a noble history buries a "sufficient quiet and passive concentration"[3] required for expressions of space: for the deep meaning of mutual relationships, of time becoming space, and of space becoming time. A place, says Wright Morris, "where the dreams crossed, a point in time rather than in space."[4] Or perhaps, we might say, a point where space and time are no longer separable, because they are no longer artifactual, because they have not become the property of a historicity: a place of several dimensions but no direction,[5] because the direction, the thrust of a chronology, has always been imposed upon the several choices of the space. The figures and moments of these spaces, and of the language they imply and exude, are "remote from anything the proper historian understands as history."[6]

These spaces have no history, and their dialect, their idiom, is of the soul, and of the experiences in and of that soul. And this knowledge, this possibility for knowing the greatness of the spaces, is not histor-ical, but what the physicians of the eighteenth century identified as philosophical:[7] knowledge involving origins, principles, and causes. The knowing of history is a preface. The knowing of history is a crowding preface: a gloss. The knowing of cultural, of human spaces is a restful textuality. Separation and obscuring of the human space has been a condition of science, and of a historicity. Mythological space and myth-ological time were not only separated from scientific space and time,[8] but obliterated by them. Thus the voices of the elemental spaces have been silent, and we have been taught not to listen to their voices. If "the chief aim of magic is to control spirits, [by] controlling their time and space,"[9] then when cultural space is dulled, even nullified, the spirit is not liberated, but made amorphous, wandering. The formless spaces of Los Angeles do not release, they terrify. The city wanders, and so does the spirit. The spaces are dark, salable, enigmatic, violent. The spirit is afforded no protection; magic dwindles and dies—but we have a clear history of the city, a knowledge of the preface.

Culture yearns for perceptions of space. Whether those perceptions agree that the most beautiful thing in the wilderness is a road,[10] or a stunted juniper at the edge of a cliff,[11] space and perceptions of space are crucial; space is culture, and a culture must be spaces. A crowd becomes a crowd within and because of its spaces. And the essence of crowds or cultures is expressed in their respective spaces. The very real differences between nations[12] may be read in the differences between their cultural spaces. Language is space, and space is language. "It is true that those who are brought up in a particular linguistic and cultural tradition see the world in a different way from those who belong to other traditions."[13] But such views are expressed in a culture's spaces.

Studies of space, because of the resistance of the subject not only to standard scholarly approaches, but also to the discourse of scholarship, or of normal scholarship, are relatively non-existent. Michel Foucault, however, in several of his important works, has dealt with perceptions of space surrounding the human body, within which the body is defined and given a meaning. The space of hysteria, for example, defined the body "in the coherence of its organic and its moral values."[14] The "theme" of certain diseases is found in perceptions of space surrounding the body, so that a common theme for both hysteria and hypochondria is constriction:[15] a space which presses in upon the body. The asylum itself, the place of confinement, is also perceived and defined according to its spaces, the doctor residing in the space of preponderance.[16] Such spaces are neither natural nor predictable. These spaces are determined by certain cultural institutions and their perceptions of what is real, desirable, and reprehensible. To write of the clinic, then, is to write about space and about language,[17] at least from the point of view of an archaeologist of space rather than a historian of places. Problems of shifting perceptions of patients and of their diseases (when and if the two were actually separable) are read only in the spaces they vacate,[18] and in the reappearance, re-perception, of other spaces. What has changed in such situations is not the intelligence or humanity of the group, but "the silent configuration in which language finds support."[19] Spaces change and fluctuate only with the language that expresses them, that creates them. The supposed empiricism of modern medicine, says Foucault, is based upon a "reorganization of manifest and secret space" that occurred when a different view of suffering was taken.[20] We might say, then, that suffering equals space, that suffering from culture to culture, even expressed within something as varied and changeable as the built landscape, is expressed, made meaningful and acceptable, through spatiality. Suffering signifies what a culture determines and is expressed in the spaces a culture has provided. This is as true, as crucial, in the sufferings of the Donner Party as it is in the sufferings of apoplectics in eighteenth-century Europe.

The image of space expressed in the family genealogical tree[21] (that the essence of a family summed by a close relationship of progenitors within a certain closed space) is the image that determines the importance and meaning of a family. This is not logical, and it is not rational; it is the pure expression of the power of spaces. In such an instance, the family becomes "a social space conceived in its most natural, most primitive, most morally secure form, both enclosed upon itself and entirely transparent."[22] The family, like its genealogy, becomes what its spaces demand. Perceptions of space transform the family from a biological unit to a moral unit.

Likewise, other human institutions are also transformed. Meanings, for example, of sexuality are determined within the space a culture allots them. A wide space: sexuality is a biology, a force. A narrow space: sexuality is confined; it moves into the home. "A single locus of sexuality was acknowledged in social space as well as at the heart of every household."[23] Sexuality may have a short history, but it has a long space, a space revealing the remembered past, a space constricting or illuminating. And in some rare cases in which the culture provides no spaces for certain of its members, spaces must be created. McLuhan says that "in a culture that assigns roles instead of jobs to people—the dwarf, the skew, the child create their own spaces."[24] Without some determined space there is no such thing as human existence, and the spaces of existence are determined by the language those who inhabit the spaces have been forced, coaxed, or allowed to speak. A destruction of space is a destruction of humanity, and also of the space itself. Patrick White speaks quite literally when he writes that "in Greece the enchanted distance is often destroyed by close acquaintance."[25] Space is destroyed by altering whatever it includes or excludes, as well as the limits (or boundaries) of those inclusions or exclusions.

Gadamer also writes of space and its totality when he says "language is not just one of man's possessions in the world, but on it depends the fact that man has a world at all."[26] Man's world is a manifestation of the language of his spaces, and without these spaces there is no world. "Matters of fact come into language,"[27] and these matters of fact are matters of space. One cannot separate a culture's language and its spaces. One determines the other. "Like animal environments the world in which man lives is built up out of elements that are available to human senses."[28] But human perceptions of space go far beyond territoriality. The animal environment is essentially a closed space. The human environment submits space to an endless variety of transformations, transformations which both define and move a culture. Human space is defined not by its vastness or territoriality, but by its ability to transform, to exude and incorporate a language. Therefore, "whoever has language 'has' the world."[29]

Language implies space, and space is the human world. Differences between cultural spaces and cultural forms are linguistic. Such a linguistic differences (and therefore spatial differences) Frazer assumed when he wrote that "every faith has its appropriate music, and the difference between the creeds might almost be expressed in musical notation."[30] Cultural space is the music of language; it is a notation expressly reflecting the world of a people. Therefore, Witherspoon's book about language and art in the Navajo universe is, primarily, a book about cultural space,[31] in which language determines spaces,[32] and spaces determine action or non-action. Emerson believed that time and space relations vanish as laws are known,[33] but time and space determine laws, and laws fluctuate with altered perceptions of time and space, just as the landscape, the horizon, has no owner even though it may be composed of parcels of land subject to illusions of ownership. Horizon is a space in total defiance of ownership. A crowd may equal its space, but some spaces cannot be humanized, and are un-ownable. Those which are humanized, which have and speak a language, imply a hierarchy, and that hierarchy can only be disturbed through "the violation of generally established and universally visible and valid distances."[34] To alter space is to alter culture.

A hierarchy of spaces implies difference. There are culturally dead spaces (between a fence and a freeway, for example), lifeless spaces, untouched and untouchable—isolated by or caught between other spaces, other moments, other language. And there are also living spaces, some of supposed utility, and some of great sacrality. The holy-of-holies is a living space within other sacred spaces. The tombs of the pharoahs contained elaborate defenses to protect their sacred space.[35] Sacred space is a privileged space, and it speaks a privileged language. This privileged space is also essential space. On January 3, 1782, the Iroquois sent to England proof of their loyalty to Britain during the American War of Independence. This patriotism, this assurance, was conceived in space and expressed in the life of clearly marked symbols. The proof comprised eight pecks of scalps, cured, dried, hooped and painted with triumphal marks—spaces. All eight pecks were invoiced, their spaces described:

> No. 1—Containing 43 scalps of Congress soldiers killed in different skirmishes. These are stretched on black hoops, four-inch diameter, the inside of the skin, painted red with a small black spot to note their being killed with bullets. Also, 62 of farmers, killed in their homes, the hoops red, the skin painted brown and marked with a hoe, a black circle all around to denote their being surprised in the night and a black hatchet in the middle signifying their being killed with that weapon.[36]

These marks of triumph are sacred marks; the marks speak louder than scalps. Without the imposition of sacred space, the scalps are only carrion. Because they bear the small space of a hatchet, or of a hoe, they are a promise of cultural worth, of loyalty: the figuration of an entire culture, a space of manifest good will, the space of a language.

Foucault has shown that one way culture has determined who is mad, or what is mad, is through perceptions of sacred space. Alienation of the madman, and thus a definition of madness, occurs outside the sacred limits of the cultural ethic.[37] Other maladies, like leprosy, were not suppressed, but kept at a sacred distance, fixed in an inverse exaltation.[38] Thus disease and disorder exist only outside the limits of a sacred space; thus also the sick are given a space of their own, a space of perpetual impoverishment, a space which results in both "the protection and the preservation of disease."[39] Each space has its own language, and the world of that space is the world of its language. "It inscribes in the space of silence and in the silence of space the living time of voice."[40] Thus, voice circumscribes itself and creates itself; it is its space. And voice cannot transcend the space of itself: it is of itself and for itself. All of these spaces, these languages, are exclusive: they are vicious and inward-turning. Therefore, "the purge, the sacralization of a given space, of a *templum*, of a garden, begins by the total and radical expulsion of all species."[41] A community, a sense of community, is only possible within the exclusive limits of a space that has become sacred to its inhabitants. The world of the scalp, inscribed and delimited to the Iroquois, was a sacred space, was a world of ultimate loyalty: a gift of language.

A price, of course, is paid for sacred space; a payment is made for territory.[42] For a community a person sacrifices some of his own essential space; he is devoured, in part, by the space of community. But man also devours space by hiding in it. In it time is suspended: time becomes space, and space becomes time. And the inhabitant of the sacred space devours both. It is history (the gloss of events, the denier of space) that hides "the fact that man is the universal parasite, that everything and everyone around him is a hospitable space."[43] But such space has also devoured man's space: a price is paid for community; a hiding place within a hiding place is made partly visible. Cultural spaces display a "harmonious geometry";[44] the holy place is purified by a sense of order, by an act of community. The unclean is made clean, and the unholy is made holy. "The founding of the naked, empty field, virgin once more, is the oldest work of the human world,"[45] because the creation and recreation of sacred space is an act of purification; its virginity and age create a holy, white space. But that space is exclusive. And the individual space dwindles. Frye notes that "as the Bible goes on, the area of sacred space shrinks."[46] And as the sacred space dwindles, the space of the individual expands; thus, Jesus is not only a wanderer, but the only major figure in the Bible with a voice clearly his own, with a discourse that transcends the cultural space. He was crucified for his voice, which denied the shrinking sacred space, the temple, the holy-of-holies. The voice of the individual space is antithetical to the language of the cultural space.

To find oneself is to find oneself excluded: beyond the boundaries of cultural sacrality. "All sacred things must have their place. . . . being in their place is what makes them sacred."[47] Sacred objects within their sacred spaces therefore maintain the order of the universe simply by being in place. Community in such a sense implies stasis; the individual always threatens the place of order with a disorder, with a voice. But both the communal and the individual space elude history. Spaces are the past, and the past is enclosed within spaces, but there is no history of the space, of the isolated image, or of the communal image. "Space that has been seized upon by the imagination cannot remain indifferent space subject to the measures and estimates of the surveyor."[48] Space that has been inhabited is a space of imagination. Since it cannot be measured, such space has no history, but it has a language, and it is a language.

In a sense, all cultural spaces are sacred spaces, no matter their smell or their appearance; they are sacred because they are language-mirrors. Even the forgotten spaces speak a forgotten language. Spaces are fixed, and spaces fix.

Therefore, I see in the profusion of my scars, in each white field, the past fixed and immeasurable in the luminous, clear details of imagination. I read my past in and through these spaces. I live my life, and I re-live my life, through these spaces, these symbols of experience. The meaning of these spaces exists for no one but me; these spaces are channels to a past without a language, but with a voice. In spite of my language, I search for a voice, for a voice of the inner spaces, a voice of the white fields: a voice to match the immensity and the intensity of experience, of the vastness of a past discoverable only through its spaces. Of a past that, finally, is of its spaces and for its spaces, and made vital through an existential wilderness.

Chapter Fifteen

Of Night in a Wilderness:
Let Us Now Praise
Famous Men

All history is modern history.
Wallace Stevens
"Adagia"

It would be better to write the grim, stupid, tragic
history of all the pleasures which societies object to
or renounce.
Roland Barthes
The Pleasure of the Text

The Man Who Lives Here is a Loony.
Neighborhood children, 1938

There is a wilderness of ideas, or a wilderness which resists the idea:
the inroads of the category, of the methodical illusion. But this wilderness persists while the close and careful category revolves about it.
Wilderness is darkness to the category, and the category is darkness to
wilderness. The two are exactly antithetical. One's light is the other's
darkness. Truth is not a grand totality, but an array of fragments, a
texture of the non-categorical.

When James Agee's *Let Us Now Praise Famous Men* is viewed from
the pedestal of totality, a place of the careful accumulation of facts, it
is beyond illumination: it is a work of darkness surrounded by darkness:
a buffoon of literary historicity. But *Let Us Now Praise Famous Men* cannot be viewed from the special vantage point of historicity; views

from that place have prompted an obscurantism and a dismissal,[1] not an attempt to interpret or understand what may well be the most important text ever published in the United States, as well as the most important work of cultural assessment and cultural sensibility—a will-to-man—ever published. Agee must be seen through images of space and trans-formation—not history—if we are to come to terms with his disturbing book. (Coming to terms, by the way, does not mean coming to classifica-tion.) We must enter a wilderness, in which the book is only a book by necessity (convenience, habit, convention), in which the book becomes "an effort in human actuality."[2] And the supreme question becomes not merely what do we know, what can we know—but what is human actuality? The question is one of existence—of the presence of not only flesh and blood, but spittle, excrement, vermin, racial prejudice, and cotton. Such problems cannot be booked, and exist only in a space and through a transformation. As Agee wrote: "A piece of the body torn out by the roots might be more to the point" (p. 13). The problem is that "in the wish for brilliance and emphasis and propriety, everything is overstepped" (p. 283).

And since the really crucial problems are ignored or subordinated, they come to be seen as an ultimate obscenity: a movement against both cultural and artistic categories. The obscene is that which defiles history: the emphasis, the sense of propriety. Consider, for example, the cultured avoidance of not only *Let Us Now Praise Famous Men*, but all of Agee's work, by the apotheosis of American literary studies, or the study of American Literature: the journal *American Literature*. Since the journal runs on a careful historicity, it cannot afford to deal with the obscene. Its own special subversion is to ignore that which is really good. The not-said of avoidance is a special lesson in censorship, which is itself an act of pornography. When Agee writes of the "hideous jokes of education" (p. 109), he brutalizes the category and its system: the subordinating principles which place books before people. Education functions largely to keep one in one's place by teaching acceptance and respect (p. 308), by raising the category to a cultural verity.

According to Robert Phelps, *Let Us Now Praise Famous Men* is "at the same time one of the most vulnerable perversities and surest glories of American literature."[3] The book is neither perverse nor indigenously American; it only seems to be so when measured in the shadows of history, whether that history be nationalistic or literary. But that which seems to deny a sense of historicity is ultimately obscene, perhaps, as noted in earlier chapters, because we have no language to describe events which lack a sense of history. Such seems to be the case in one critic's search for words to describe *Let Us Now Praise Famous Men*, words which are confused in their inability to arrange a consensus: the book is "an appalling inventory of the irrelevant, the incidental, and the relevant"; it is pretentiously whimsical.[4] Another reviewer found the book repetitious, obscene, and "obsessed with irrelevant detail."[5] Within this disorder of words is a sense of terror, a terror of the disorder itself, a frightening inability to make sense of a work without predictable boundaries. The work was "an American literary freak,"[6] even though Winfield Townley Scott admitted that those, after all, are our greatest books.

If greatness, freakishness, and the obscene are synonymous in these contexts, what are the implications for Agee's book? Perhaps it is the one book, or one of few, that has placed itself completely beyond the possibility of parasitism: of categorization, of respectability, of compromise, of the possibility for symbiosis. Such a disturbing lack of access is certainly obscene; we seem comfortable only in a world where parasitism, the warm exchange of adulation, is the rule of the day. And nationalism is a prime form of parasitism. Critics have reasoned that if Agee's book defies classification, at least the author doesn't; at least he is an American. And since he is American, hopefully his book will be also. "He was," wrote a friend, "American to the marrow." And further: "What being an American meant for an imaginative writer was very much on his mind."[7] The problem, of course, is that we have no idea what being American means; even if we could define or isolate an indigenous American crowd symbol, we would have no idea to what extent Americans may be prompted by that symbol. *Let Us Now Praise Famous Men* is only incidentally American, but it is human to the core: too human, in fact, for comfort. It was the quest for a nationalism which prompted Agee critics to strongly fault the book; because the situation of tenant farmers had improved, they reasoned, Americans were helping themselves.[8] God indeed helps those who help themselves.

The book itself defies an implied Americanism. Says Agee: "I despise and deplore the middle-class American worship of sterility and worship-fear of its own excrement" (p. 211). And he later deplored "the American genius for sterility, unimagination, and general gutlessness in meeting any opportunity for 'reform' or 'improvement'" (p. 297). Of course, renunciation of these American externals does not mean the author has rejected his own Americanism or that he can reject it. But he makes a jagged cut along a deeper, more tender nerve when he describes Americans as "creatures of a nation which has never learned loving and happy living" (p. 391). These are the genuine obscenities of *Let Us Now Praise Famous Men*: sins against the mother-country, which are sins against a glorious history, even sins against a manifest destiny which had never been manifest in the depths of American poverty. (Not that the book is a social invective—it isn't—but the ideation of movement does have its limits.)

Agee's book is the one text, written by a person who happened to be an American, that most clearly deals with a human past while it remains totally beyond the auspices of historicity. In *Let Us Now Praise Famous Men*, "all the logical small change" of history, that *is* history, is in the interstices.[9] The book is as illogical as it is ahistorical; the two do not seem separable. The book is an "uncomfortably original work,"[10] because it denies us access to the historical as it simultaneously denies us access to the subordinating transformations of cultural logic. The book is logical only in the sense that it is human. But critics have demanded a history–biography, and have assumed that the text can be intelligible only when measured by the life of its author. "The book demands, as few other books do, a reading in the light of the writer's own life."[11] This is the ultimate mistrust, and takes the form of a plea to the historical, of a plea for the retrievable events of an author's life, to take the place of his work. Such a retrieval of the subordinated past leads to speculations, assertions, that Agee was "born in the wrong time and place,"[12] when in fact he was born in exactly the right time and place, not because of a providential fortuitousness, but because of his book. The right time and the right place for a book to be written is when and where it was written. Aesthetics seldom keep pace with historicity, at least not the aesthetics of a remembered, not a taught, past.

The book itself brings us to a past, the significance of reverie: "The truest way to treat a piece of the past is as such: as if it were no longer the present" (p. 243). This is the past, continues Agee, not of chronological progression, but of un-ordered recall and free association "forward and backward upon the then past and the then future, across that expanse of experience" (p. 244). This is a past of the reverie and the timeless and unpredictable subordination of the mind: what the mind is, what it re-creates from the chaos of events. So that "all of the past one finds useful is 'usable' because it is of the present and because both present and past are essentially irrelevant to the whole manner of 'use'" (p. 353). The word is *use*, not utility. Usable people, says Agee, are timeless. They are timeless because their use is a use of reverie. The "'actual,' 'unrecreated' world of personal or speculative experience" (p. 353) has nothing whatsoever to do with the chronology of events, with the particular illusions of historical systems. And the materials of this past, this apolitical place of movement and of the unpredictable, are "a universe of things which should be accepted and recorded for its own sake" (p. 467). Such materials can never be part of a history *for*, since they always exist beyond the utility of the system in a place labeled obscene, where the past and the present are no longer distinguishable (p. 471). The past is a major moment in Agee's book; it is the natural, indelible validator of human experience.

But this past is impervious to the inroads of history: there are no systems here, only people, only the obscene, only acts of being human.[13] Since the language of normal criticism has grounded itself firmly in the historical mainstream, in the flow of institutional events, we have no critical language for *Let Us Now Praise Famous Men*. The book is ahistorical; the langage of normal criticism is thoroughly historical. Here, there is no "cohabitation of languages *working side by side*."[14] There is, rather, a language and a not-language. The poet is the priest of the invisible,[15] of the not-language, the obscene rather than the pro-prietous, the clear, the cleanly chronological. About Agee's book of poems, published when he was twenty-five, one interpreter has observed that "it was as if the interests and pressures of the time made it inaudible."[16] Actually, the inaudibility of the text was (and continues to be) the condition of *Let Us Now Praise Famous Men*. Because we have no language for Agee's book, we are deaf to the language it speaks. *Let Us Now Praise Famous Men*, therefore, is not a satisfactory or a satisfying book. Satisfaction and greatness are antithetical. What Agee has done is project meaning and a kind of order into the chaos of human affairs by his language.[17] But his transformations remain inaudible because they defy every cultural prescription and human formula we have known. And yet the book has a clear and present voice. Critical language for this voice beyond criticism: beyond the dead language of the status quo, within the invulnerability of a thoroughly predictable world, sees the expression of "self-destructive guilt and creative overreaching."[18] What the voice has whispered is that "all values must remain vulnerable, and those that do not are dead."[19] Agee's voice is always vulnerable, and *Let Us Now Praise Famous Men* therefore remains disturbingly alive.

What most have searched for in this book is the possibility of structure,[20] the blessed rage for the order of the overt transformation, not the possibility of meaning. Meaning always eludes structures both imposed and implied. Agee cannot be understood through the application of a methodology, but by learning the subtle language of *human* voice. *Let Us Now Praise Famous Men* is not a social document,[21] as the language of invulnerability would have us believe. On the contrary, it is an existential document, a chaotic reverie, a text of vulnerability. The voice in Agee's text does not speak a language of "a shameless lack of responsibility."[22] The voice is eminently responsible; but it is responsible for an expression of human essence, the highly vulnerable, not a structure or a category. His language is shameless because it is vulnerable and ahistorical. Lionel Trilling's answer for this disturbing sense of vulnerability is to call the book a piece of "American liberal writing."[23] But the book is not American. And it is not liberal—that is, it is apolitical rather than aligned. The respectable noise of normal criticism attempts a transformation of the vulnerable to the invulnerable. In Agee's words, "All of this, I repeat, seems to me curious, obscene, terrifying, and unfathomably mysterious" (p. 8). The voice hears itself; it can admit chaos beyond the transformation. This is, I repeat, not a "normal" social document. Agee hears in the half-wakened mutterings of these people a cadence and comfort "which anneals all fence of language and surpasses music" (p. 58). This work is a particle of the chaos of existence: the unvanquishable poetry of the oppressed (p. 215). The book is not art; it is its antithesis: a piece of flesh torn out by the roots. So that the scarcely-visible becomes not only visible, but omnipresent. "Of milk," writes Agee, "I hardly know how to say; it is skimmed, blue-lighted; to a city palate its warmth and odor are somehow

dirty and at the same time vital, a little as if one were drinking blood"
(p. 416). The drinking of milk has no history, and it seems to have no
politics: a nameless activity which forms part of an image of humanity.

This image is not classifiable. The act of milk drinking, like virtually
every other act and action in the book, is ahistorical. We can neither
classify nor codify, and because of this the book remains vulnerable: it
remains a great human document. "What relation can there be between
the pleasure of the text and the institutions of the text? Very slight."[24]
The essence of a text and its politicization have nothing in common. The
Classification: a distinguished failure.[25] The essence: a piece of flesh torn
out by the roots. While we search for a "coherence in Agee's life and
writing,"[26] the book persists in its chaos. Ironically, critics are able to
say, in sentences that are almost back-to-back, that Agee defied categorization, while they search to "determine the extent to which James Agee
used autobiographical writing."[27] The chaos of context must have a
predictable (discoverable) content. The morphology (truth) of the critic
is his own image.

Greatness, however, has little to do with logical thought and disci-
plined action.[28] At least, these do not seem discoverable in actual
context, but only in a feigned reflection—not of the writer, but of an
imposed category, the category which fails to enclose the text itself,[29]
because its language is beyond classification—even the implied classification of comparing *Let Us Now Praise Famous Men* to *Moby Dick*.[30]
Except that both Agee's and Melville's books deal with a chaos, they
seem to me to have little in common. One defines itself within a wilderness of symbols; the other within a wilderness of human emotions. And
while symbol and emotion may be synonymous, their portrayal in literature is not: symbols can be frozen in space; human emotions cannot. An
objectivity of thought and intent may swirl about the arrested symbol;
human emotions are as unobjective as they are ahistorical.

And Agee has been faulted for his lack of objectivity. Critics uncomfortably admit that the subject of *Let Us Now Praise Famous Men* is
Agee himself.[31] But it is this lack of objectivity which makes the book
forever vulnerable. The real liars, whether they hide in the robes of
ethnologist or novelist, are those who claim an unbiased objectivity in
their work. This illusion of objectivity comes from a happy awareness of
the scientific method: simply one face of a cultural transformation which

sees life and the world as thoroughly predictable. Of course Agee is not objective. The wilderness of human emotions is a difficult space for the science of measurement—at least prejudices here have other faces, faces which seem boundless. So Agee's compassion, writes one critic, "so lacked boundaries that it was tantamount to masochism."[32] Passion is always suspect, whether its boundaries can be discovered or not. The problem is that passion, like other emotions, is boundless. And passion is always vulnerable, perhaps because it is not objective. Problems of sharecropping may be timely or untimely,[33] but problems of passion are in no way bounded by time. They have a place and they don't have a place. The point is, how does one not simply portray passion in a book, but actually get the flesh torn out by the roots onto the pages? This is accomplished not through propriety or compromise,[34] but through passion. Of course, Agee worked within the confines of his own reality.[35] But with Agee, the transformations he imposed upon the perceived suffering of tenant farmers were transformations of and by his own passions, not of or by political, historical, or social systems. His transformations, then, were ultimately obscene.

And yet there is a major push in Agee criticism to label *Let Us Now Praise Famous Men* as religious or moral. This is the genuine obscenity, for if the term religion (L. *religio*) implies not only reverence for the gods, but a system of religious belief, then Agee's book is as irreligious as it is ahistorical. Wright Morris says the book defies imitation, and he speaks of the "presence of life in worn-out objects, made holy by use," but sees the burden of intent in Agee's book as religious.[36] The objects are not holy, and the intent is not religious. Parts of Agee's book only seem this way because his method of explication is beyond our cultural transformations, in the place we ambivalently define as either obscene or religious, terms we use for the inexplicable, and thus the threatening: spaces beyond the boundaries of our tranformations.

Other writers have concurred with this sense of the religious: "A religious sense of life, in short—moved James Agee in his best work."[37] And yet it is a sense of the human, the obscene, which seems to have moved Agee. Father Flye, to whom Agee wrote many letters, praised *Let Us Now Praise Famous Men* as deeply religious,[38] but Father Flye had an investment at stake in a profession which generally refers not only to the unknown, but to the unexperienced, as religious. So from this point of view, if Agee wrote of the tenant farmer (the human being) and his accoutrements with passion and sympathy, then "the denim and fertilizer sacks of the tenant man and woman become virtually religious garments."[39] Or they become obscene; at any rate, transformed—not by Agee, but by those to whom the invisible-becoming-visible is a menacing experience, "a peculiarly hopeless form,"[40] written by "a twentieth-century Saint Francis,"[41] "a failure of 'moral realism.'"[42] These labels seems to have little to do with the actualities of Agee's book. Likewise, there are those who saw in the construct of the book a "very basic religious structure,"[43] a religious service "with verses, preamble, inductions, and recessional," even though "the work as a whole does not fall on any established church service structure."[44] Despite effusive religious pronouncements, the anti-structure of the book continues to menace critics, those to whom meaning cannot exist beyond codification.

This religious fervor, this rage for structure continues: "A proper response to the book, again on its own terms, might be: to pray, to join the Peace Corps, to make love, to listen to Beethoven, to eat a good meal."[45] This disgusting, self-indulgent list is thoroughly misleading. If there is a proper response to the book, an admonition of sorts, it is to look in your own drawer, to *look*. We confuse the amorphous with the untransformed; one is shapeless, the other has no possibility of shape. "A work of great moral intensity"[46] does not have, and cannot have a morphology; a religious work is guided by and enclosed within a morphology. Agee saw his book as sinful because it fell short of the mark;[47] he meant the mark of intensity, not the mark of morphology. The religious sense and the moral sense are antithetical: one craves and defines itself by a structure, the other is defined, obscene, ahistorical: beyond the auspices of form. It is the quest for form which suppresses the Moral Voice; that is why systematized thought "can never arrive at a real definition of life."[48] That is also why some purposes are justifiable (they exist within a form), while others are pure (they exist in spite of form).[49] Morality implies conflict; religion implies concordance. There is no unity in morality (only a voice);[50] there is supreme unity in religion (with its accompanying language—or noise). From a religious point of view, morality is obscene because morality shuns the form. From the religious, the group point of view, the moral site (always immaculately defined and described) is "cleansed of any linguistic sensuality."[51] The holy-of-holies is thoroughly predictable, and thoroughly exclusive. The moral space becomes filled; it assumes the structure of a religious icon.

If there is a holiness in *Let Us Now Praise Famous Men*, it is "a holiness of silence" (p. 51): a holiness of space, not a holiness of structure: "there can be more beauty and more deep wonder in the standings and spacings of mute furnishings on a bare floor beween the squaring bourns of walls than in any music ever made" (p. 134). The voice of holiness (and of the moral) is a voice of spaces, not a voice of places. And morality, space, beauty are as inseparable as they are unformed. It is that which is, which is holy (p. 459), not that which shall become. The *is* is the moral; the *shall* is religious. If this book is holy it is because it approaches that which *is* not, that which will become. So that in Agee beauty is anger, and anger is moral. Wallace Stevens seems to have had Agee, or the nonmorphological sense of morality, in mind when he wrote: "There is nothing beautiful in life except life."[52] That is the disturbing core of Agee's book: the obscene is that, and only that, which is beautiful. And that which is true is therefore not only disturbing, but unbearable. Agee spoke of *things* as "full of vitality and of the ardor of their own truth,"[53] a truth of things as they are, not as they will or must become: the truth of the individual space of transformation as opposed to the structure, the worshipped form of the transformation of the group.[54] When one critic timidly wrote of Agee's book that he thought "there was a bit too much expression of self-consciousness and speaking of [Agee's] feelings,"[55] he rightly figured the voice of truth, which obviously embarrassed him with its formlessness and its avoidance of the scientific method, which has erased the individual from interpretation.[56] If this book is a young man's book,[57] it is because the young have not yet been taught to forget, to obscure, to disguise their own voice. Such a disguise is applauded by one critic, who writes:

> Agee, I suspect, eventually came to realize his mistaken judgment when writing *Let Us Now Praise Famous Men* and, for that reason, soon turned to fiction. It is only there, he must have seen, that the "truth" that comes from artistic discipline and from finding the right words in the right order, for example, the truth that is revealed in *A Death in the Family*, shines forth.[58]

The acceptable truth is the truth portrayed in and through the careful and the predictable structure.

Agee, of course, did not concur. "The deadliest blow," he wrote, "the enemy of the human soul can strike is to do fury honor. . . . Official acceptance is the one unmistakable symptom that salvation is beaten again" (p. 15). In every way imaginable, this book resists categorization. It pleases no one (no group, at least); it unmercifully focuses on the thing and the moral idea of the thing, not of its structure, but of its texture, for Agee's book is a book of textures, of feelings, not forms. It is texture we feel in "the subtle almost strangling strong asymmetries of that which has been hand wrought toward symmetry" (p. 38), as in the wood of "a texture and look like that of weathered bone" (p. 132). It is the texture we feel, not the structure we see. The particular quality of things hand-made[59] (p. 144) is the quality of texture. An item is judged by its form, but appreciated by its texture. To feel the thing, one must feel its texture:

> The first is this: In any house, standing in any one room of it, or standing disembodied in remembrance of it, it is possible, by sufficient quiet and passive concentration, to realize for a little while at a time the simultaneity in existence of all of its rooms in their exact structures and mutual relationships in space and in all they contain; and to realize this not merely with the counting mind, nor with the imagination of the eye, which is no realization at all, but with the whole of the body and being, and in translations of the senses so that in part at least they become extrahuman, become a part of the nature and being of these rooms and their contents and of this house. (P. 183)

This texture is a-social, a-historical, a-ethnographic, but deeply human, deeply obscene, and deeply beautiful. "A chain of truths did actually weave itself and run through: it is their texture that I want to represent, not betray, nor pretty up into art" (p. 240). A book about texture is a book about truth. "The more intensely one feels something that one likes the more one is willing for it to be what it is."[60] And what a thing is in *Let Us Now Praise Famous Men* is its texture, is the warm, bloody feel of milk running down a throat, and the fine, weathered grain of a pine board. What matters is the feel of truth, its texture, which is totally beyond a limit or a definition. On the level of the morphological, truth is the self-image reflected everywhere, but on the level of the existential, it is a texture. Truth only matters as it assumes, as it is, a texture. And textures are obscene. But they are also powerful, threatening. "The Mississippi has such power," writes Agee, "that men who have never seen it use its language in their work" (p. 329). A texture of riverness, of an un-seen language, motivates most thoroughly a work. A promise of wage only transforms work to commodity.

Thus language is a texture; the language of this book is a texture. Wilderness is a texture; and wilderness persists. Texture is an array of fragments, and in the non-form of this array lies the human meaning James Agee so painfully touched and spoke about in a book whose greatness lies in pieces—not in the cohesion of a moment of place, but in the space of the thousand voices of night in a wilderness.

Notes

Preface

1. Wright Morris, *Fire Sermon* (Lincoln: University of Nebraska Press, 1979), p. 120.

2. Elias Canetti, *The Torch in My Ear* (New York: Farrar, Straus and Giroux, 1982), p. 308.

3. Wallace Stevens, "Like Decorations in a Nigger Cemetery," in *The Collected Poems* (New York: Random House, Vintage Books, 1982), p. 151.

Chapter One   History and Folklore

1. See Mircea Eliade, *Myth and Reality*, trans. William Trask (New York: Harper and Row, Harper Colophon Books, 1963), p. 1.

2. Alexander Haggerty Krappe, *The Science of Folk-lore* (London: Methuen, 1930), p. ix.

3. Ibid., p. 1.

4. Richard M. Dorson, "Rejoinder to 'American Folklore vs. Folklore in America: A Fixed Fight?'" *Journal of the Folklore Institute* 17 (January–April 1980): 87.

5. Ibid., p. 86.

6. Alan Dundes, "The American Concept of Folklore," *Journal of the Folklore Institute* 3 (December 1966): 241.

7. Dundes' term. Ibid.

8. Ibid.

9. Hayden White, *Tropics of Discourse: Essays in Cultural Criticism* (Baltimore: Johns Hopkins University Press, 1978), p. 59. White's term elsewhere is "exploitive" (see p. 5) rather than "manipulative."

10. Ibid., p. 70. As White notes, he owes a debt to theories developed by Stephen C. Pepper in his *World Hypotheses: A Study in Evidence* (1942;

reprint, Berkeley and Los Angeles: University of California Press, 1970). For a full development and discussion of White's modes of explotment see his *Metahistory: The Historical Imagination in Nineteenth-Century Europe* (1973; reprint, Baltimore: Johns Hopkins University Press, 1975). The book is one of the most valuable discussions of the meaning of the historical method to be published in this century.

11. See White, *Tropics of Discourse*, p. 40.

12. This trend is evident in the nationwide movement to establish folk art programs, largely in conjunction with historical societies and mainly for public consumption.

13. Jean-Paul Sartre, *Being and Nothingness: An Essay in Phenomenological Ontology*, trans. Hazel E. Barnes (1956; reprint, Secaucus, N.J.: Citadel Press, 1974), p. 89.

14. White, *Tropics of Discourse*, p. 39.

15. Ibid.

16. Ibid., p. 82.

17. Ibid., p. 136.

18. Richard M. Dorson, *America in Legend: Folklore from the Colonial Period to the Present* (New York: Random House, Pantheon Books, 1973), p. xiv.

19. Richard M. Dorson, *American Folklore and the Historian* (Chicago: University of Chicago Press, 1971), p. ix.

20. See Carl G. Jung's discussion of this problem in *Man and His Symbols* (New York: Dell, Laurel Books, 1964), pp. 55–56.

21. See Dorson, *American Folklore and the Historian*, p. 28.

22. For a discussion of the "myth meaning" Cooper gave the landscape of the American West, see my article "Fenimore Cooper and the Exploration of the Great West," *Heritage of Kansas: A Journal of the Great Plains* 10 (Spring 1977): 15–24.

23. See John K. Townsend, *Narrative of a Journey Across the Rocky Mountains* (Philadelphia: Henry Perkins, 1839), reproduced in vol. 21 of *Early Western Travels: 1748–1846*, ed. Reuben Gold Thwaites (Cleveland: Arthur H. Clark Co., 1905), p. 244.

24. See D. H. Lawrence, *Studies in Classic American Literature* (New York: Thomas Seltzer, 1923), p. 84.

25. Stephen Stern and Simon J. Bronner, "American Folklore vs. Folklore in America: A Fixed Fight?" *Journal of the Folklore Institute* 17 (January–April

1980): 79. For further thoroughly historicized "objections" to a certain historical methodology in folklore studies see *Western Folklore* 41 (January 1982), for a special section of related articles. In a somewhat historicized article, Barbara Allen sees, nonetheless, the personal transcending the historical. See "The Personal Point of View in Orally Communicated History," *Western Folklore* 38 (April 1979): 110–18.

26. Tom Carter, "Folk Design in Utah Architecture: 1849–90," in *Utah Folk Art*, ed. Hal Cannon (Provo, Utah: Brigham Young University Press, 1980), p. 36.

27. Ibid., p. 56.

28. See my chapter "History and Meaning: The Limitations of Chronology," in my *The Pure Experience of Order: Essays on the Symbolic in the Folk Material Culture of Western America* (Albuquerque: University of New Mexico Press, 1982).

29. Carter's ideas follow Henry Glassie's historical approach in *Folk Housing in Middle Virginia* (Knoxville: University of Tennessee Press, 1975). For a non-historical approach to material culture in which the items are assessed on other terms, see Michael Owen Jones' *The Hand Made Object and Its Maker* (Berkeley and Los Angeles: University of California Press, 1975).

30. Dundes, "American Concept of Folklore," p. 245.

31. Dundes also notes that "American anthropological folklorists under the influence of Franz Boas have also favored a historical approach to folklore." Ibid., p. 241.

32. White, *Tropics of Discourse*, p. 43.

33. Ibid., p. 28.

34. Norman O. Brown, *Life against Death: The Psychoanalytic Meaning of History* (1959; reprint, Middletown, Conn.: Wesleyan University Press, 1970), p. 16.

35. Dundes, "American Concept of Folklore," p. 242.

36. Ibid., p. 243.

37. Michel Foucault, *The Archaeology of Knowledge*, trans. A. M. Sheridan Smith (New York: Harper and Row, Harper Colophon Books, 1976), p. 3.

38. For a discussion of these jokes and several of their implications, see William A. Wilson and Richard C. Poulsen, "The Curse of Cain and Other Stories: Blacks in Mormon Folklore," *Sunstone* 5 (November–December 1980): 9–13.

39. John G. Neihardt, *Black Elk Speaks: Being the Life Story of a Holy Man of the Oglala Sioux* (Lincoln: University of Nebraska Press, Bison Book, 1961).

40. Claude Lévi-Strauss, *The Savage Mind* (Chicago: University of Chicago Press, 1966), p. 258.

41. Thomas S. Kuhn, *The Structure of Scientific Revolutions*, 2d ed. (Chicago: University of Chicago Press, 1970), p. 55.

42. Ernst Cassirer, *An Essay on Man: An Introduction to a Philosophy of Human Culture* (1944; reprint, New Haven: Yale University Press, 1962), p. 175.

43. Ibid., p. 178.

44. Although Clifford Geertz disparages what he calls "blurring genres," such a process, in my opinion, is requisite to genuine discovery. See Clifford Geertz, "Blurred Genres: The Refiguration of Social Thought," *The American Scholar* 49 (Spring 1980): 165–79. Such a process leads to revolutionary rather than normal science, where real discovery (in the revolution) takes place.

45. See White, *Tropics of Discourse*, p. 42.

46. Ibid., p. 50.

47. Ibid., p. 99. Erich Neumann writes of the establishment of a "psycho-history" and contends that normal history is unable to assess or deal with basic human problems. See *The Great Mother: Analysis of the Archetype*, trans. Ralph Manheim (reprint, Princeton: Princeton University Press, 1974), pp. 89–90.

48. See René Girard, *Violence and the Sacred*, trans. Patrick Gregory (Baltimore: Johns Hopkins University Press, 1977), p. 9.

49. See Jacques Lacan, *Ecrits: A Selection*, trans. Alan Sheridan (New York: Norton, 1977), p. 103.

50. Brown, *Life against Death*, p. ix.

51. Ibid., p. 12.

52. Sartre, *Being and Nothingness*, p. lxii.

53. Ibid., p. 45.

54. Ibid., p. 85.

55. Ibid., p. 92.

56. See Michel Foucault, *Discipline and Punish: The Birth of the Prison*, trans. Alan Sheridan (New York: Random House, Vintage Books, 1979), p. 31.

57. Alberto Busignani, *Pollock* (Feltham, Middlesex, England: Hamlyn, 1971), cover flap.

58. Gary Witherspoon, *Language and Art in the Navajo Universe* (Ann Arbor: University of Michigan Press, 1977), p. 175.

59. See my article, "'This is the Place': Myth and Mormondom," *Western Folklore* 36 (July 1977): 246–52.

60. The same conflict, I believe, was responsible on a conscious level for the infamous Mountain Meadows Massacre, in which Mormons murdered Missouri immigrants on their way to California through Utah. See Juanita Brooks, *The Mountain Meadows Massacre* (1950; reprint, Norman: University of Oklahoma Press, 1962).

Chapter Two   The Enigma of the Puritan Mind

1. Cotton Mather, *Magnalia Christi Americana; or, The Ecclesiastical History of New England* (Hartford: Silas Andrus and Son, 1853), vol. 1, p. 145.

2. Cotton Mather, *The Wonders of the Invisible World* (London: John Russell Smith, 1862), p. 27. The third chapter of Colossians exhorts the community to godliness. There is no fifteenth chapter.

3. Ibid., p. 51.

4. Thus Perry Miller and Thomas H. Johnson call him "a case for a psychiatrist" who was, fortunately, not "very representative of Puritanism as a whole." *The Puritans* (New York: American Book, 1938), p. 46.

5. Perry Miller, *The New England Mind: The Seventeenth Century* (New York: Macmillan, 1939), p. 10.

6. Ibid., p. 196.

7. Ibid., p. 5.

8. See Katherine Anne Porter's three chapters on Mather printed in *The Collected Essays and Occasional Writings of Katherine Anne Porter* (New York: Delacorte Press, 1970), p. 314.

9. Ibid., p. 335.

10. Robert Middlekauff, *The Mathers: Three Generations of Puritan Intellectuals, 1596–1728* (1971; reprint, New York: Oxford University Press, 1976), p. 194.

11. Ibid.

12. Ibid. Samuel Eliot Morison, *Harvard College in the Seventeenth Century* (Cambridge: Harvard University Press, 1936), vol. 2, p. 417. Philip Gura,

adding to the long string of diatribes against Mather, writes that "recent criticism supports Calef's observation and has stressed the degree to which many of Mather's public pronouncements were scarcely veiled psychological projections which resolved tensions arising from his imaginative identification with New England and his almost hysterical awareness that upon him had developed the unenviable task of maintaining the purity of the New England churches." See Philip F. Gura, "Cotton Mather's *Life of Phips*: 'A Vice With the Vizard of Vertue Upon It,'" *The New England Quarterly* 50 (September 1977): 440.

13. Kenneth B. Murdock, ed., *Cotton Mather* (New York: Hafen Publishing, 1965), p. xiv.

14. Ibid., p. xxiv.

15. Ibid., p. xxv.

16. Barrett Wendell, *Cotton Mather: The Puritan Priest* (Cambridge: Harvard University Press, 1926), p. 1.

17. Sacvan Bercovitch, "'Nehemias Americanus': Cotton Mather and the Concept of the Representative American," *Early American Literature* 8 (Winter 1974): 235–36.

18. Gustaaf Van Cromphout, "Cotton Mather: The Puritan Historian as Renaissance Humanist," *American Literature* 49 (November 1977): 327.

19. David Levin, "The Hazing of Cotton Mather: The Creation of a Biographical Personality," *The New England Quarterly* 36 (June 1963): 153.

20. Ibid., p. 149.

21. By "historical fallacy" I refer to the assumption that truths of the past can eminently and ultimately be discovered by historical approaches. For a discussion of this problem, see Hayden White, *Metahistory: The Historical Imagination in Nineteenth-Century Europe* (1973; reprint, Baltimore: Johns Hopkins University Press, 1975). See also his *Tropics of Discourse: Essays in Cultural Criticism* (Baltimore: Johns Hopkins University Press, 1978).

22. Miller, *New England Mind*, p. 214.

23. Ibid., p. 229.

24. Pershing Vartanian, "Cotton Mather and the Puritan Transition into the Enlightenment," *Early American Literature* 7 (Winter 1973): 222.

25. Middlekauff, *The Mathers*, p. 194.

26. Gustaaf Van Cromphout's article "Cotton Mather as Plutarchan Biographer," *American Literature* 46 (January 1975): 465–81, is a comparison of

the world-views of Plutarch and Mather. The article is well researched and written, but clearly shows that Mather cannot be understood by perceiving him as historian. Van Cromphout calls Mather "a pathetic Plutarch" (p. 481), a term borrowed from Peter Gay in his *A Loss of Mastery: Puritan Historians in Colonial America* (Berkeley and Los Angeles: University of California Press, 1966), p. 65.

27. Levin, "Hazing," p. 170.

28. Ibid., p. 148.

29. Ibid., p. 171.

30. See Murdock, *Cotton Mather*, p. xvi.

31. See Franz Boas, *The Religion of the Kwakiutl*, Columbia University Contributions to Anthropology (New York: Columbia University Press, 1930), vol. 10, part 2, pp. 1–41.

32. See Claude Lévi-Strauss, "The Sorcerer and His Magic," chap. 10 in *Structural Anthropology*, trans. Claire Jacobson and Brooke Grundfest Schoepf (New York: Basic Books, 1963), p. 180. Henceforth, all references to Lévi-Strauss will be to this essay, and page numbers will be included in the text.

33. Ibid., p. 181. About normal and pathological thought, Lévi-Strauss writes: "In a universe which it strives to understand but whose dynamics it cannot fully control, normal thought continually seeks the meaning of things which refuse to reveal their significance. So-called pathological thought, on the other hand, overflows with emotional interpretations and overtones, in order to supplement an otherwise deficient reality. For normal thinking there exists something which cannot be empirically verified and is, therefore, 'claimable.' For pathological thinking there exist experiences without object, or something 'available.' We might borrow from linguistics and say that so-called normal thought always suffers from a deficit of meaning, whereas so-called pathological thought (in at least some of its manifestations) disposes of a plethora of meaning."

34. When Theodore Hornberger writes: "The significant point about Mather's interest in science would seem, however, to be its paradoxical character. From the very beginning of his career, his attitude towards the external world is curiously confused," he is mistaken in claiming Mather's attitudes were confused. See Theodore Hornberger, "The Date, the Source, and the Significance of Cotton Mather's Interest in Science," *American Literature* 6 (January 1935): 419.

35. Mather believed deeply, privately, personally in witchcraft. See *Diary of Cotton Mather* (New York: Frederick Ungar, [1957]), vol. 1, pp. 150–52.

36. Murdock, *Cotton Mather*, p. x.

37. Wendell, *Cotton Mather*, p. 2.

38. Ibid., p. 109.

39. Middlekauff, *The Mathers*, p. 206.

40. Ibid., p. 207.

Chapter Three   Violence and the Sacred

1. See Leonard J. Arrington and Davis Bitton, *The Mormon Experience: A History of the Latter-day Saints* (New York: Alfred A. Knopf, 1979), p. 324.

2. Sigmund Freud, *Jokes and Their Relation to the Unconscious*, trans. James Strachey (New York: Norton, 1963), p. 178.

3. The implication is that since blacks may now enter the temples, they may also marry there—perhaps even marry those of the white middle class.

4. See Mary Douglas, "The Social Control of Cognition: Some Factors in Joke Perception," *Man* 3 (September 1968): 365.

5. Freud, *Jokes*, p. 132.

6. Ibid., p. 96. Freud explained that tendentiousness in the joke-work is grounded either in obscurity or hostility: they are synonymous (p. 97).

7. Douglas, "Social Control," p. 368.

8. Ibid., p. 375.

9. See H. A. Wolff, C. E. Smith, and H. A. Murray, "The Psychology of Humor: A Study of Responses to Race-Disparagement Jokes," *The Journal of Abnormal and Social Psychology* 28 (January–March 1934): 342.

10. Freud, *Jokes*, p. 15.

11. Ibid., p. 134.

12. See Alan Dundes, "A Study of Ethnic Slurs: The Jew and the Polack in the United States," *Journal of American Folklore* 84 (April–June 1971): 186.

13. See Daniel Katz and Kenneth W. Braly, "Verbal Stereotypes and Racial Prejudice," in *Readings in Social Psychology*, ed. Eleanor E. Maccoby, Theodore M. Newcomb, and Eugene L. Hartley, 3d ed. (New York: N.p., 1958). The

authors note that "it is not necessary to have a well worked out set of such rationalizations [of the undesirable qualities of a group] to obtain expressions of extreme prejudice" (pp. 45–46).

14. See Walter P. Zenner, "Joking and Ethnic Stereotyping," *Anthropological Quarterly* 43 (April 1970): 111.

15. See Frank C. Miller, "Humor in a Chippewa Tribal Council," *Ethnology* 6 (July 1967): 267.

16. Douglas, "Social Control," pp. 371–72.

17. Freud, *Jokes*, p. 103.

18. Zenner, "Joking," p. 96.

19. Mary Douglas, *Natural Symbols* (New York: Vintage Books, 1973), p. 111.

20. Mary Douglas, "Social Control," p. 369.

21. Ibid., p. 370.

22. Ibid., p. 373.

23. Américo Paredes, "Folk Medicine and the Intercultural Jest," in *Spanish Speaking People in the United States*, ed. June Helm, Proceedings of the 1968 Annual Spring Meeting of the American Ethnological Society, pp. 104–19.

24. Thus, when Elliott Oring, writing of *chizbat* humor among the Israelis, says, "The *chizbat* reveals that, for the Palmakhniks, there was a cognitive discrepancy between their ideal and their real self-image, a discrepancy that generated incongruity throughout their repertory. This is the nature of *chizbat* truth," he seems to be writing of rite and anti-rite, not social incongruity. See "'Hey, You've Got No Character': Chizbat Humor and the Boundaries of Israeli Identity," *Journal of American Folklore* 86 (October–December 1973): 366.

25. Freud, *Jokes*, p. 101.

26. Ibid., p. 105.

27. Douglas, "Social Control," p. 363.

28. Michel Foucault, *Discipline and Punish: The Birth of the Prison*, trans. Alan Sheridan (New York: Random House, Vintage Books, 1979), p. 216.

29. René Girard, *Violence and the Sacred*, trans. Patrick Gregory (Baltimore: Johns Hopkins University Press, 1977), p. 10.

30. Ibid., p. 8.

31. Quoted in Girard, *Violence*, p. 9.

32. Ibid., p. 20.

33. Ibid., p. 23.

34. Ibid., p. 31.

35. Wolff, Smith, and Murray, "Psychology of Humor," p. 341.

36. See Thomas S. Kuhn, *The Structure of Scientific Revolutions*, 2d ed. (Chicago: University of Chicago Press, 1970).

37. Girard, *Violence*, p. 66.

38. Douglas, "Social Control," p. 365.

39. Ibid., p. 368.

40. Ibid., p. 373.

41. Victor Turner, *Chihamba, The White Spirit: A Ritual Drama of the Ndembu*, Rhodes-Livingstone Papers, no. 33 (Manchester, England: Manchester University Press, 1962), p. 87.

42. Writing of his discovery of mythological systems, Roland Barthes notes: "At that time, I still used the word 'myth' in its traditional sense. But I was already certain of a fact from which I later tried to draw all the consequences: myth is a language." *Mythologies*, trans. Annette Lavers (New York: Hill and Wang, 1972), p. 11.

43. Freud, *Jokes*, p. 132.

44. Ibid., p. 180.

Chapter Four   Speech as Liminality

1. Claude Lévi-Strauss, *Structural Anthropology* (New York: Basic Books, 1963), p. 206.

2. John Milton, "Areopagitica," in *John Milton: Complete Poems and Major Prose*, ed. Merrit Y. Hughes (New York: Odyssey Press, 1957), p. 720.

3. Lévi-Strauss, *Structural Anthropology*, p. 213.

4. This narrow stance was illustrated forcefully by Geoffrey Kirk in a symposium on mythology at Brigham Young University, fall 1981, when he stated that the quality of Greek tales is that they are extraordinary and literary. Such dilletantism has done little to nurture an understanding of mythology.

5. Mircea Eliade, *Myth and Reality*, trans. William Trask (New York: Harper and Row, Harper Colophon Books, 1975), p. 200.

6. Vladimir Propp, *Morphology of the Folktale*, trans. Laurence Scott, 2d ed. (Austin: University of Texas Press, 1968), p. 15.

7. Ibid., p. 5.

8. Roland Barthes, *S/Z*, trans. Richard Miller (New York: Hill and Wang, 1974), p. 7.

9. Lévi-Strauss, *Structural Anthropology*, p. 209.

10. Ibid., p. 210.

11. Ibid., p. 211.

12. See Mary Douglas, *Purity and Danger* (London: Routledge and Kegan Paul, 1966).

13. Roland Barthes, *Mythologies*, trans. Annette Lavers (New York: Hill and Wang, 1972), p. 11.

14. Ibid., p. 142.

15. Gary Witherspoon, *Language and Art in the Navajo Universe* (Ann Arbor: University of Michigan Press, 1977), p. 91.

16. A controlled, perceptive study needs to be made of this problem. Peter L. Berger and Thomas Luckmann note: "Language marks the co-ordinates of my life in society and fills that life with meaningful objects." *The Social Construction of Reality: A Treatise in the Sociology of Knowledge* (New York: Doubleday, Anchor Books, 1967), p. 22.

17. Ibid., p. 39.

18. Victor Turner, *The Ritual Process: Structure and Anti-Structure* (Ithaca: Cornell University Press, Cornell Paperbacks, 1977), p. 110.

19. Arnold van Gennep, *The Rites of Passage*, trans. Monika B. Vizedom and Gabrielle L. Caffee (Chicago: University of Chicago Press, Phoenix Books, 1960), p. 10.

20. Turner, *Ritual Process*, p. 94.

21. See, for example, Kenneth Burke, *Language as Symbolic Action: Essays on Life, Literature, and Method* (Berkeley and Los Angeles: University of California Press, 1966), and the chapter "The Language of Symbol" in my *The Pure Experience of Order* (Albuquerque: University of New Mexico Press, 1982).

22. Turner, *Ritual Process*, p. 95.

23. Ibid., p. 128.

24. Ibid., p. 129.

25. Ibid., p. 103.

26. Ibid., p. 106.

27. See, for example, Claude Lévi-Strauss, "Categories, Elements, Species, Numbers," chap. 5 in *The Savage Mind* (Chicago: University of Chicago Press, 1966).

28. Ibid., p. 245.

29. Turner, *Ritual Process*, p. 127.

30. Ibid., pp. 153–54.

31. Victor Turner, *The Forest of Symbols: Aspects of Ndembu Ritual* (Ithaca: Cornell University Press, 1967), p. 97.

32. Victor Turner, *Dramas, Fields, and Metaphors: Symbolic Action in Human Society* (Ithaca: Cornell University Press, 1974), p. 274.

33. Michel Foucault, *The Order of Things: An Archaeology of the Human Sciences* [orig. title *Les Mots et les choses*] (New York: Random House, Vintage Books, 1973), p. xx.

34. Ibid.

35. Ibid., p. xxi.

36. Turner, *Dramas*, p. 277.

37. Turner, *Forest of Symbols*, p. 95.

Chapter Five   Nihilism on the Plains

1. See "Cultural Invisibility: The Self-Consuming Artifact," chap. 7 in my *The Pure Experience of Order* (Albuquerque: University of New Mexico Press, 1982).

2. Marshall McLuhan, *Understanding Media: The Extensions of Man* (New York: New American Library, Mentor Books, 1964), p. 30.

3. Simon Patrick, *A Discourse About Tradition: Shewing What is Meant by it, and What Tradition Is to be Received, and What Tradition Is to be Rejected* (London: Miles Flesher, 1683), p. 5.

4. Ibid., p. 3.

5. Ibid., p. 23.

6. Quoted in David Biale, *Gershom Scholem: Kabbalah and Counter-History* (Cambridge: Harvard University Press, 1979), p. 107.

7. Marvin Fox, "Secularism Denied," review of *Tradition and Reality: The Impact of History on Modern Jewish Thought*, by Nathan Rotenstreich, *Commentary* 55 (February 1973): 92.

8. Ibid.

9. David Levy, "Reality, Utopia, and Tradition," *Modern Age* 20 (Spring 1976): 162. My emphasis.

10. Nathan Rotenstreich, *Tradition and Reality: The Impact of History on Modern Jewish Thought* (New York: Random House, 1972), p. 15.

11. Louis B. Wright, *Tradition and the Founding Fathers* (Charlottesville: University Press of Virginia, 1975), p. 106.

12. Ronald Cohen, foreword to *Tradition and Identity in Changing Africa*, by Mark A. Tessler, William M. O'Barr, and David H. Spain (New York: Harper and Row, 1973), p. vii.

13. Arthur Mandelbaum, "Threats to the Modern Family," *Science Digest* 65 (March 1969): 59.

14. Walter Greenwood Beach, *The Growth of Social Thought* (1939; reprint, Port Washington, N.Y.: Kennikat Press, 1967), p. 8.

15. David E. Ward, "Eliot, Murray, Homer, and the Idea of Tradition: 'So I Assumed a Double Part . . . ,'" in *Essays in Criticism* 18 (January 1968): 47.

16. See Carl J. Friedrich, *Tradition and Authority* (London: Pall Mall Press, 1972), p. 14.

17. J. G. A. Pocock, "Time, Institutions and Action: An Essay on Traditions and Their Understanding," in *Politics and Experience*, ed. Preston King and B. C. Parekh (Cambridge: Cambridge University Press, 1968), p. 210.

18. Robert Redfield, *The Folk Culture of Yucatan* (Chicago: University of Chicago Press, 1941), p. 343.

19. The word *tradition* is not discussed in Maria Leach, ed., *Standard Dictionary of Folklore, Mythology, and Legend* (New York: Funk and Wagnalls, 1950). Other works purporting to deal with tradition, but which take the terms almost entirely for granted, include Margaret Stacey, *Tradition and Change: A Study of Banbury* (London: Oxford University Press, 1960), and Ole Vesterholt, *Tradition and Individuality: A Study in Slavonic Oral Epic Poetry* (Copenhagen: Rosenkilde and Bagger, 1973).

20. Michel Foucault, *The History of Sexuality*, vol. 1, *An Introduction*, trans. Robert Hurley (New York: Vintage Books, 1980), p. 85.

21. Peter L. Berger and Thomas Luckmann, *The Social Construction of Reality: A Treatise in the Sociology of Knowledge* (New York: Doubleday, Anchor Books, 1967), p. 49.

22. Ibid., p. 50.

23. Ibid., p. 58.

24. Paul J. Magnarella, *Tradition and Change in a Turkish Town* (New York: John Wiley and Sons, 1974), p. 8.

25. Paul de Man, *Blindness and Insight: Essays in the Rhetoric of Contemporary Criticism* (New York: Oxford University Press, 1971), p. 147.

26. Berger and Luckmann, *Social Construction of Reality*, p. 52.

27. For a discussion of normal science, the science of cumulation, of burgeoning truth, and its illusion, see Thomas S. Kuhn, *The Structure of Scientific Revolutions*, 2d ed. (Chicago: University of Chicago Press, 1970).

28. Berger and Luckmann, *Social Construction of Reality*, p. 134.

29. Ibid., p. 115.

30. Ibid., p. 161.

31. Stacey, *Tradition and Change*, p. 16.

32. Levy, "Reality," p. 162.

33. Berger and Luckmann, *Social Construction of Reality*, p. 163.

34. According to Robert Plant Armstrong, "since inquiry proceeds from erroneous views, it cannot produce relevant information and it can only obscure our fuller views of man." *The Affecting Presence: An Essay in Humanistic Anthropology* (Urbana: University of Illinois Press, 1971), p. xxi.

35. Berger and Luckmann, *Social Construction of Reality*, p. 60.

Chapter Six   The Equilibrium of Presence

1. See my "Bosom Serpentry among the Puritans and Mormons," *Journal of the Folklore Institute* 16 (September–December 1979): 176–89.

2. For various examples of these tales, see my "Bosom Serpentry" as well as the articles catalogued in it.

3. See Thomas Hill, *The Gardener's Labyrinth* (1563; reprint, London: Jane Bell, 1652), p. 81.

4. Victor Turner refers to water as the master symbol of fertility; among the Ashanti, it symbolizes semen. See Victor Turner, *The Ritual Process: Structure and Anti-Structure* (Ithaca: Cornell University Press, Cornell Paperbacks, 1977), p. 122.

5. Wolfram Eberhard, ed., *Folktales of China*, rev. ed. (Chicago: University of Chicago Press, 1965), pp. 26–29.

6. Ibid., p. 29.

7. Sir James George Frazer, *The Golden Bough: A Study in Magic and Religion* (New York: Macmillan, 1963), p. 168.

8. Ibid., p. 169.

9. Ibid.

10. Claude Lévi-Strauss, *Totemism*, trans. Rodney Needham (Boston: Beacon Press, 1963), p. 37.

11. Ibid., p. 3.

12. Ibid., p. 37.

13. Michel Foucault, *Madness and Civilization: A History of Insanity in the Age of Reason*, trans. Richard Howard (New York: Random House, Vintage Books, 1973), p. 189.

14. Ibid.

15. Ibid.

16. Ibid., pp. 189–90.

17. Sigmund Freud, *The Interpretation of Dreams*, trans. James Strachey (New York: Avon Books, Discus Books, 1965), p. 392.

18. Carl G. Jung, *Symbols of Transformation*, trans. R. F. C. Hull, 2d ed. (Princeton: Princeton University Press, 1976), p. 378.

19. Ibid., p. 436.

20. Ibid., p. 379.

21. Ibid., p. 326.

22. Robert Graves, *The White Goddess* (New York: Farrar, Straus and Giroux, 1948), pp. 387–88.

23. Lévi-Strauss, *Totemism*, pp. 73–74.

24. M. Fortes, *The Dynamics of Clanship among the Tallensi* (Oxford: Oxford University Press, 1945), p. 143; quoted in Lévi-Strauss, *Totemism*, p. 74.

Chapter Seven   The Hero as Cultural Mirror

1. Joseph Campbell, *The Hero with a Thousand Faces*, 2d ed. (1968; reprint, Princeton: Princeton University Press, 1972), p. 381.

2. Dixon Wecter, *The Hero in America: A Chronicle of Hero-Worship* (New York: Scribners, 1941), p. 7.

3. Roger D. Abrahams, "Some Varieties of Heroes in America," *Journal of the Folklore Institute* 3 (December 1966): 350.

4. Ibid., p. 360.

5. Michael Owen Jones, "(PC + CB) × SD (R + I + E) = HERO," *New York Folklore Quarterly* 27 (September 1971): 244.

6. Pete Axthelm, "Where Have All the Heroes Gone?" *Newsweek* 94 (August 6, 1979): 44.

7. Orrin E. Klapp, *Heroes, Villains, and Fools* (Englewood Cliffs, N.J.: Prentice-Hall, 1962), p. 123.

8. William J. Bennett, "Let's Bring Back Heroes," *Newsweek* 90 (August 25, 1977): 3.

9. Gertrude Jobes, *Dictionary of Mythology, Folklore, and Symbols* (New York: Scarecrow Press, 1962), part 1, p. 762.

10. William W. Savage, Jr., *The Cowboy Hero: His Image in American History and Culture* (Norman: University of Oklahoma Press, 1979), p. 109.

11. Northrop Frye, *Anatomy of Criticism* (1957; reprint, Princeton: Princeton University Press, 1971), p. 33.

12. Lord Raglan, *The Hero: A Study in Tradition, Myth, and Drama* (1956; reprint, Westport, Conn.: Greenwood Press, 1975), p. 38.

13. Ibid., p. 37.

14. Ibid., p. v.

15. Ibid., p. 3.

16. Ibid., p. 4.

17. Ibid., p. 35.

18. Ibid., p. 38.

19. For an explicit discussion of fantasy-thinking, see C.G. Jung, *Symbols of Transformation*, trans. R. F. C. Hull, 2d ed. (Princeton: Princeton University

Press, 1976), p. 18. See also "Repetition in Folk Artifacts," chap. 8 in my *The Pure Experience of Order* (Albuquerque: University of New Mexico Press, 1982).

20. Raglan, *Hero*, p. 215.

21. Ibid., p. 53.

22. Ibid., p. 29.

23. Savage, *Cowboy Hero*, p. 38.

24. Ibid.

25. Paul A. Hutton, "From Little Bighorn to Little Big Man: The Changing Image of a Western Hero in Popular Culture," *Western Historical Quarterly* 7 (1976): 45.

26. Marshall W. Fishwick, "The Making of a Hero," *Saturday Review* 47 (August 1, 1964): 12.

27. Jones, "HERO," p. 246.

28. Raglan, *Hero*, p. 12.

29. Ibid., p. 43.

30. Campbell, *Hero*, p. 16.

31. Bruce A. Rosenberg, "Custer and the Epic of Defeat," *Journal of American Folklore* 88 (April–June 1975): 177.

32. Orrin E. Klapp, "The Creation of Popular Heroes," *American Journal of Sociology* 54 (1948–49): 138.

33. Robert Plant Armstrong, *The Affecting Presence: An Essay in Humanistic Anthropology* (Urbana: University of Illinois Press, 1971), p. 4.

34. Ibid., p. 31.

35. Ibid., p. 23.

36. Ibid., p. 31.

37. Don Ward, "April 3, 1882: An Outlaw Dies and a Hero Is Born," *Folklore and Mythology*, UCLA Center for the Study of Comparative Folklore and Mythology, 1 (April 1982): 1.

38. Ibid., p. 5.

39. Campbell, *Hero*, p. 246.

40. Raglan, *Hero*, p. 174.

41. Ibid., p. 203.

42. Roland Barthes, *A Lover's Discourse: Fragments*, trans. Richard Howard (New York: Hill and Wang, 1978), p. 209.

43. Campbell, *Hero*, p. vii.

Chapter Eight   Legend

1. For a vital discussion of this problem, see Don D. Walker, *Clio's Cowboys: Studies in the Historiography of the Cattle Trade* (Lincoln: University of Nebraska Press, 1981).

2. Gary Witherspoon, *Language and Art in the Navajo Universe* (Ann Arbor: University of Michigan Press, 1977).

3. Robert Scholes and Robert Kellogg, *The Nature of Narrative* (1966; reprint, New York: Oxford University Press, 1968), p. 10.

4. Ibid., p. 13.

5. Ibid., p. 17.

6. Alan Dundes, "On the Psychology of Legend," in Wayland D. Hand, ed., *American Folk Legend: A Symposium* (Berkeley and Los Angeles: University of California Press, 1971), p. 25.

7. Witherspoon, *Language and Art*, p. 5.

8. Scholes and Kellogg, *The Nature of Narrative*, p. 12. In his book *Of Grammatology*, trans. Gayatri Chakravorty Spivak (Baltimore: Johns Hopkins University Press, 1976), Jacques Derrida derides Claude Lévi-Strauss' assertion in *Tristes Tropiques*, in the section titled "A Writing Lesson," that written discourse is an evolutionary extension of spoken discourse. Since history does not exist outside books, traditional narratives cannot be historical.

9. Patrick B. Mullen, "The Relationship of Legend and Folk Belief," *Journal of American Folklore* 84 (October–December 1971): 411.

10. Linda Dégh, "The 'Belief Legend' in Modern Society: Form, Function, and Relationship to Other Genres," in Hand, *American Folk Legend*, p. 62.

11. Richard M. Dorson, "How Shall We Rewrite Charles M. Skinner Today?" in Hand, *American Folk Legend*, p. 88.

12. William Bascom, "The Forms of Folklore: Prose Narratives," *Journal of American Folklore* 78 (January–March 1965): 4.

13. Katharine Luomala, "Disintegration and Regeneration, the Hawaiian Phantom Hitchhiker Legend," *Fabula* 13 (1972): 22.

14. Robert A. Georges, "The General Concept of Legend: Some Assumptions to Be Reexamined and Reassessed," in Hand, *American Folk Legend*, p. 1.

15. Ibid., p. 4.

16. Ibid., p. 12.

17. Américo Paredes, "Mexican Legendry and the Rise of the Mestizo: A Survey," in Hand, *American Folk Legend*, p. 98.

18. Paul Ricoeur discusses metaphor as repression in his *Freud and Philosophy: An Essay on Interpretation*, trans. Denis Savage (New Haven: Yale University Press, 1970), pp. 396, 403.

19. Georges, "Legend," p. 18.

20. Luomala, "Disintegration," p. 24.

21. Bascom, "Prose Narratives," p. 7.

22. Jacob Grimm, *Teutonic Mythology*, 4th ed., trans. James Steven Stallybrass (London, 1883), vol. 3, pp. xvi–xvii.

23. See Jan Harold Brunvand, *The Vanishing Hitchhiker: American Urban Legends and Their Meanings* (New York: Norton, 1981), pp. 40–41.

24. Mullen, "Legend and Folk Belief," p. 413.

25. See Richard M. Dorson, *American Folklore* (Chicago: University of Chicago Press, 1959), pp. 250–51.

26. Stith Thompson, *Motif-Index of Folk-Literature*, rev. ed. (Bloomington: Indiana University Press, 1955).

27. See, for example, motifs E332.3.2, ghost rides in carriage, disappears suddenly at certain spot; E272.1, ghost rides in cart; E299.3, ghost upsets farmers' wagons; E332.3.3, ghost asks for ride in automobile; E338, non-malevolent ghost haunts building; G265.8.3.2, witch bewitches wagon. I am, by the way, not forgetting the profound limitations of indexes (as archives) here.

28. See my "The Ghost Ship: A Legend among Airline Personnel," *Indiana Folklore* 11, no. 1 (1978): 63–70.

Chapter Nine   The Journey of Renewal

1. William A. Douglass, "Peasant Emigrants: Reactors or Actors?" in *Migration and Anthropology*, Proceedings of the 1970 Annual Spring Meeting of the American Ethnological Society (Seattle: University of Washington Press, 1970), p. 21.

2. Stuart B. Philpott, "The Implications of Migration for Sending Societies: Some Theoretical Considerations," in *Migration and Anthropology*, p. 9.

3. Hoyt S. Alverson, "Labor Migrants in South African Industry: The Human Dimension," in *Migration and Anthropology*, p. 50.

4. Ole Gade, "Geographic Research and Human Spatial Interaction Theory: A Review of Pertinent Studies in Migration," in *Migration and Anthropology*, p. 74.

5. Clifford J. Jansen, "Migration: A Sociological Problem," in Clifford J. Jansen, ed., *Readings in the Sociology of Migration* (Oxford: Pergamon Press, 1970), p. 3.

6. See Gyorgy Kepes, ed., *Sign, Image, Symbol* (New York: George Braziller, 1966), p. 206.

7. H. Harcourt Horn, *An English Colony in Iowa* (Boston: N.p., 1931), p. 24.

8. P. George, "Types of Migration of the Population according to the Professional and Social Composition of Migrants," in Jansen, *Sociology of Migration*, pp. 39–40.

9. A Castilian proverb wails: "Bad things, already familiar, are preferable to good things, still unknown." Stanley H. Brandes, *Migration, Kinship, and Community: Tradition and Transition in a Spanish Village* (New York: Academic Press, 1975), p. xi.

10. Elias Canetti attributes essential meaning to nations through what he calls crowd symbols. See *Crowds and Power*, trans. Carol Stewart (reprint, New York: Continuum, 1978), pp. 169–79.

11. See my article "'This Is the Place': Myth and Mormondom," *Western Folklore* 36 (July 1977): 246–52.

12. George Kingsley Zipf, *Human Behavior and the Principle of Least Effort: An Introduction to Human Ecology* (New York: Addison-Wesley Press, 1949), p. 1.

13. O. D. Duncan, "Population Redistribution and Economic Growth: A Review," *Economic Development and Cultural Change* 7 (1958–59): 90.

14. Claude Lévi-Strauss coined the term *mytheme* in his important essay "The Structural Study of Myth," in *Structural Anthropology*, trans. Claire Jacobsen and Brooke Grundfest Schoepf (New York: Basic Books, 1963). Unlike Lévi-Strauss, however, I am not using *mytheme* as a mathematical, but as a mythological unit.

15. It is true that biblical Jews regained the Promised Land—but with great terror and sacrifice. And their out-migration was not a migration at all, but a chaotic dispersal into bondage.

16. Philpott, "Implications of Migration," p. 12.

17. The best book to date on the subject is Juanita Brooks' *The Mountain Meadows Massacre* (1950; reprint, Norman: University of Oklahoma Press, 1962). For a discussion of the problem in its "mythical context," see my "Fate and the Persecutors of Joseph Smith: Transmutations of an American Myth," *Dialogue* 11 (Winter 1978): 63–70.

18. Peter A. Morrison and Judith P. Wheeler, "The Image of 'Elsewhere' in the American Tradition of Migration," in *Human Migration: Patterns and Policies*, ed. William H. McNeill and Ruth S. Adams (Bloomington: Indiana University Press, 1978), p. 76.

19. Albert S. Gatschet, *A Migration Legend of the Creek Indians* (Philadelphia: D. G. Brinton, 1884; reprint, New York: AMS Press, 1969), vol. 1, p. 187.

20. Ibid., pp. 187–88.

21. Ibid., p. 214.

22. See Joseph Campbell, "The Keys," part 1, chap. 4 in *The Hero with a Thousand Faces*, 2d ed. (Princeton: Princeton University Press, 1972), pp. 245–51.

23. Gatschet, *Migration Legend*, p. 215.

24. Their own in-house documents, such as Joseph Smith, *History of the Church of Jesus Christ of Latter-day Saints*, ed. B. H. Roberts (Salt Lake City: Deseret News Press, 1932–51), show that the trip west was very well planned in most particulars, and that the valley of the Great Salt Lake was well known. See, for example, vol. 7, p. 439.

Chapter Ten   Manifest Destiny

1. Vladimir Propp, *Morphology of the Folktale*, trans. Laurence Scott, 2d ed. (Austin: University of Texas Press, 1968), pp. 5, 15.

2. Julius W. Pratt, "The Origin of 'Manifest Destiny,'" *American Historical Review* 32 (July 1927): 798.

3. Frederick Merk, *Manifest Destiny and Mission in American History: A Reinterpretation* (New York: Alfred A. Knopf, 1963), pp. 24–25.

4. Editorial, *New-York Evening Post*, January 28, 1803; quoted in Albert K. Weinberg, *Manifest Destiny: A Study of Nationalistic Expansionism in American History* (Baltimore: Johns Hopkins Press, 1935), p. 31. Original emphasis.

5. Historians conclude that O'Sullivan's editorial was the first widely noted use of the term *manifest destiny*.

6. Editorial, *New York Morning News*, October 13, 1845; quoted in Merk, *Manifest Destiny*, p. 25.

7. Merk, *Manifest Destiny*, p. 51.

8. Ibid., p. 52.

9. Weinberg, *Manifest Destiny*, p. ix.

10. Merk, *Manifest Destiny*, p. ix.

11. Ibid., p. 266.

12. Ibid., p. 261.

13. Ibid., p. ix.

14. John S. Chipman, January 14, 1846, *Congressional Globe*, 29th Cong., 1st sess., p. 207; quoted in Graebner, *Manifest Destiny*, p. xxi.

15. Merk, *Manifest Destiny*, p. 227. My emphasis.

16. Cotton Mather, *The Wonders of the Invisible World* (London: John Russell Smith, 1862), p. 51.

17. Merk writes: "A sense of mission to redeem the Old World by high example was generated in pioneers of idealistic spirit on their arrival in the New World. It was generated by the potentialities of a new earth for building a new heaven." *Manifest Destiny*, p. 3.

18. Ibid., p. 47.

19. See ibid., p. 55, for a discussion of elements of manifest destiny. Despite what he says, all the components of manifest destiny he lists in his book are products and manifestations of nationalism.

20. Ibid., pp. 256–57.

21. Weinberg, *Manifest Destiny*, p. 8. My emphasis.

22. A term used by Jesse S. Reeves, *American Diplomacy under Tyler and Polk* (Baltimore: Johns Hopkins University Press, 1907), p. 58.

23. Weinberg, *Manifest Destiny*, p. 15.

24. Ibid., p. 17.

25. Ibid., p. 12.

26. Norman A. Graebner, ed., introduction to *Manifest Destiny* (Indianapolis: Bobbs-Merrill, 1968), p. xxi.

27. Ralph Waldo Emerson, "The Young American," *Dial* 4 (April 1844): 484, 492.

28. See Richard H. Peterson, *Manifest Destiny in the Mines: A Cultural Interpretation of Anti-Mexican Nativism in California, 1848-1853* (San Francisco: R and E Research Associates, 1975), pp. 10–11.

29. Merk, *Manifest Destiny*, p. 50.

30. See Leo Marx, *The Machine in the Garden: Technology and the Pastoral Ideal in America* (1964; reprint, New York: Oxford University Press, 1967).

31. Merk, *Manifest Destiny*, p. 51.

32. Ibid., p. 3.

33. Ibid., p. 4.

34. Kenneth W. McNaught, with John C. Ricker and John T. Saywell, *Manifest Destiny: A Short History of the United States* (Toronto: Clarke, Irwin, 1963), p. 194.

35. See Joseph Campbell, "The Keys," part 1, chap. 4 in *The Hero with a Thousand Faces*, 2d ed. (1968; reprint, Princeton: Princeton University Press, 1973).

36. Charles Brockden Brown, in a footnote added to his translation of C. F. Volney, *A View of the Soil and Climate of the United States* (Philadelphia: 1804; reprint, New York: Hafner, 1968), wrote: "Instead of anticipating the extension of this great empire merely to the sea on the south, and to the *great river* [the St. Lawrence] on the north, we may be sure that, in no long time,

it will stretch east and west from sea to sea, and from the north pole to the Isthmus of Panama" (p. 2).

37. Robert Michels, *Der Patriotismus; Prolegomena zu seiner soziologischen Analyse* (Munich, 1929), p. 40; quoted in Weinberg, *Manifest Destiny*, p. 17.

38. Weinberg, *Manifest Destiny*, pp. 8–9.

39. Ibid., p. 24.

40. Emerson, "The Young American," p. 484.

41. Sacvan Bercovitch, foreword to *Puritans, Indians, and Manifest Destiny*, by Charles M. Segal and David C. Stineback (New York: G. P. Putnam's Sons, 1977), p. 15.

42. Mircea Eliade, *Myth and Reality*, trans. Willliam Trask (New York: Harper and Row, Harper Colophon Books, 1975), pp. 183–84.

43. Weinberg, *Manifest Destiny*, p. 34.

44. Graebner, *Manifest Destiny*, p. xxv.

45. James Buchanan to Thomas O. Larkin, October 17, 1845, *The Works of James Buchanan*, ed. John Bassett Moore (Philadelphia: J. B. Lippincott, 1909), vol. 6, p. 275; quoted in Graebner, *Manifest Destiny*, p. xlix.

46. Despite what Merk suggests, *Manifest Destiny*, p. 55.

47. Emerson, "The Young American," p. 491.

48. Bercovitch, foreword, p. 16.

49. Henry David Thoreau, "Walking," in *The Writings of Henry David Thoreau* (Boston: Houghton Mifflin, 1906), vol. 5, pp. 217–18.

50. Lévi-Strauss writes of "that cosmic rhythm which, since the beginning of the human race, has imbued mankind with the unconscious belief that to move with the sun is positive, and to move against it negative, one direction expressing order, the other disorder." *Tristes Tropiques*, trans. John Weightman and Doreen Weightman (New York: Atheneum Books, 1974), p. 122.

Chapter Eleven   The Donner Party

1. Michel Foucault, *The Archaeology of Knowledge*, trans. A. M. Sheridan Smith (New York: Harper and Row, Harper Colophon Books, 1976), p. 3.

2. Because, as Jacques Derrida says, "This gossipy small talk of history reduces *the thing itself* . . . to the form of a particular, finite object." *Dissemination*, trans. Barbara Johnson (Chicago: University of Chicago Press, 1981), p. 10.

3. Michel Serres, *The Parasite*, trans. Lawrence R. Schehr (Baltimore: Johns Hopkins University Press, 1982), p. 121.

4. John Breen, "Memories of a Pioneer," *Pony Express Courier* 7 (January 1941): 7.

5. Eliza W. Farnham, *California, In-Doors and Out; or, How We Farm, Mine, and Live Generally in the Golden State* (New York: Dix, Edwards and Co., 1856), p. 454.

6. James Reed, "The Journal of James Frazier Reed," ed. J. Roderick Korns, *Utah Historical Quarterly* 19 (1951): 186. This is a special issue of the journal, titled *West From Fort Bridger: The Pioneering of the Immigrant Trails across Utah, 1846–1850*, ed. J. Roderick Korns.

7. Ibid.

8. Ibid.

9. *California Star*, April 10, 1847; quoted in Reed, "Journal," p. 187.

10. George R. Stewart, *Ordeal by Hunger: The Classic Story of the Donner Party* (New York: Pocket Books, 1971), p. 5.

11. Ibid., p. 205. My emphasis.

12. Bernard De Voto, *The Year of Decision, 1846* (Boston: Houghton Mifflin, 1942), p. 340. My emphasis.

13. Ibid., p. 344.

14. Ibid., p. 345.

15. Homer Croy, *Wheels West* (New York: Hastings House, 1955), p. ix.

16. Ibid.

17. C. F. McGlashan, *History of the Donner Party: A Tragedy of the Sierras* (Truckee, Calif.: Crowley and McGlashan, 1879), p. 5.

18. Quoted in ibid., p. 127.

19. Ibid., p. 15.

20. Ibid., p. 145.

21. James Agee and Walker Evans, *Let Us Now Praise Famous Men* (Boston: Houghton Mifflin, 1939), p. 15.

22. Eliza P. Donner Houghton, *The Expedition of the Donner Party and Its Tragic Fate* (Los Angeles: Grafton, 1920), p. ix. My emphasis.

23. Hoffman Birney, *Grim Journey* (New York: Minton, Balch, 1934), p. 127.

24. Ibid., p. 171.

25. Reed, "Journal," p. 203.

26. Ibid., p. 207. My emphasis.

27. Thomas F. Andrews, "Lansford W. Hastings and the Promotion of the Salt Lake Desert Cutoff: A Reappraisal," *Western Historical Quarterly* 4 (April 1973): 150. My emphasis.

28. Joseph Pigney, *For Fear We Shall Perish: The Story of the Donner Party Disaster* (New York: E. P. Dutton, 1961), p. 17.

29. Ibid., p. 159.

30. Ibid., p. 157.

31. Croy, *Wheels West*, p. x.

32. Ibid.

33. George Keithley, *The Donner Party* (New York: George Braziller, 1972), dust jacket.

34. De Voto, *Year of Decision*, p. 353.

35. Louis Dupree, "The Retreat of the British Army from Kabul to Jalalabad in 1842: History and Folklore," *Journal of the Folklore Institute* 4 (1967): 50–74.

36. Virginia E. B. Reed to Mary Gillespie, Napa Valley, California, May 16, 1847; quoted in Reed, "Journal," p. 223.

37. Virginia Reed Murphy, "Across the Plains in the Donner Party (1846): A Personal Narrative of the Overland Trip to California," *Century Magazine* 42 [vol. 20, new series] (July 1891): 422. My emphasis.

38. Ibid., p. 423.

39. Ibid., p. 425.

40. Houghton, *Expedition*, p. viii.

41. Ibid., pp. ix–x.

42. Ibid., p. 231.

43. McGlashan, *History*, p. 6.

44. De Voto, *Year of Decision*, p. 341.

45. Elias Canetti, *Crowds and Power*, trans. Carol Stewart (reprint, New York: Continuum, 1978), p. 262.

46. Ibid.

47. Breen, "Memories of a Pioneer," p. 7.

48. Houghton, *Expedition*, p. 70.

49. Wright Morris, *Will's Boy: A Memoir* (New York: Harper and Row, 1981), p. 129.

50. Murphy, "Across the Plains," p. 426.

51. "The Diary of Patrick Breen," in *Academy of Pacific Coast History Publications* (Berkeley: University of California, 1910), vol. 1, p. 273.

52. De Voto, *Year of Decision*, p. 344.

53. Georg Lukacs, *The Theory of the Novel: A Historico-Philosophical Essay on the Forms of Great Epic Literature*, trans. Anna Bostock (1971; reprint, Cambridge: MIT Press, 1973), p. 45.

54. Keithley, *Donner Party*, p. 125.

55. Ibid., p. 232.

56. Ibid., p. 239.

57. Vardis Fisher, *The Mothers: A Documentary Novel of the Donner Party* (Chicago: Swallow Press, Sage Books, 1971), p. 287.

58. Keithley, *Donner Party*, p. 195.

59. Annie Dillard, *Holy the Firm* (New York: Harper and Row, 1977), p. 60.

Chapter Twelve   The Fracture of Mormonism

1. *New York Tribune*, November 17, 1873; quoted in Charles Schuchert and Clara Mae LeVene, *O. C. Marsh: Pioneer in Paleontology* (New Haven: Yale University Press, 1940), pp. 125, 136–37.

2. *Journal of Discourses* (Liverpool: Albert Carrington, 1872), vol. 14, p. 115.

3. See Linda P. Wilcox, "The Imperfect Science: Brigham Young on Medical Doctors," *Dialogue* 12 (Fall 1979): 26–36.

4. Ibid., p. 30.

5. N. Lee Smith, "Herbal Remedies: God's Medicine?" *Dialogue* 12 (Fall 1979): 39.

6. Ibid., p. 38.

7. Ibid., p. 39.

8. *The Doctrine and Covenants of The Church of Jesus Christ of Latter-day Saints* (Salt Lake City: Deseret Book, 1921) 42:43.

9. *Doctrine and Covenants* 89:10.

10. See my article "Some Botanical Cures in Mormon Folk Medicine: An Analysis," *Utah Historical Quarterly* 44 (Fall 1976): 379–88. On p. 388 I discuss "a nearly invisible culture within a culture within a culture."

11. See L. Kay Gillespie, "Cancer Quackery in the State of Utah" (1976), p. 62. Prepared privately for the Utah Department of Social Services, Office of Comprehensive Health Planning.

12. Michel Serres, *The Parasite*, trans. Lawrence R. Schehr (Baltimore: Johns Hopkins University Press, 1982), p. 74.

13. Ibid., p. 75.

14. Francis Bacon, *Novum Organum*, in *The Works of Francis Bacon*, vol. 8, ed. J. Spedding, R. L. Ellis, and D. D. Heath (New York: Hurd and Houghton, 1864), p. 210.

15. The haunting statement "all truth is unbearable" is made by the Rector in William Faulkner, *Soldiers' Pay* (New York: New American Library, Signet Books, 1968), p. 220.

16. Hans-Georg Gadamer, *Truth and Method* (New York: Continuum, 1975), p. 22.

17. Ibid., p. 23.

18. Michel Foucault, *Discipline and Punish: The Birth of the Prison*, trans. Alan Sheridan (New York: Random House, Vintage Books, 1979), p. 3.

19. Ibid., p. 5.

20. Friedrich Nietzsche, *The Birth of Tragedy* and *The Genealogy of Morals*, trans. Francis Golffing (New York: Doubleday, Anchor Books, 1956), p. 68.

21. Duane E. Jeffrey, "Seers, Savants and Evolution: The Uncomfortable Interface," *Dialogue* 8, nos. 3/4 (1973): 68.

22. Robert Rees, "Science, Religion, and Man," *Dialogue* 8, nos. 3/4 (1973): 5.

23. Ibid., p. 6.

24. Richard F. Haglund, "Science and Religion: A Symbiosis," *Dialogue* 8, nos. 3/4 (1973): 24.

25. Ibid., p. 25.

26. Ibid.

27. Ibid., p. 31.

28. Ibid., p. 37.

29. Thomas S. Kuhn describes normal science as "research firmly based upon one or more past scientific achievements, achievements that some particular scientific community acknowledges for a time as supplying the foundation for its further practice." *The Structure of Scientific Revolutions*, 2d ed. (Chicago: University of Chicago Press, 1970), p. 10.

30. Jeffrey, "Seers," p. 43.

31. David O. McKay, "A Message for LDS College Youth," Brigham Young University Speeches of the Year [Provo, Utah, October 10, 1952].

32. Joseph Fielding Smith, *Man: His Origin and Destiny* (Salt Lake City: eseret Book, 1954). See also Jeffrey, "Seers," pp. 65–66.

33. Jeffrey, "Seers," p. 68.

34. Orson Pratt, *Key to the Universe, or a New Theory of Its Mechanism* (Salt Lake City: Orson Pratt, 1879).

35. Henry Eyring, "Science and Faith," in *Science and Your Faith in God* (Salt Lake City: Bookcraft, 1958), p. 11. The book is a selected compilation of ritings and talks by prominent Latter-day Saint scientists on the subjects of science and religion.

36. Carl J. Christensen, "Man's Three Dimensional Future," in *Science and Your Faith*, p. 41.

37. Ibid., p. 42.

38. Eyring, "Science and Faith," p. 11. Eyring actually uses a form of the word *harmony*.

39. Franklin S. Harris, "Seek Truth in Science and Religion," in *Science and Your Faith*, p. 91.

40. John A. Widtsoe, "What Is the Attitude of the Church toward Science?" in *Science and Your Faith*, p. 212.

41. Ibid., p. 213.

42. This synonymous discourse of symbiosis, which reflects the same image, uses even the same manifest language, irrespective of the *position* or *education* of the writer, is precisely what Freud discovered in the discourse of dreams, the dream-work. The expression of wish found in the dream is antithetical to the "historical" experience of the writer, although that past may trigger the starting point of the dream. *The Interpretation of Dreams*, trans. James Strachey (New York: Avon Books, 1965), p. 140. The dream content is, however, the fulfillment of a wish (p. 151). The rhetoric of symbiosis seems also a wish fulfillment. For a discussion of the importance of language to Freud (besides the work of Jacques Lacan), see Bruno Bettelheim, *Freud and Man's Soul* (New York: Alfred A. Knopf, 1983).

43. Statement by Harvey Fletcher in *Deseret News*, Church News section, May 24, 1958.

44. Milton Jenkins Jones, *Science and Religion Agree!* (Salt Lake City: Deseret News Press, 1949), p. 18. Jones' emphasis.

45. John A. Widtsoe, *Joseph Smith as Scientist: A Contribution to Mormon Philosophy* (Salt Lake City: General Board, Young Men's Mutual Improvement Associations, 1908), p. 1.

46. Ibid., p. 95.

47. John A. Widtsoe, *Evidences and Reconciliations: Aids to Faith in a Modern Day*, 3d ed. (Salt Lake City: Bookcraft, 1943), p. 125.

48. N. Lee Smith, "Herbal Remedies: God's Medicine?" *Dialogue* 12 (Fall 1979): 56.

49. Northrop Frye, *The Great Code: The Bible and Literature* (New York: Harcourt Brace Jovanovich, 1982), p. 30.

50. Frye also says: "The need to unify [synthesize?], we suggested, is an indication of the finiteness of the human mind, unity and the finite being aspects of the same thing." Ibid., p. 228.

51. Kuhn, *Scientific Revolutions*, p. 69.

52. Jacques Derrida, *Dissemination*, trans. Barbara Johnson (Chicago: University of Chicago Press, 1981), p. 129.

53. Widtsoe, *Evidences and Reconciliations*, p. 3.

Chapter Thirteen The Transforming Image

1. See John Charles Frémont, *The Expeditions of John Charles Frémont*, vol. 1, *Travels from 1838 to 1844*, ed. Donald Jackson and Mary Lee Spence (Urbana: University of Illinois Press, 1970). Average frost dates recorded by Frémont were the same then as now.

2. Elias Canetti, *Crowds and Power*, trans. Carol Stewart (reprint, New York: Continuum, 1978), p. 337.

3. Claude Lévi-Strauss, *Tristes Tropiques*, trans. John Weightman and Doreen Weightman (New York: Atheneum Books, 1974), p. 85.

4. Or, the archaeologist of space; see Lévi-Strauss, *Tristes Tropiques*, p. 43.

5. Franz Kafka, "Prometheus," trans. Willa Muir and Edwin Muir, in *The Complete Stories*, ed. Nahum N. Glatzer (New York: Schocken Books, 1971), p. 432.

6. Peter L. Berger and Thomas Luckmann, *The Social Construction of Reality: A Treatise in the Sociology of Knowledge* (New York: Doubleday, Anchor Books, 1967), p. 90.

7. Northrop Frye, *The Great Code: The Bible and Literature* (New York: Harcourt Brace Jovanovich, 1982), p. 72.

8. Michel Serres, *The Parasite*, trans. Lawrence R. Schehr (Baltimore: Johns Hopkins University Press, 1982), p. 99.

9. Although science has become a specious magic—or at least its technology has.

10. Georg Lukacs, *The Theory of the Novel: A Historico-Philosophical Essay on the Forms of Great Epic Literature*, trans. Anna Bostock (1971; reprint, Cambridge: MIT Press, 1973), p. 65.

11. Claude Lévi-Strauss, *The Savage Mind* (Chicago: University of Chicago Press, 1966), p. 97.

12. Canetti, *Crowds and Power*, p. 108.

13. Ibid., p. 380.

14. Ibid., p. 383.

15. Hans-Georg Gadamer, *Truth and Method* (New York: Continuum, 1975), p. 54.

16. Lévi-Strauss, *Savage Mind*, p. 95.

17. Jacques Derrida, *Dissemination*, trans. Barbara Johnson (Chicago: University of Chicago Press, 1981), p. 53.

18. Ibid., p. 54.

19. In my book *The Pure Experience of Order: Essays on the Symbolic in the Folk Material Culture of Western America* (Albuquerque: University of New Mexico Press, 1982), I discuss the symbol without meaning, which I view as the essence of cultural invisibility. See p. 103.

20. Lukacs, *Theory of the Novel*, p. 126.

21. Lévi-Strauss, *Savage Mind*, p. 76.

22. Ibid., p. 78.

23. Serres, *The Parasite*, p. 63.

24. Ibid., p. 72.

25. Mircea Eliade, *Rites and Symbols of Initiation: The Mysteries of Birth and Rebirth*, trans. William Trask (New York: Harper and Row, Harper Colophon Books, 1975), p. 11.

26. Ibid., p. 13.

27. Canetti, *Crowds and Power*, p. 109.

28. Ibid., p. 294. Here, Canetti claims that silence isolates, that silence inhibits self-transformation.

29. Ibid., p. 342.

30. Gadamer, *Truth and Method*, p. 100.

31. Ibid.

32. Canetti, *Crowds and Power*, p. 90.

33. Lord Raglan, *The Hero: A Study in Tradition, Myth, and Drama* (1956; reprint, Westport, Conn.: Greenwood Press, 1975), p. 32.

34. Ibid., p. 33.

35. Gadamer asserts that from a particular viewpoint, "'reality' is defined as what is untransformed." *Truth and Method*, p. 102.

36. Serres, *The Parasite*, p. 73.

37. Ibid., p. 215.

38. Gadamer, *Truth and Method*, p. 101.

39. Ibid., p. 103.

40. Lévi-Strauss, *Tristes Tropiques*, p. 272.

41. Canetti, *Crowds and Power*, p. 110.

42. Ibid., p. 340.

43. Canetti speaks of cannibalism and transformation having "entered into a close alliance." *Crowds and Power*, p. 357. Actually, the two are synonymous.

44. Ibid., p. 382.

Chapter Fourteen   Human Spaces

1. Joseph Conrad, *Lord Jim* (New York: New American Library, Signet Classics, 1961), p. 169.

2. James Agee and Walker Evans, *Let Us Now Praise Famous Men* (Boston: Houghton Mifflin, 1939), p. 155.

3. Ibid., p. 183.

4. Wright Morris, *Ceremony in Lone Tree* (Lincoln: University of Nebraska Press, Bison Book, 1973), p. 232.

5. Georg Lukacs, *The Theory of the Novel: A Historico-Philosophical Essay of the Forms of Great Epic Literature*, trans. Anna Bostock (1971; reprint, Cambridge: MIT Press, 1973), p. 122.

6. Elias Canetti, *Crowds and Power*, trans. Carol Stewart (reprint, New York: Continuum, 1978), p. 170.

7. Michel Foucault, *The Birth of the Clinic: An Archaeology of Medical Perception*, trans. A. M. Sheridan Smith (New York: Random House, Pantheon Books, 1973), p. 5.

8. Northrop Frye, *The Great Code: The Bible and Literature* (New York: Harcourt Brace Jovanovich, 1982), p. 15.

9. Ibid., p. 227.

10. Wright Morris, *Man and Boy* (Lincoln: University of Nebraska Press, Bison Book, 1974), p. 165.

11. Edward Abbey writes: "My lone juniper stands half-alive, half-dead, the silvery wind-rubbed claw of wood projected stiffly at the sun. A single cloud floats in the sky to the northeast, motionless, a magical coalescence of vapor where a few minutes before there was nothing visible but the hot, deep,

black-grained blueness of infinity." *Desert Solitaire: A Season in the Wilderness* (New York: McGraw Hill, 1968), p. 135.

12. Canetti, *Crowds and Power*, p. 170.

13. Hans-Georg Gadamer, *Truth and Method* (New York: Continuum, 1975), p. 405.

14. Michel Foucault, *Madness and Civilization: A History of Insanity in the Age of Reason*, trans. Richard Howard (New York: Random House, Vintage Books, 1973), p. 143.

15. Ibid., p. 154.

16. Ibid., p. 170.

17. Foucault, *Birth of the Clinic*, p. ix.

18. Ibid., p. x.

19. Ibid., p. xi.

20. Ibid., p. xii.

21. Ibid., p. 4.

22. Ibid., p. 18.

23. Michel Foucault, *The History of Sexuality*, vol. 1, *An Introduction*, trans. Robert Hurley (New York: Random House, Vintage Books, 1980), p. 3.

24. Marshall McLuhan, *Understanding Media: The Extensions of Man* (New York: New American Library, Mentor Books, 1964), p. 31.

25. Patrick White, *Flaws in the Glass: A Self-Portrait* (New York: Viking Press, 1982), p. 176.

26. Gadamer, *Truth and Method*, p. 401.

27. Ibid., p. 403.

28. Ibid., p. 409.

29. Ibid., p. 411.

30. Sir James George Frazer, *The Golden Bough: A Study in Magic and Religion*, abridged ed. (New York: Macmillan, 1963), p. 389.

31. Gary Witherspoon, *Language and Art in the Navajo Universe* (Ann Arbor: University of Michigan Press, 1977).

32. According to Ludwig Wittgenstein, "The truth is, we could not say of an 'unlogical' world how it would look. To present in language anything which 'contradicts logic' is as impossible as in geometry to present by its

coordinates a figure which contradicts the laws of space." See *Tractatus Logico-Philosophicus*, trans. C. K. Ogden, rev. ed. (1955; reprint, London: Routledge and Kegan Paul, 1981), p. 43.

33. Ralph Waldo Emerson, "Nature," in *The Selected Writings of Ralph Waldo Emerson*, ed. Brooks Atkinson (New York: Random House, Modern Library, 1950), p. 22.

34. Canetti, *Crowds and Power*, p. 19.

35. Frye, *Great Code*, p. 159.

36. Alma Greene (Gah-wonh-nos-doh), *Forbidden Voice: Reflections of a Mohawk Indian* (London: Hamlyn, n.d.), p. 124.

37. Foucault, *Madness and Civilization*, p. 58.

38. Ibid., p. 6.

39. Foucault, *Birth of the Clinic*, p. 19.

40. Jacques Derrida, *Dissemination*, trans. Barbara Johnson (Chicago: University of Chicago Press, 1981), p. 137.

41. Michel Serres, *The Parasite*, trans. Lawrence R. Schehr (Baltimore: Johns Hopkins University Press, 1982), p. 177.

42. Ibid., p. 22.

43. Ibid., p. 24.

44. Ibid., p. 143.

45. Ibid., p. 178.

46. Frye, *Great Code*, p. 158.

47. Claude Lévi-Strauss, *The Savage Mind* (Chicago: University of Chicago Press, 1966), p. 10.

48. Gaston Bachelard, *The Poetics of Space*, trans. Maria Jolas (reprint, Boston: Beacon Press, 1969), p. xxxii.

Chapter Fifteen   Of Night in a Wilderness

1. Or worse, a cultish adulation.

2. James Agee and Walker Evans, *Let Us Now Praise Famous Men* (Boston: Houghton Mifflin, 1939), p. xvi. Henceforth, references to this book will be indicated by page numbers in the text of the chapter.

3. Robert Phelps, "James Agee," in *Letters of James Agee to Father Flye*, 2d ed. (Dunwoody, Ga.: Norman S. Berg, 1978), p. 1.

4. The critic: George Barker, quoted in Peter H. Ohlin, *Agee* (New York: Ivan Obolensky, 1966), p. 51.

5. Ibid., pp. 51–52.

6. Winfield Townley Scott, quoted in ibid., p. 54.

7. Robert Fitzgerald, ed., *The Collected Short Prose of James Agee* (London: Calder and Boyars, 1972), p. 10.

8. Ohlin, *Agee*, p. 54.

9. Roland Barthes, *The Pleasure of the Text*, trans. Richard Miller (New York: Hill and Wang, 1975), p. 9.

10. Ohlin, *Agee*, p. 55.

11. Erling Larsen, *James Agee*, University of Minnesota Pamphlets on American Writers, no. 95 (Minneapolis: University of Minnesota Press, 1971), p. 26.

12. Dwight Macdonald, quoted in Kenneth Seib, *James Agee: Promise and Fulfillment* (Pittsburg: University of Pittsburg Press, 1968), p. ix.

13. Agee writes: "And meanwhile the landowner had loosened the top two buttons of his trousers, and he now reached his hand in to the middle of the forearm, and, squatting with bent knees apart, clawed, scratched and rearranged his genitals" (p. 28).

14. Barthes, *Pleasure of the Text*, p. 4.

15. Wallace Stevens, *Opus Posthumous*, ed. Samuel French Morse (New York: Alfred A. Knopf, 1957), p. 169.

16. Fitzgerald, *Short Prose*, p. 23.

17. Ohlin, *Agee*, pp. 10–11.

18. David Madden, "On the Mountain with Agee," in David Madden, ed., *Remembering James Agee* (Baton Rouge: Louisiana State University Press, 1974), p. 10.

19. Gaston Bachelard, *The Poetics of Space*, trans. Maria Jolas (reprint, Boston: Beacon Press, 1969), p. 59.

20. Robert Fitzgerald, "A Memoir," in Madden, *Remembering James Agee*, pp. 47–48.

21. Ibid., p. 53.

22. Seib, *James Agee*, p. 56.

23. Ibid., p. 137.

24. Barthes, *Pleasure of the Text*, p. 60.

25. Fitzgerald, *Short Prose*, pp. 48–49.

26. Mark A. Doty, *Tell Me Who I Am: James Agee's Search for Selfhood* (Baton Rouge: Louisiana State University Press, 1981), p. xii.

27. Ibid., pp. xii–xiii.

28. Louis Kronenberger, "A Real Bohemian," in Madden, *Remembering James Agee*, pp. 111–12.

29. Seib, *James Agee*, p. ix.

30. Ibid., p. 41.

31. Doty, *Tell Me Who I Am*, p. 39.

32. Ibid., p. 40.

33. Ohlin, *Agee*, p. 53.

34. Says Agee: "The essence of the trouble is that compromise is held to be a virtue of itself" (p. 309).

35. Seib, *James Agee*, p. 45.

36. Wright Morris, *About Fiction: Reverent Reflections on the Nature of Fiction with Irreverent Observations on Writers, Readers, and Other Abuses* (New York: Harper and Row, 1975), p. 167.

37. Fitzgerald, *Short Prose*, p. 23.

38. Agee, *Letters*, p. 252.

39. Doty, *Tell Me Who I Am*, p. 49.

40. Dwight Macdonald, quoted in ibid., p. 52.

41. Ibid., pp. 51–52.

42. Ibid., p. 67.

43. Ohlin, *Agee*, pp. 54–55.

44. Ibid., pp. 57–58.

45. Ibid., p. 65.

46. Alfred Kazin, quoted in ibid., p. 66.

47. Larsen, *James Agee*, p. 27.

48. Georg Lukacs, *The Theory of the Novel: A Historico-Philosophical Essay on the Forms of Great Epic Literature*, trans. Anna Bostock (1971; reprint, Cambridge: MIT Press, 1973), p. 48.

49. Stevens, *Opus Posthumous*, p. 157.

50. Barthes: "What is overcome, split, is the *moral unity* that society demands of every human product." *Pleasure of the Text*, p. 31.

51. Ibid., p. 54.

52. Stevens, *Opus Posthumous*, p. 162.

53. Fitzgerald, *Short Prose*, p. 21.

54. Says Fitzgerald, Agee was "after the truth, the truth about specific events or things, and the truth about his own impressions and feelings. By truth I mean what he would chiefly mean: correspondence between what is said and what is the case—but what is the case at the utmost reach of consciousness." *Short Prose*, pp. 24–25.

55. Agee, *Letters*, p. 252.

56. For a treatment of this problem see David Bleich, *Subjective Criticism* (1978; reprint, Baltimore: Johns Hopkins University Press, 1981).

57. Dwight Macdonald, "Jim Agee, a Memoir," in Madden, *Remembering Agee*, p. 142.

58. Seib, *James Agee*, p. 57.

59. For a thoughtful discussion of the hand-made object, but not of texture, see Michael Owen Jones, *The Hand Made Object and Its Maker* (Berkeley and Los Angeles: University of California Press, 1975).

60. Stevens, *Opus Posthumous*, p. 175.

Selected Bibliography

Abbey, Edward. *Desert Solitaire: A Season in the Wilderness*. New York: McGraw Hill, 1968.

Abrahams, Roger D. "Some Varieties of Heroes in America." *Journal of the Folklore Institute* 3 (December 1966): 341–62.

Agee, James. "The Last Letter of James Agee to Father Flye." Boston: David R. Godine, Mandragora Press, 1969.

———. *Letters of James Agee to Father Flye*, 2d ed. Dunwoody, Ga.: Norman S. Berg, 1978.

Agee, James, and Evans, Walker. *Let Us Now Praise Famous Men*. Boston: Houghton Mifflin, 1939.

Allen, Barbara. "The Personal Point of View in Orally Communicated History." *Western Folklore* 38 (April 1979): 110–18.

Alverson, Hoyt S. "Labor Migrants in South African Industry: The Human Dimension." In *Migration and Anthropology*.

Ander, O. Fritiof, ed. *In the Trek of the Immigrants: Essays Presented to Carl Wittke*. Rock Island, Ill.: Augustana College Library, 1964.

Andrews, Thomas. "Lansford W. Hastings and the Promotion of the Salt Lake Desert Cutoff: A Reappraisal." *Western Historical Quarterly* 4 (April 1973): 133–50.

Armstrong, Robert Plant. *The Affecting Presence: An Essay in Humanistic Anthropology*. Urbana: University of Illinois Press, 1971.

Arrington, Leonard J., and Bitton, Davis. *The Mormon Experience: A History of the Latter-day Saints*. New York: Alfred A. Knopf, 1979.

Axthelm, Pete. "Where Have All the Heroes Gone?" *Newsweek* 94 (August 6, 1979): 44–50.

Bachelard, Gaston. *The Poetics of Space*. Translated by Maria Jolas. Reprint. Boston: Beacon Press, 1969.

———. *The Poetics of Reverie: Childhood, Language, and the Cosmos*. Translated by Daniel Russell. Reprint. Boston: Beacon Press, 1971.

Bacon, Francis. *The Works of Francis Bacon*. Edited by J. Spedding, R. L. Ellis, and D. D. Heath. 12 vols. New York: Hurd and Houghton, 1864.

Barth, Fredrik. *Models of Social Organization*. Royal Anthropological Institute Occasional Paper no. 23. Glasgow: Royal Anthropological Institute of Great Britain and Ireland, University Press, 1966.

Barthes, Roland. *Mythologies*. Translated by Annette Lavers. New York: Hill and Wang, 1972.

———. *S/Z*. Translated by Richard Miller. New York: Hill and Wang, 1974.

———. *The Pleasure of the Text*. Translated by Richard Miller. New York: Hill and Wang, 1975.

———. *A Lover's Discourse: Fragments*. Translated by Richard Howard. New York: Hill and Wang, 1978.

Bascom, William. "The Forms of Folklore: Prose Narratives." *Journal of American Folklore* 78 (January–March 1965): 3–20.

Beach, Walter Greenwood. *The Growth of Social Thought*. 1939. Reprint. Port Washington, N.Y.: Kennikat Press, 1967.

Beard, Charles A. *The Idea of National Interest: An Analytical Study in American Foreign Policy*. New York: Macmillan, 1934.

Bennett, William. "Let's Bring Back Heroes." *Newsweek* 90 (August 15, 1977): 3.

Bercovitch, Sacvan. "'Nehemias Americanus': Cotton Mather and the Concept of the Representative American." *Early American Literature* 8 (Winter 1974): 220–38.

———. Foreword to *Puritans, Indians, and Manifest Destiny*, by Charles M. Segal and David C. Stineback. New York: G. P. Putnam's Sons, 1977.

Berger, Peter L., and Luckmann, Thomas. *The Social Construction of Reality: A Treatise in the Sociology of Knowledge*. New York: Doubleday, Anchor Books, 1967.

Bettelheim, Bruno. *Freud and Man's Soul*. New York: Alfred A. Knopf, 1983.

Biale, David. *Gershom Scholem: Kabbalah and Counter-History*. Cambridge: Harvard University Press, 1979.

Biebuyck, Daniel P. *Hero and Chief: Epic Literature from the Banyanga Zaire Republic*. Berkeley and Los Angeles: University of California Press, 1978.

Birney, Hoffman. *Grim Journey*. New York: Minton, Balch, 1934.

Bleich, David. *Subjective Criticism*. 1978. Reprint. Baltimore: Johns Hopkins University Press, 1981.

Boaz, Franz. *The Religion of the Kwakiutl Indians*. Columbia University Contributions to Anthropology, vol. 10. New York: Columbia University Press, 1930.

Brandes, Stanley H. *Migration, Kinship, and Community: Tradition and Transition in a Spanish Village*. New York: Academic Press, 1975.

Breen, John. "Memories of a Pioneer." *Pony Express Courier* 7 (January 1941): 3–16.

Breen, Patrick. "The Diary of Patrick Breen." In *Academy of Pacific Coast History Publications*, vol. 1. Berkeley: University of California, 1910.

Brooks, Juanita. *The Mountain Meadows Massacre*. 1950. Reprint. Norman: University of Oklahoma Press, 1962.

Brown, Charles Brockden, trans. *A View of the Soil and Climate of the United States*, by C. F. Volney. 1804. Reprint. New York: Hafner, 1968.

Brown, Norman O. *Life Against Death: the Psychoanalytic Meaning of History*. 1959. Reprint. Middletown, Conn.: Wesleyan University Press, 1970.

Brunvand, Jan Harold. *The Vanishing Hitchhiker: American Urban Legends and Their Meanings*. New York: Norton, 1981.

Buchanan, James. *The Works of James Buchanan*. Edited by John Bassett Moore. Philadelphia: J. B. Lippincott, 1909.

Burke, Kenneth. *Language as Symbolic Action: Essays on Life, Literature, and Method*. Berkeley and Los Angeles: University of California Press, 1966.

Busignani, Alberto. *Pollock*. Feltham, Middlesex, England: Hamlyn, 1971.

Campbell, Joseph. *The Hero with a Thousand Faces*, 2d ed. Princeton: Princeton University Press, 1972.

Camus, Albert. *The Myth of Sisyphus and Other Essays*. Translated by Justin O'Brien. New York: Random House, Vintage Books, 1955.

Canetti, Elias. *Crowds and Power*. Translated by Carol Stewart. Reprint. New York: Continuum, 1978.

———. *The Torch in My Ear*. Translated by Joachim Neugroschel. New York: Farrar, Straus and Giroux, 1982.

Carter, Tom. "Folk Design in Utah Architecture: 1849–90." In *Utah Folk Art*. Edited by Hal Cannon. Provo, Utah: Brigham Young University Press, 1980.

Cassirer, Ernst. *An Essay on Man: An Introduction to a Philosophy of Human Culture*. 1944. Reprint. New Haven: Yale University Press, 1962.

Cather, Willa. *My Antonia*. Boston: Houghton Mifflin, 1918.

Christensen, Carl J. "Man's Three Dimensional Future." In *Science and Your Faith in God*.

Christiansen, Reidar Th. *The Migratory Legends: A Proposed List of Types with Systematic Catalogue of the Norwegian Variants*. FF Communications, vol. 71, no. 175. Helsinki: Academia Scientiarum Fennica, 1958.

Coan, Richard W. *Hero, Artist, Sage, or Saint?* New York: World Publishing, 1969.

Cohen, Ronald. Foreword to *Tradition and Identity in Changing Africa*, by Mark A. Tessler, William M. O'Barr, and David H. Spain. New York: Harper and Row, 1973.

Conrad, Joseph. *Lord Jim*. New York: New American Library, Signet Classics, 1961.

Croy, Homer. *Wheels West*. New York: Hastings House, 1955.

Dégh, Linda. "The 'Belief Legend' in Modern Society: Form, Function, and Relationship to Other Genres." In Hand, *American Folk Legend*.

de Man, Paul. *Blindness and Insight: Essays in the Rhetoric of Contemporary Criticism*. New York: Oxford University Press, 1971.

Derrida, Jacques. *Of Grammatology*. Translated by Gayatri Chakravorty Spivak. Baltimore: Johns Hopkins University Press, 1976.

———. *Dissemination*. Translated by Barbara Johnson. Chicago: University of Chicago Press, 1981.

De Voto, Bernard. *The Year of Decision, 1846*. Boston: Houghton Mifflin, 1942.

Dillard, Annie. *Holy the Firm*. New York: Harper and Row, 1977.

The Doctrine and Covenants of The Church of Jesus Christ of Latter-day Saints. Salt Lake City: Deseret Book, 1921.

Dorson, Richard M. *American Folklore*. Chicago: University of Chicago Press, 1959.

———. *American Folklore and the Historian*. Chicago: University of Chicago Press, 1971.

———. "How Shall We Rewrite Charles M. Skinner Today?" In Hand, *American Folk Legend*.

———. *America in Legend: Folklore from the Colonial Period to the Present*. New York: Random House, Pantheon Books, 1973.

———. "Rejoinder to 'American Folklore vs. Folklore in America: A Fixed Fight?'" *Journal of the Folklore Institute* 17 (January–April 1980): 85–89.

Doty, Mark A. *Tell Me Who I Am: James Agee's Search for Selfhood*. Baton Rouge: Louisiana State University Press, 1981.

Douglas, Mary. *Purity and Danger: An Analysis of the Concepts of Pollution and Taboo*. London: Routledge and Kegan Paul, 1966.

———. "The Social Control of Cognition: Some Factors in Joke Perception." *Man* 3 (September 1968): 361–76.

———. *Natural Symbols*. New York: Random House, Vintage Books, 1973.

Douglass, William A. "Peasant Emigrants: Reactors or Actors?" In *Migration and Anthropology*.

Duncan, O. D. "Population Redistribution and Economic Growth: A Review." *Economic Development and Cultural Change* 7 (1958–59): 90–94.

Dundes, Alan. "The American Concept of Folklore." *Journal of the Folklore Institute* 3 (December 1966): 226–49.

———. "A Study of Ethnic Slurs: The Jew and the Polack in the United States." *Journal of American Folklore* 84 (April–June 1971): 186–203.

———. "On the Psychology of Legend." In Hand, *American Folk Legend*.

Dupree, Louis. "The Retreat of the British Army from Kabul to Jalalabad in 1842: History and Folklore." *Journal of the Folklore Institute* 4 (June 1967): 50–74.

Eberhard, Wolfram, ed. *Folktales of China*. Rev. ed. Chicago: University of Chicago Press, 1965.

Edman, Irwin. *The Contemporary and His Soul*. New York: Jonathan Cape and Harrison Smith, 1931.

Edmonson, Munro S. *Lore: An Introduction to the Science of Folklore and Literature*. New York: Holt, Rinehart and Winston, 1971.

Eliade, Mircea. *Myth and Reality*. Translated by William Trask. New York: Harper and Row, Harper Colophon Books, 1963.

———. *Rites and Symbols of Initiation: The Mysteries of Birth and Rebirth*. New York: Harper and Row, Harper Colophon Books, 1975.

Emerson, Ralph Waldo. "The Young American." *Dial* 4 (April 1844): 484–507.

———. *The Selected Writings of Ralph Waldo Emerson*. Edited by Brooks Atkinson. New York: Random House, Modern Library, 1950.

Eyring, Henry. "Science and Faith." In *Science and Your Faith in God*.

Farnham, Eliza W. *California, In-Doors and Out; or, How We Farm, Mine, and Live Generally in the Golden State*. New York: Dix, Edwards and Co., 1856.

Faulkner, William. *Soldiers' Pay*. New York: New American Library, Signet Books, 1968.

Fisher, Vardis. *The Mothers: A Documentary Novel of the Donner Party*. Chicago: Swallow Press, Sage Books, 1971.

Fishwick, Marshall W. "The Making of a Hero." *Saturday Review* 47 (August 1, 1964): 12–14.

Fitzgerald, Robert, ed. *The Collected Short Prose of James Agee*. London: Calder and Boyars, 1978.

Foucault, Michel. *The Birth of the Clinic: An Archaeology of Medical Perception*. Translated by A. M. Sheridan Smith. New York: Random House, Pantheon Books, 1973.

———. *Madness and Civilization: A History of Insanity in the Age of Reason*. Translated by Richard Howard. New York: Random House, Vintage Books, 1973.

———. *The Order of Things: An Archaeology of the Human Sciences*. [Orig. title *Les Mots et les choses*.] New York: Random House, Vintage Books, 1973.

———. *The Archaeology of Knowledge*. Translated by A. M. Sheridan Smith. New York: Harper and Row, Harper Colophon Books, 1976.

————. *Discipline and Punish: The Birth of the Prison*. Translated by Alan Sheridan. New York: Random House, Vintage Books, 1979.

————. *The History of Sexuality*. Vol. 1, *An Introduction*. Translated by Robert Hurley. New York: Random House, Vintage Books, 1980.

Fox, Marvin. "Secularism Denied." Review of *Tradition and Reality: The Impact of History on Modern Jewish Thought*, by Nathan Rotenstreich. *Commentary* 55 (February 1973): 92–93.

Frank, Philipp. *Einstein: His Life and Times*. New York: Alfred A. Knopf, 1947.

Frazer, Sir James George. *The Golden Bough: A Study in Magic and Religion*. Abridged ed. New York: Macmillan, 1963.

Frémont, John Charles. *The Expeditions of John Charles Frémont*. Vol. 1, *Travels from 1838 to 1844*. Edited by Donald Jackson and Mary Lee Spence. Urbana: University of Illinois Press, 1970.

Freud, Sigmund. *Jokes and Their Relation to the Unconscious*. Translated by James Strachey. New York: Norton, 1963.

————. *The Interpretation of Dreams*. Translated by James Strachey. New York: Avon Books, Discus Books, 1965.

Friedrich, Carl J. *Tradition and Authority*. London: Pall Mall Press, 1972.

Frye, Northrop. *Anatomy of Criticism*. 1957. Reprint. Princeton: Princeton University Press, 1971.

————. *The Great Code: The Bible and Literature*. New York: Harcourt Brace Jovanovich, 1982.

Fullerton, Kemper. *Essays and Sketches: Oberlin, 1904–1934*. New Haven: Yale University Press, for Oberlin College, 1938.

Gadamer, Hans-Georg. *Truth and Method*. New York: Continuum, 1975.

Gade, Ole. "Geographic Research and Human Spatial Interaction Theory: A Review of Pertinent Studies in Migration." In *Migration and Anthropology*.

García Márquez, Gabriel. *The Autumn of the Patriarch*. Translated by Gregory Rabassa. New York: Harper and Row, 1976.

Gatschet, Albert S. *A Migration Legend of the Creek Indians*. Philadelphia: D. G. Brinton, 1884. Reprint. New York: AMS Press, 1969.

Gay, Peter. *A Loss of Mastery: Puritan Historians in Colonial America*. Berkeley and Los Angeles: University of California Press, 1966.

Geertz, Clifford. "Blurred Genres: The Refiguration of Social Thought." *American Scholar* 49 (Spring 1980): 165–79.

Gennep, Arnold van. *The Rites of Passage*. Translated by Monica B. Vizedom and Gabrielle L. Caffee. Chicago: University of Chicago Press, Phoenix Books, 1960.

George, P. "Types of Migration of the Population according to the Professional and Social Composition of Migrants." In Jansen, *Sociology of Migration*.

Georges, Robert A. "The General Concept of Legend: Some Assumptions to be Reexamined and Reassessed." In Hand, *American Folk Legend*.

Gillespie, L. Kay. "Cancer Quackery in the State of Utah." Prepared privately for the Utah Department of Social Services, Office of Comprehensive Health Planning, 1976.

Girard, René. *Violence and the Sacred*. Translated by Patrick Gregory. Baltimore: Johns Hopkins University Press, 1977.

Glassie, Henry. *Folk Housing in Middle Virginia: A Structural Analysis of Historic Artifacts*. Knoxville: University of Tennessee Press, 1975.

Graebner, Norman A., ed. Introduction to *Manifest Destiny*. Indianapolis: Bobbs-Merrill, 1968.

Graves, Robert. *The White Goddess*. Rev. ed. New York: Farrar, Straus and Giroux, 1966.

Greene, Alma (Gah-wonh-nos-doh). *Forbidden Voice: Reflections of a Mohawk Indian*. London: Hamlyn, n.d.

Grimm, Jacob. *Teutonic Mythology*. 4th ed. Translated by James Steven Stallybrass. 4 vols. London, 1883–88.

Gura, Philip F. "Cotton Mather's *Life of Phips*: 'A Vice With the Vizard of Vertue Upon It.'" *New England Quarterly* 50 (September 1977): 440–57.

Haglund, Richard. "Science and Religion: A Symbiosis." *Dialogue* 8, nos. 3/4 (1973): 23–40.

Hand, Wayland D., ed. *American Folk Legend: A Symposium*. Berkeley and Los Angeles: University of California Press, 1971.

Handlin, Oscar. *Immigration as a Factor in American History*. Englewood Cliffs, N.J.: Prentice-Hall, 1959.

Harlan, Jacob Wright. *California, '46 to '88*. Oakland: Jacob Wright Harlan, 1896.

Harris, Franklin S. "Seek Truth in Science and Religion." In *Science and Your Faith in God*.

Hill, Thomas. *The Gardener's Labyrinth*. 1563. Reprint. London: Jane Bell, 1652.

Honko, Lauri. "Memorates and the Study of Folk Beliefs." *Journal of the Folklore Institute* 1 (1964): 5–19.

Horn, H. Harcourt. *An English Colony in Iowa*. Boston: 1931.

Hornberger, Theodore. "The Date, the Source, and the Significance of Cotton Mather's Interest in Science." *American Literature* 6 (January 1935): 413–20.

Houghton, Eliza P. Donner. *The Expedition of the Donner Party and Its Tragic Fate*. Los Angeles: Grafton, 1920.

Hutton, Paul A. "From Little Bighorn to Little Big Man: The Changing Image of a Western Hero in Popular Culture." *Western Historical Quarterly* 7 (January 1976): 19–46.

Jansen, Clifford J., ed. *Readings in the Sociology of Migration*. Oxford: Pergamon Press, 1970.

———. "Migration: A Sociological Problem." In Jansen, *Sociology of Migration*.

Jeffrey, Duane E. "Seers, Savants and Evolution: The Uncomfortable Interface." *Dialogue* 8, nos. 3/4 (1973): 41–75.

Jobes, Gertrude. *Dictionary of Mythology, Folklore, and Symbols*. 2 parts. New York: Scarecrow Press, 1962.

Jones, Michael Owen. "(PC + CB) × SD (R + I + E) = HERO." *New York Folklore Quarterly* 27 (September 1971): 243–60.

———. *The Hand Made Object and Its Maker*. Berkeley and Los Angeles: University of California Press, 1975.

Jones, Milton Jenkins. *Science and Religion Agree!* Salt Lake City: Deseret News Press, 1949.

Journal of Discourses. 26 vols. Liverpool: Franklin D. Richards, 1855–86.

Joyce, James. *Ulysses*. Rev. ed. New York: Random House, 1961.

Jung, Carl G. *Symbols of Transformation*. Translated by R. F. C. Hull. 2d ed. Princeton: Princeton University Press, 1976.

———. *Man and His Symbols*. New York: Dell, Laurel Books, 1968.

Kafka, Franz. *The Complete Stories*. Edited by Nahum N. Glatzer. New York: Schocken Books, 1971.

Katz, Daniel, and Braly, Kenneth W. "Verbal Stereotypes and Racial Prejudice." In *Readings in Social Psychology*, edited by Eleanor E. Maccoby, Theodore M. Newcomb, and Eugene L. Hartley. 3d ed. New York, 1958.

Katz, Jacob. *Tradition and Crisis: Jewish Society at the End of the Middle Ages*. 1961. Reprint. New York: Schocken Books, 1971.

Keithley, George. *The Donner Party*. New York: George Braziller, 1972.

Kepes, Gyorgy, ed. *Sign, Image, Symbol*. New York: George Braziller, 1966.

Kierkegaard, Soren. *Fear and Trembling* and *The Sickness unto Death*. Translated by Walter Lowrie. Rev. ed. Princeton: Princeton University Press, 1968.

King, Preston, and Parekh, B. C., eds. *Politics and Experience*. Cambridge: Cambridge University Press, 1968.

Klapp, Orrin E. "The Creation of Popular Heroes." *American Journal of Sociology* 54 (1948–49): 135–41.

———. "The Folk Hero." *Journal of American Folklore* 62 (January–March 1949): 17–25.

———. *Heroes, Villains, and Fools*. Englewood Cliffs, N.J.: Prentice-Hall, 1962.

———. *Symbolic Leaders: Public Dramas and Public Men*. Chicago: Aldine, 1964.

Krappe, Alexander Haggerty. *The Science of Folk-lore*. London: Methuen, 1930.

Kuhn, Thomas S. *The Structure of Scientific Revolutions*. 2d ed. Chicago: University of Chicago Press, 1970.

Lacan, Jacques. *Ecrits: A Selection*. Translated by Alan Sheridan. New York: Norton, 1977.

Larsen, Erling. *James Agee*. University of Minnesota Pamphlets on American Writers, no. 95. Minneapolis: University of Minnesota Press, 1968.

Lawrence, D. H. *Studies in Classic American Literature*. New York: Thomas Seltzer, 1923.

Leach, Maria, ed. *Standard Dictionary of Folklore, Mythology, and Legend*. New York: Funk and Wagnalls, 1950.

Lévi-Strauss, Claude. *Structural Anthropology*. Translated by Claire Jacobson and Brooke Grundfest Schoepf. New York: Basic Books, 1963.

———. *Totemism*. Translated by Rodney Needham. Boston: Beacon Press, 1963.

———. *The Savage Mind*. Chicago: University of Chicago Press, 1966.

———. *Tristes Tropiques*. Translated by John Weightman and Doreen Weightman. New York: Atheneum Books, 1974.

Levin, David. "The Hazing of Cotton Mather: The Creation of a Biographical Personality." *New England Quarterly* 36 (June 1963): 147–71.

Levy, David. "Reality, Utopia, and Tradition." *Modern Age* 20 (Spring 1976): 153–63.

Lukacs, Georg. Translated by Anna Bostock. *The Theory of the Novel: A Historico-Philosophical Essay on the Forms of Great Epic Literature*. 1971. Reprint. Cambridge: MIT Press, 1973.

Luomala, Katharine. "Disintegration and Regeneration, the Hawaiian Phantom Hitchhiker Legend." *Fabula* 13 (1972): 20–59.

Maamary, Samir N. *Attitude towards Migration among Rural Residents: Stages and Factors Involved in the Decision to Migrate*. San Francisco: R and E Research Associates, 1976.

Madden, David, ed. *Remembering James Agee*. Baton Rouge: Louisiana State University Press, 1974.

Magnarella, Paul J. *Tradition and Change in a Turkish Town*. New York: John Wiley and Sons, 1974.

Mandelbaum, Arthur. "Threats to the Modern Family." *Science Digest* 65 (March 1969): 57–60.

Marcuse, Herbert. "Repressive Tolerance." In *A Critique of Pure Tolerance*. Edited by Robert Paul Wolff, Barrington Moore, Jr., and Herbert Marcuse. Boston: Beacon Press, 1965.

————. *Eros and Civilization: A Philosophical Inquiry into Freud.* 1966. Reprint. Boston: Beacon Press, 1974.

Marx, Leo. *The Machine in the Garden: Technology and the Pastoral Ideal in America.* 1964. Reprint. New York: Oxford University Press, 1967.

Mather, Cotton. *Magnalia Christi Americana; or, The Ecclesiastical History of New England.* Hartford: Silas Andrus and Son, 1853.

————. *The Wonders of the Invisible World.* London: John Russell Smith, 1862.

————. *Diary of Cotton Mather.* 2 vols. New York: Frederick Ungar, [1957].

McGlashan, C. F. *History of the Donner Party: A Tragedy of the Sierras.* Truckee, Calif.: Crowley and McGlashan, 1879.

McKay, David O. "A Message for LDS College Youth." Brigham Young University Speeches of the Year [Provo, Utah, October 10, 1952].

McLuhan, Marshall. *Understanding Media: The Extensions of Man.* New York: New American Library, Mentor Books, 1964.

McNaught, Kenneth W., with John C. Ricker and John T. Saywell. *Manifest Destiny: A Short History of the United States.* Toronto: Clarke, Irwin, 1963.

McNeill, William H., and Adams, Ruth S., eds. *Human Migration: Patterns and Policies.* Bloomington: Indiana University Press, 1978.

Merk, Frederick. *Manifest Destiny and Mission in American History: A Reinterpretation.* New York: Alfred A. Knopf, 1963.

Middlekauff, Robert. *The Mathers: Three Generations of Puritan Intellectuals, 1596–1728.* 1971. Reprint. New York: Oxford University Press, 1976.

Migration and Anthropology. Proceedings of the 1970 Annual Spring Meeting of the America Ethnological Society. Seattle: University of Washington Press, 1970.

Miller, Frank C. "Humor in a Chippewa Tribal Council." *Ethnology* 6 (July 1967): 263–71.

Miller, Perry. *The New England Mind: The Seventeenth Century.* New York: Macmillan, 1939.

Miller, Perry, and Johnson, Thomas H. *The Puritans.* New York: American Book, 1938.

Milton, John. "Areopagitica." In *John Milton: Complete Poems and Major Prose*, edited by Merrit Y. Hughes. New York: Odyssey Press, 1957.

Morison, Samuel Eliot. *Harvard College in the Seventeenth Century.* 2 vols. Cambridge: Harvard University Press, 1936.

Morris, Wright. *Ceremony in Lone Tree.* Lincoln: University of Nebraska Press, Bison Book, 1973.

————. *Man and Boy.* Lincoln: University of Nebraska Press, Bison Book, 1974.

————. *About Fiction: Reverent Reflections on the Nature of Fiction with Irreverent Observations on Writers, Readers, and Other Abuses*. New York: Harper and Row, 1975.

————. *Fire Sermon*. Lincoln: University of Nebraska Press, Bison Book, 1979.

————. *Plains Song: For Female Voices*. 1980. Reprint. New York: Penguin Books, 1981.

————. *Will's Boy: A Memoir*. New York: Harper and Row, 1981.

Morrison, Peter A., and Wheeler, Judith P. "The Image of 'Elsewhere' in the American Tradition of Migration." In *Human Migration: Patterns and Policies*, edited by William H. McNeill and Ruth S. Adams. Bloomington: Indiana University Press, 1978.

Mullen, Patrick B. "The Relationship of Legend and Folk Belief." *Journal of American Folklore* 84 (October–December 1971): 406–13.

Mullin, Robert N., and Welch, Charles E., Jr. "Billy the Kid: The Making of a Hero." *Western Folklore* 32 (April 1973): 104–11.

Murdock, Kenneth B., ed. *Cotton Mather*. New York: Hafen Publishing, 1965.

Murphy, Virginia Reed. "Across the Plains in the Donner Party (1846): A Personal Narrative of the Overland Trip to California." *Century Magazine* 42 [vol. 20, new series] (July 1891): 409–26.

Murray, Albert. *The Hero and the Blues*. University of Missouri Press, 1973.

Neihardt, John G. *Black Elk Speaks: Being the Life Story of a Holy Man of the Oglala Sioux*. Lincoln: University of Nebraska Press, Bison Book, 1961.

Neumann, Erich. *The Great Mother: An Analysis of the Archetype*. Translated by Ralph Manheim. Reprint. Princeton: Princeton University Press, 1972.

Nietzsche, Friedrich. *The Birth of Tragedy* and *The Genealogy of Morals*. Translated by Francis Golffing. New York: Doubleday, Anchor Books, 1956.

————. *The Use and Abuse of History*. Translated by Adrian Collins. 2d ed. New York: Bobbs-Merrill, Library of Liberal Arts, 1957.

Nisbet, Robert A. *Tradition and Revolt: Historical and Sociological Essays*. New York: Random House, 1968.

Norman, Dorothy. *The Hero: Myth/Image/Symbol*. New York: World Publishing, 1969.

Ohlin, Peter H. *Agee*. New York: Ivan Obolensky, 1966.

Oring, Elliott. "'Hey, You've Got No Character': Chizbat Humor and the Boundaries of Israeli Identity." *Journal of American Folklore* 86 (October–December 1973): 359–66.

Paredes, Américo. "Folk Medicine and the Intercultural Jest." In *Spanish Speaking People in the United States*, edited by June Helm. Proceedings of the 1968 Annual Spring Meeting of the American Ethnological Society.

———. "Mexican Legendry and the Rise of the Mestizo: A Survey." In Hand, *American Folk Legend*.

Parsons, Gerald. "Second Thoughts on a 'Folk Hero': or, Sam Patch Falls Again." *New York Folklore Quarterly* 25 (June 1969): 83–92.

Patrick, Simon. *A Discourse About Tradition: Shewing What is Meant by it, and What Tradition Is to be Received, and What Tradition Is to be Rejected*. London: Miles Flesher, 1683.

Pepper, Steven C. *World Hypotheses: A Study in Evidence*. 1942. Reprint. Berkeley and Los Angeles: University of California Press, 1970.

Peterson, Richard H. *Manifest Destiny in the Mines: A Cultural Interpretation of Anti-Mexican Nativism in California, 1848-1853*. San Francisco: R and E Research Associates, 1975.

Phelps, Robert. "James Agee." In Agee, *Letters*.

Philpott, Stuart B. "The Implications of Migration for Sending Societies: Some Theoretical Considerations." In *Migration and Anthropology*.

Pigney, Joseph. *For Fear We Shall Perish: The Story of the Donner Party Disaster*. New York: E. P. Dutton, 1961.

Pocock, J. G. A. "Time, Institutions and Action: An Essay on Traditions and Their Understanding." In *Politics and Experience*, edited by Preston King and B. C. Parekh. Cambridge: Cambridge University Press, 1968.

Popper, Karl. *The Open Society and Its Enemies*. Rev. ed. Princeton: Princeton University Press, 1950.

Porter, Katherine Anne. *The Collected Essays and Occasional Writings of Katherine Anne Porter*. New York: Delacorte Press, 1970.

Poulsen, Richard C. "Some Botanical Cures in Mormon Folk Medicine: An Analysis." *Utah Historical Quarterly* 44 (Fall 1976): 379–88.

———. "Fenimore Cooper and the Exploration of the Great West." *Heritage of Kansas: A Journal of the Great Plains* 10 (Spring 1977): 15–24.

———. "'This is the Place': Myth and Mormondom." *Western Folklore* 36 (July 1977): 246–52.

———. "Fate and the Persecutors of Joseph Smith: Transmutations of an American Myth." *Dialogue* 11 (Winter 1978): 63–70.

———. "The Ghost Ship: A Legend among Airline Personnel." *Indiana Folklore* 11, no. 1 (1978): 63–70.

———. "Bosom Serpentry among the Puritans and Mormons." *Journal of the Folklore Institute* 16 (September–December 1979): 176–89.

————. *The Pure Experience of Order: Essays on the Symbolic in the Folk Material Culture of Western America*. Albuquerque: University of New Mexico Press, 1982.

Pratt, Julius W. "The Origin of 'Manifest Destiny.'" *American Historical Review* 32 (July 1927): 795–98.

Pratt, Orson. *Key to the Universe, or a New Theory of Its Mechanism*. Salt Lake City: Orson Pratt, 1879.

Press, Irwin. *Tradition and Adaptation: Life in a Modern Yucatan Maya Village*. Westport, Conn.: Greenwood Press, 1975.

Price, Reynolds. *A Palpable God*. New York: Atheneum, 1978.

Propp, Vladimir. *Morphology of the Folktale*. Translated by Laurence Scott. 2d ed. Austin: University of Texas Press, 1968.

Raglan, Lord. *The Hero: A Study in Tradition, Myth, and Drama*. 1956. Reprint. Westport, Conn.: Greenwood Press, 1975.

Redfield, Robert. *The Folk Culture of Yucatan*. Chicago: University of Chicago Press, 1941.

Reed, James. "The Journal of James Frazier Reed," edited by J. Roderick Korns. *Utah Historical Quarterly* 19 (1951): 186–223.

Rees, Robert. "Science, Religion, and Man." *Dialogue* 8, nos. 3/4 (1973): 4–6.

Reeves, Jesse S. *American Diplomacy under Tyler and Polk*. Baltimore: Johns Hopkins University Press, 1907.

Ricoeur, Paul. *Freud and Philosophy: An Essay on Interpretation*. Translated by Denis Savage. New Haven: Yale University Press, 1970.

Rosenberg, Bruce A. "Custer and the Epic of Defeat." *Journal of American Folklore* 88 (April–June 1975): 165–77.

Rotenstreich, Nathan. *Tradition and Reality: The Impact of History on Modern Jewish Thought*. New York: Random House, 1972.

Sartre, Jean-Paul. *Being and Nothingness: An Essay in Phenomenological Ontology*. Translated by Hazel E. Barnes. 1956. Reprint. Secaucus, N.J.: Citadel Press, 1974.

————. *Existentialism and Human Emotions*. Secaucus, N.J.: Castle Books, n.d.

Savage, William W., Jr. *The Cowboy Hero: His Image in American History and Culture*. Norman: University of Oklahoma Press, 1979.

Scholes, Robert, and Kellogg, Robert. *The Nature of Narrative*. 1966. Reprint. New York: Oxford University Press, 1976.

Schuchert, Charles, and LeVene, Clara Mae. *O. C. Marsh: Pioneer in Paleontology*. New Haven: Yale University Press, 1940.

Science and Your Faith in God. Salt Lake City: Bookcraft, 1958.

Seib, Kenneth. *James Agee: Promise and Fulfillment*. Pittsburg: University of Pittsburg Press, 1968.

Serres, Michel. *The Parasite*. Translated by Lawrence R. Schehr. Baltimore: Johns Hopkins University Press, 1982.

Singham, A. W. *The Hero and the Crowd in a Colonial Polity*. New Haven: Yale University Press, 1968.

Smith, Joseph. *History of The Church of Jesus Christ of Latter-day Saints*. Edited by B. H. Roberts. 2d ed. 7 vols. Salt Lake City: Deseret News Press, 1932–51.

Smith, Joseph Fielding. *Man: His Origin and Destiny*. Salt Lake City: Deseret Book, 1954.

Smith, N. Lee. "Herbal Remedies: God's Medicine?" *Dialogue* 12 (Fall 1979): 37–60.

Stacey, Margaret. *Tradition and Change: A Study of Banbury*. London: Oxford University Press, 1960.

Stern, Stephen, and Bronner, Simon J. "American Folklore vs. Folklore in America: A Fixed Fight?" *Journal of the Folklore Institute* 17 (January–April 1980): 76–84.

Stevens, Wallace. *Opus Posthumous*. Edited by Samuel French Morse. New York: Alfred A. Knopf, 1957.

———. *The Collected Poems*. New York: Random House, Vintage Books, 1982.

Stewart, George R. *Ordeal by Hunger: The Classic Story of the Donner Party*. New York: Pocket Books, 1971.

Thompson, Stith. *Motif-Index of Folk-Literature*. Rev. ed. Bloomington: Indiana University Press, 1955.

Thoreau, Henry David. "Walking." In *The Writings of Henry David Thoreau*, vol. 4. Boston: Houghton Mifflin, 1906.

Townsend, John K. *Narrative of a Journey Across the Rocky Mountains*. Philadelphia: Henry Perkins, 1839. Reproduced in *Early Western Travels: 1748–1846*, vol. 21, edited by Reuben Gold Thwaites. Cleveland: Arthur H. Clark, 1905.

Turner, Victor. *Chihamba, the White Spirit: A Ritual Drama of the Ndembu*. Rhodes-Livingstone Papers, no. 33. Manchester: Manchester University Press, 1962.

———. *The Forest of Symbols: Aspects of Ndembu Ritual*. Ithaca: Cornell University Press, Cornell Paperbacks, 1970.

———. *Dramas, Fields, and Metaphors: Symbolic Action in Human Society*. Ithaca: Cornell University Press, Cornell Paperbacks, 1975.

———. *The Ritual Process: Structure and Anti-Structure*. Ithaca: Cornell University Press, Cornell Paperbacks, 1977.

Van Cromphout, Gustaaf. "Cotton Mather as Plutarchan Biographer." *American Literature* 46 (January 1975): 465–81.

———. "Cotton Mather: The Puritan Historian as Renaissance Humanist." *American Literature* 49 (November 1977): 327–37.

Vartanian, Pershing. "Cotton Mather and the Puritan Transition into the Enlightenment." *Early American Literature* 7 (Winter 1973): 213–24.

Vesterholt, Ole. *Tradition and Individuality: A Study in Slavonic Oral Epic Poetry*. Copenhagen: Rosenkilde and Bagger, 1973.

Walker, Don D. *Clio's Cowboys: Studies in the Historiography of the Cattle Trade*. Lincoln: University of Nebraska Press, 1981.

Ward, David E. "Eliot, Murray, Homer, and the Idea of Tradition: 'So I Assumed a Double Part . . .'" *Essays in Criticism* 18 (January 1968): 47–59.

Ward, Don. "April 3, 1882: An Outlaw Dies and a Hero Is Born." *Folklore and Mythology*. UCLA Center for the Study of Comparative Folklore and Mythology 1 (April 1982): 1–5.

Wecter, Dixon. *The Hero in America: A Chronicle of Hero-Worship*. New York: Scribners, 1941.

Weinberg, Albert K. *Manifest Destiny: A Study of Nationalist Expansionism in American History*. 1935. Reprint. Gloucester, Massachusetts: Peter Smith, 1958.

Wendell, Barrett. *Cotton Mather: The Puritan Priest*. Cambridge: Harvard University Press, 1926.

White, Hayden. *Metahistory: The Historical Imagination in Nineteenth-Century Europe*. 1973. Reprint. Baltimore: Johns Hopkins University Press, 1975.

———. *Tropics of Discourse: Essays in Cultural Criticism*. Baltimore: Johns Hopkins University Press, 1978.

White, Patrick. *The Twyborn Affair*. New York: Viking Press, 1980.

———. *Flaws in the Glass: A Self-Portrait*. New York: Viking Press, 1982.

Widtsoe, John A. *Joseph Smith as Scientist: A Contribution to Mormon Philosophy*. Salt Lake City: General Board, Young Men's Mutual Improvement Associations, 1908.

———. *Evidences and Reconciliations: Aids to Faith in a Modern Day*. 3d ed. Salt Lake City: Bookcraft, 1943.

———. "What Is the Attitude of the Church toward Science?" In *Science and Your Faith in God*.

Wilcox, Linda P. "The Imperfect Science: Brigham Young on Medical Doctors." *Dialogue* 12 (Fall 1979): 26–36.

Will, George F. "Fashions in Heroes." *Newsweek* 94 (August 6, 1979): 84.

Wilson, William A., and Poulsen, Richard C. "The Curse of Cain and Other Stories: Blacks in Mormon Folklore." *Sunstone* 5 (November–December 1980): 9–13.

Witherspoon, Gary. *Language and Art in the Navajo Universe*. Ann Arbor: University of Michigan Press, 1977.

Wittgenstein, Ludwig. *Tractatus Logico-Philosophicus*. Translated by C. K. Ogden. Rev. ed. 1955. Reprint. London: Routledge and Kegan Paul, 1981.

Wolff, H. A., Smith, C. E., and Murray, H. A. "The Psychology of Humor: A Study of Responses to Race Disparagement Jokes." *Journal of Abnormal and Social Psychology* 28 (January–March 1934): 341–65.

Wright, Louis B. *Tradition and the Founding Fathers*. Charlottesville: University Press of Virginia, 1975.

Young Men's Mutual Improvement Associations Manual. Salt Lake City: Deseret News, General Board of the Young Men's Mutual Improvement Associations, 1904–05, 1905–06.

Zenner, Walter P. "Joking and Ethnic Stereotyping." *Anthropological Quarterly* 43 (April 1970): 93–113.

Zipf, George Kingsley. *Human Behavior and the Principle of Least Effort: An Introduction to Human Ecology*. New York: Addison-Wesley Press, 1949.

Index

Motif-Index of Folk-Literature, 83, 173 n. 27

Murdock, Kenneth, 17, 22

Muses, Greek and Roman, 5, 14

Myth, 37–45; beyond empiricism, 63, 64; embalmed in literature, 38, 164 n. 4; and language, 39–41, 45, 164 n. 42; no morphology of, 39, 45; and time, 39; voice of, 42, 44; and world-view, 43

Nihilism, 54–57; in jokes, 29

Pepper, Steven C., *World Hypotheses*, 38–39

Pollock, Jackson, view of past, 13

Puritans, 19, 21; Mather a stereotype of, 18; world-view, 14, 24

Quesalid (Indian shaman), 19–20, 22–23

Raglan, Lord, 71, 74; hero, 69–70, 72, 75

Reed, James, journal of, 108

Science, normal, 54, 122, 168 n. 27, 183 n. 29

Shaman (sorcerer): and deception, 20, 22; powerless without congregation, 19–20; transforms chaos, 23–24; unity of thought and action, 23

Smith, Joseph, 118–19

Space, 135–42, 188 n. 32; of body, 137; and community, 141–42; and language, 139; meaning in, 136; mythological and scientific, 136; sacred, 140, 142; sexual, 138; of time, 2

Stevens, Wallace, 2

Stewart, George R., 105

Symbiosis, 184 n. 42; of science and religion, 120–24

Thoreau, Henry David, 101

Tradition: definitions of, 48, 53, 167 n. 19; and historicity, 51–52; and individual, 53; and nihilism, 54, 56; and religion, 50

Transformation: and chaos, 127; an image, 131; in initiation rites, 130; of landscape, 125–33; and mood, 128, 129; and predictability, 127; of self, 129–30; through sex, 128

Truth: Agee's, 143, 154, 192 n. 54; religion and, 119–20, 123, 124; unbearable, 120, 182 n. 15

Turner, Victor, 35, 42

Wendell, Barrett, 17, 22

White, Hayden: historical fallacy, 160 n. 21; historical manipulation, 7, 155 n. 9, 156 n. 10; history an escape, 12; history not a science, 9

Witherspoon, Gary, 14, 41, 79

World-view, 5, 24

Young, Brigham, 118

Richard C. Poulsen

THE MOUNTAIN MAN VERNACULAR
Its Historical Roots, Its Linguistic Nature, and Its Literary Uses

American University Studies: Series IV (English Language and Literature). Vol. 22
ISBN 0-8204-0197-8   336 pages   hardback US $ 36.00*

*Recommended price – alterations reserved

The book is about the speech of the mountains: its historical evidence and implications, its linguistic nature (insofar as that can be determined), and its uses in and importance to the literature of the American West.
No historical dialect has been given so exhaustive and complete treatment. The model the book provides for determining the authenticity of oral narrative establishes a key of verisimilitude never provided before. Literary criticism is here based upon the rigor of historical exactitude and a linguistic and stylistic model.

«A surprise and a delight.» Barre Toelken
«... important for those interested in symbolism». Roger L. Welsch, New Mexico Historical Review

PETER LANG PUBLISHING, INC.
62 West 45th Street
USA — New York, NY 10036